The Ayatollah's Gaze

unbound

Unbound is a publisher which champions bold, unexpected books.

We give readers the opportunity to support books directly, so our authors are empowered to take creative risks and write the books they really want to write. We help readers to discover new writing they won't find anywhere else.

We are building a community in which authors engage directly with people who love what they do. It's a place where readers and writers can connect with and support one another, enjoy unique experiences and benefits, and make books that matter.

This book is in your hands because readers made it possible. Everyone who pledged their support is listed below. Join them by visiting unbound.com and supporting a book today.

Azeta, @ukbook_reviewer
Shahin Bekhradnia
Carolyn Braby
Susanne Emde
Noel Healy
Alex Lambert
Shirley Mawer
Andrew Nunn
James Penha
Smehur
Rick Smith
Simon Smith
Fiona Stocker
Tamara
Mike and Alan Wright

The Ayatollah's Gaze

A Memoir of the Forbidden and the Fabulous

Majid Parsa

Neem Tree Press

Published by Neem Tree Press Limited, 2025

Copyright © Majid Parsa, 2025

1 3 5 7 9 10 8 6 4 2

Neem Tree Press
An imprint of Boundless Publishing Group
c/o Ketton Suite, The King Centre, Main Road,
Barleythorpe, Rutland, LE15 7WD
www.unbound.com
All rights reserved

A catalogue record for this book is available from the British Library.

ISBN 978-1-915584-46-5 Hardback
ISBN 978-1-915584-47-2 Ebook

All rights reserved. No part of this publication may be reproduced, distributed, or transmitted in any form or by any means, including photocopying, recording, or other electronic or mechanical methods, without the prior written permission of the publisher, except in the case of brief quotations embodied in critical reviews and certain other non-commercial uses permitted by copyright law. For permission requests, write to the publisher at the address above.

Printed and bound by Clays Ltd, Elcograf S.p.A.

Iran: what does the word conjure?

Political unrest, Islamic revolution, something nuclear, international sanctions.

Fists thrown in the air, chanting, "Death to America! Death to Israel!"

Or a country of deserts and ancient ruins, often mistaken for its neighbour, Iraq?

Some say Iran is a country of culture, history, and exotic food. The swelling pride often associated with this portrayal is difficult to miss when you speak to someone from Iran in the West, whether they refer to themselves as an 'Iranian' or a 'Persian'. Some left for a better life, some escaped, others exiled.

Which description is more accurate?

All of the above, perhaps.

There are many tales to be told about Iran: its culture, people, history, and politics. However, some stories are lost between the cracks, left untold.

Ignored.

This is the story of a boy growing up in that country, a boy who realized he was different from others.

It is the story of one person's struggle with identity, sexuality, tradition, and religion, in a place where the word *gay* remains unheard among all the other noises and chants.

Prologue

He hugged me tight, my head on his chest.

His arms wrapped around me, like he'd never let go. I could not make out his face. I squinted, but it remained a blur.

Somehow, I knew him. I had always known him.

Where was I? The sofa we sat on, the maroon carpet with its curved lines and flowers—as if they were also in an embrace—and the thick beige curtain, drawn closed: all appeared familiar, yet alien.

It felt calm.

Private.

Safe.

He ran his fingers through my hair. I smiled. Up until that moment, I could only smell *him*, his warm sweet scent.

The smell was being replaced by an uninvited intruder. It tingled my nostrils and made my stomach churn.

Rice.

I shook my head side to side to get rid of it, to have him back. It only got stronger, like a thick fog descending on us, occupying every corner. A distant voice called my name like an echo. And then a pull.

My head detached from his chest. I tried to stay. I tried hard. I couldn't. I was being pulled away with a force I had no strength to fight against. He was becoming smaller, merging with the beige of the curtains, the maroon of the carpet, a distorted and distant smudge. I opened my mouth and shouted, but I had no voice. I stretched my arm towards him.

My stomach made another moan.

The second shake on my foot woke me up.

"Majid, get up. Everyone is up, come on," whispered Maman.

When I opened my eyes, I could make out her chador silhouette in the dark. I groaned and pulled the duvet over my head. I closed my eyes, screwed them tight, hoping to see him again. To feel him again.

It was too late. He was gone.

Maman left the room, careful not to wake up Sina, my little brother. I looked at the window. Pitch black. The humming sounds of cutlery and the TV through the closed bedroom door were getting louder. I had to get up.

I flinched as I entered the bright TV room. Our *sofreh*, a pale plastic sheet with pink flowers printed on, was spread in the middle of the carpet. Five plates with mismatching forks and spoons on each, lined the edges of it. Pictures of flowers and an Arabic prayer crawled across the top of the TV screen, next to a clock: 4.00 a.m. The musical sound of the man reciting the prayer on TV was mournful and melancholic. I knew the prayer by heart. His voice was what we heard every night before dawn during Ramadan, it was a countdown timer to the morning prayer call, the *azaan*.

Baba was sitting cross-legged at the *sofreh* already, along with Saman. He looked grumpy, like always. Maman put a tray of tea on the floor.

"Majid, go get the rice. I'll serve the *khoresht*."

I obeyed, carefully placing the steaming rice dish in the middle of the *sofreh* on a hotplate, to stop it from melting a new hole in the plastic.

Maman sat on the carpet opposite Baba, placing the stew next to the rice, her floral prayer chador skilfully twisted around her head, keeping her hands free. She glanced at the clock on TV, saying, "Quick. Eat. I almost missed my alarm this morning; not much time left till *azaan*," as she served us rice and stew.

We all ate in silence while the sombre prayer continued on TV in the background.

I kept remembering my dream and smiled to myself, how vivid it was. I believed, after offering my prayer and going back to bed, he would be waiting for me. I already longed to have his arms around me again.

I was fourteen.

My morning prayer, the one on the TV, the prayers of Maman or Baba—none could stop the pull in my gut.

A pull by a monster.

Little did I know, this monster I was feeding was insatiable.

Little did I know, this feeling I was nurturing innocently was punishable by death.

Part I

Faded Hue

June 2018, London

"Syphilis? Again?"

He looks at me as if I have not only given him his diagnosis, but the disease itself. He sounds like a child who's just dropped his ice cream.

"Yes. I know," I sympathize. "It's not what you want to hear."

He grunts. "But I have been so careful; I don't understand." There, that voice again.

I glance at the clock on my computer screen: nearly five p.m. I'd really like to leave on time today. I'm going out for drinks this evening, finally. Ben and I have been trying for several weeks to set a second date, and I do not want to be late—least of all because someone else has had an unfortunate result for having too much fun. *Deep breath.*

I turn to him again, smiling. "It's difficult to know exactly how you got it, or who you got it from. Have you been using condoms for oral sex, too?"

His eyebrows form a frown as he pulls his chin close to his neck, creating an unattractive double chin. I would have thought of him as "acceptably handsome" up until then. I fight back the temptation to roll my eyes.

"Of course not; who does that?" he says, voice back to normal.

"Well, some do. There are flavoured condoms out there for a reason."

"Would *you*?"

Like a tightrope walker being hit by a gust of wind, my footing is lost for a second, as the hair on the back of my neck stands up. I look at his smug face, his perfectly raised eyebrow saying, *I can see through you.* Suddenly, I wish the tiny room had a window.

My cheeks a little bit warmer, I clear my throat. "I don't think that is relevant."

Images of the past flash in front of my eyes for a second. Have I ever? Did I use condoms for any kind of sex, back then? An uncomfortable sense of shame starts to bubble in my stomach. I got away with it. Perhaps there is a god who watches over me, only to punish me in the afterlife.

Feeling like a bit of a hypocrite, I gather myself and continue: "A third of syphilis is transmitted through oral sex."

He is not impressed with my answer. Neither am I. The time on the computer screen is screaming, *You're definitely going to be late!* Need to wrap up.

Once I have given a monologue listing various scientific facts about syphilis, I leave him looking baffled and give the penicillin prescription to the nurse. I hand over to the next doctor and rush out, feverishly texting Ben: **Sorry, just left. Am going to be late x.**

On the Tube, a middle-aged woman wearing hijab is sitting opposite me, holding a huge floral bag close to her chest, her face serious. I follow her gaze to a few seats down, where a girl sits in a tiny denim skirt, her straightened blond hair loose at her shoulders. She is holding a tiny pink mirror in her left hand and skilfully adding more mascara to an already heavily made-up face with the other. Her glittery lips form an O shape, as if surprised about what is happening to the rest of her face. I look back at the hijab woman, still clutching her bag, knuckles white. There is something in her eyes. Is it pity? Or envy? I can't tell. She catches my glance. I smile. She is quick to look away, releasing her grip on the bag.

I put my earphones in and close my eyes, my mind venturing into the past. I imagine what Maman would think about the girl in the denim skirt. What would she think about *my* earlier speech on oral sex, about the gay man—or, as she'd put it, "the sodomite"? Could she picture her son talking about flavoured condoms? What a strange turn of events it has been. Bobbing up and down to the gentle rocking of the Tube train, I let the floodgates of memories open.

*

Memories.

Events which made me laugh, cry, and everything in between. The tickling and the tormenting. They are like gigantic hands moulding soft clay into who I am now.

Let's start with the most distant one. It is so far, it may only be my imagination. Like dust gathered on a shelf, an itch at the back of the throat.

A soft hand. A smile.

The loud roar of an engine.

Ears popping.

They were going back.

Baba wasn't from a religious background, but he had his religious principles: he fasted, offered prayers five times a day, and so on. An architect, he was one of two children, with an older brother. I never met my paternal grandmother, who died of cancer a few years before my parents had children. Baba's father was a successful judge and lawyer, who retired before the 1979 Islamic revolution.

Maman, on the other hand, was from a big religious family, born to conservative Shia Muslim parents in Ankara, Turkey. She met Baba when he was at university in Turkey. They got married and moved back to pre-revolution Iran for a couple of years. Maman does not talk much about those days, now—in fact, she does not talk about them at all. It must have been a daunting experience, leaving her homeland and moving to a country in which she had no family or friends, and did not know the language. I look at the faded pictures from back then and see a young woman with lush black curly hair, almost like an Afro, wearing fashionable clothes and with a shy smile. The Maman I know is so different now, it is impossible to imagine her voice, her laugh, and her smell in the Polaroid photos. Was her accent stronger? Would she still tut if she saw lovers hold hands or kiss in public? Did she do those things in public?

They soon moved to the UK, to study. It was a rite of passage to obtain a Western degree. It still is. My older brother Saman and I were both born in England. I was born in Sheffield, in 1981.

I don't know at what point it happened exactly, but my mum and dad fell in love with the revolution and what it stood for. Perhaps it was the adrenaline that the radical change pumped into their hearts, or the promise that accompanied it: an ideal world. After all, don't all revolutions promise that?

The Islamic revolution emerged from frustration with the Shah, and it toppled 2,500 years of monarchy in Iran. Led by Ayatollah Khomeini, the Grand Ayatollah, religion and politics were to be made one entity, inseparable. The banner of Islam was raised, sharia became *the* law. Iran's flag changed face, the lion-and-sun emblem giving way to the word *Allah*, written in Arabic. The country was shaken from an imperial dynasty to the Islamic Republic.

In 1980, Iraq invaded Iran. A war was imposed on the newly born regime. This was when my parents decided to go back, to be home. Baba had just finished his master's, while Maman was busy looking after me and my brother.

This time round, moving to Iran was different. Maman had begun to cover her head and wore a hijab. I never saw the days when she did not wear one and can only picture what it was like sitting in her lap, while she confidently showed off that full head of hair. Now, not a single strand escaped her scarf, which hid it from the looks of men who weren't allowed to see it. Her confidence was in one thing only: Islam. The faith became her identity. It was what she now breathed, ate, and drank.

The old yellow-hued pictures also show a different-looking Baba: clean shaven, thick black unruly hair, wearing those Elvis-type boot-cut trousers, a cigarette in his hand. He was handsome.

The religious transformation was drastic. The revolution had brought out the ideologue in each of them and, in the case of Iran's revolution, that ideology was wholly Islamic. My dad grew a full beard, stopped smoking, and reinvented himself. Both of my parents devoted themselves to the new regime and renewed their religious vows.

My ears popped again.
    A soft hand caressed my face.
    We were landing.
    The Islamic Republic was two, and I was a six-month-old child sitting in Maman's lap.
    I only needed that gentle rocking, back then; I hadn't the faintest understanding of how my future was being drawn in front of me, like a mirage.

The Unholy War

1985

"Majid, come here. Quick, Baba is leaving."

I jumped up and accidentally kicked my handiwork. The perfectly arranged shell casings around the fragments of a grenade were meant to look like mountains surrounded by golden trees. I groaned in frustration and got back on my knees and elbows again, carefully standing a couple of the empty shells upright.

"MAJID!" Maman's voice had her warning tone laced into it this time, coming through gritted teeth.

I left my toys and, with a frown, stepped out of the bedroom. Baba was on one knee, tying the laces of his tired army boots. His beard looked fuller, and his uniform worn out. He had enlisted as part of the volunteer force and was sent to the front line for a few months at a time. It wasn't enlistment, in his eyes—it was pilgrimage. "The Holy Defence" was the name the Ayatollah had given it.

Maman was in her prayer chador, holding a Quran. That white cotton sheet with small pink flowers printed on it covered her from top to toe, Allah's embrace.

Saman was already standing next to her, watching Baba intently. His finger was in his nose, hunting for treasure. When I joined them, Maman put her hand on my head, and I pulled away, still angry.

"Baba, can you bring a big shell, like last time—the one which is this tall?" I asked, putting my hand next to my inflated chest.

"Sure, if I see one." He smiled as he stood up.

I looked at my mum with excitement. She wasn't looking back and seemed to be staring at the door, lost. Her lower lip was quivering as she chewed on it and her eyes were glossy. I buried my face in her chador and inhaled the familiar warm rose scent.

"Right, I'm off," said Baba as he pulled the strap of the khaki holdall over his shoulder.

Maman cleared her throat and held the Quran up above his head. We watched, transfixed, my mouth open and Saman's finger still glued. Baba walked under the holy book, turned around and, as Maman lowered the book to his face, kissed and touched his forehead on it. One final look at us three and he was gone, again.

"Can I kiss it, too?" said Saman, trying to reach for Maman's hand.

"No, you can't touch the book without *vodhu*." She pulled her hand away, her tone serious. No emotion could overcome Maman's devotion to religious routines. *Vodhu* was the act of cleansing with water prior to offering prayers.

Two years older than me, Saman was always trying to mirror Baba and craved his authority. When Baba was away, he *was* the man of the house.

Itching to return to my game with our healthy collection of war souvenirs, I ran back to my bedroom, glancing over my shoulder before entering. Maman was still standing in front of the door, perhaps hoping her husband had forgotten something.

Our first home in Tehran was a flat in the north of the city, close to one of Tehran's biggest parks, with old trees forming a green arch over our street. The neighbourhood had once been serene and lush, where birds chirped and trees danced in the wind, but I couldn't remember it that way. The sparrows had been replaced with metal birds and their chirping with deafening air-raid sirens. The fire of war was blazing in full force; the ultimate aim of "The Holy Defence" was to defend the religion.

Often, I saw Maman on her prayer mat in the middle of the night, reading the Quran in a musical tone. Forgetting I needed the loo, I stood still, watching her as she rocked back and forth, her voice breaking occasionally. I wished I knew what she was praying for.

I had learned the words to the martyrdom songs and anthems, and sang them to myself. They were catchy. I sat in front of the screen as my favourite ones were played on TV, whispering the lyrics as I watched pictures of young men in oversized uniforms smiling and joking in long queues, rifles on their shoulders, wearing headbands with Arabic chants written on them. I stared at their faces till my eyes hurt, looking for Baba.

They got on buses: their one-way chariots to the front line.

The anthems fuelled courage in their blood. A promise of heaven. Their sacrifice was like a butterfly leaping from a flower. No bullet holes were mentioned, no being torn apart by a bomb blast. Did they know that was what awaited them? Did I?

And then there were the air raids and the criss-crossed parcel tape stuck on windows to limit the spraying of shards if the glass was shattered by a blast. It was a usual sight in the city, and so were the murals: Quran verses, the Grand Ayatollah, and the martyrs.

The martyrs.

The butterflies.

When the buses returned empty, the faces on the walls of the city kept smiling, kept hoping. More and more walls revealed their faces every day. The war was when the holy stamp of the revolution took over the capital's face.

Baba had been away on the front line. I was sitting on the floor, too close to the TV, mouth open again. My favourite Iranian cartoon was on. The little girl on the screen was wearing a chador and drying dishes for her mum, her dad reading the newspaper: all happy; the perfect family. I wondered why a small girl had to wear a hijab, trying to picture her without. Did she have long black hair down to her heels? Did she tie it back? Why was she covered up if she was at home?

Suddenly, it all stopped. The change in colour on the screen was all too abrupt. I thought I had got used to it. The bright red made me squint, and the loud siren forced me to put my fingers in my ears.

"ATTENTION! ATTENTION! THE SOUND YOU ARE HEARING IS A RED ALERT! YOU MUST GO TO A SHELTER, YOU MUST—"

Maman switched the TV off and pulled my hand, yanking me up to my feet. "Quick, put your shoes on. Where is your brother? SAMAN!"

Holding hands, we ran down the stairs to our basement. In the damp room with its concrete floor, Maman greeted our next-door neighbour with a nod. She held her cooing new-born, rocking side to side, looking more tired than afraid. A single light bulb hung naked from the ceiling. The static buzz of the filament inside was the only sound in the heavy silence. Until it wasn't. The rattling sound of the not-so-distant artillery began to wax and wane, trying to fend off enemy planes like a repellent against mosquitoes.

After the first few air raids, the excitement had faded and I was only annoyed about sitting on the cold floor, hugging my knees for a few hours, and hoping cockroaches would not join us again. My mum stared at the ceiling, as if hoping her gaze would be an additional pillar, and kept a tight hold of our hands.

When we went back upstairs, we had to sleep under the large dining table in case the roof collapsed. My brother and I fought over the best spot, as if having a picnic, while Maman carefully arranged the bedding, making sure the table covered us all. She kept the lights off; we were in stealth mode. When she eventually joined us, she was wearing a head scarf.

"Why don't you take it off? Are we going out?" I asked, my eyelids heavy.

"No, I *like* to keep it on. It's more comfortable."

I didn't argue, turning my back to her and pulling the duvet close to my chin. One of my empty shells was on the floor in front of my face. I stood it up: the small golden tree. The repellent was still rattling in the distance. I drifted away.

It was only later that I realized she had kept her scarf on for her dignity, her belief. She did not want her hair showing in case, the next morning, her body was dug out of the rubble, beside her two children, one holding a shell in his hand.

1988

Bombs fell in Tehran and people died. The war lasted eight years, the scars of which would stay forever. Around 600,000 people lost their lives during those years. At the time, I could not comprehend that our usual sights and sounds, my usual toys and songs, were anything but.

When I was seven, we left our first home. The war had ended. Baba was back for good. He smiled less, and he prayed more. He had become more short-tempered. What had he seen during those years?

The country entered a long phase of recovery and rebuilding. The murals of the martyrs on the city walls, and their names on streets, buildings, and universities, were constant reminders of our debt to the regime, to what it stood for. The war gave birth to a new entity: the Revolutionary Guard, the religious armed force which kept the country together. With the unparalleled and uninhibited power it possessed, the Revolutionary Guard planted a seed in every organization, every infrastructure. It had the sharia stamp on it, rendering it untouchable and unquestionable.

Sharia's grip on the republic became tighter. Almost all politicians were now religious clerics, a true merging of religion and politics. Khomeini was the holiest of them all. Often on TV, he was shown in his home, sitting on the floor to greet world leaders, or walking in his backyard in slow motion in simple clothes and slippers, hunched, hands behind his back. He would smile at the camera. That is, his lips formed a smile; his eyes always remained rigid. A father to the nation. My mother, along many others, watched this humble religious leader and worshipped him. Every time his name was heard, we had to send three blessings in Arabic to the Prophet Mohammed and his family. I got anxious if I accidentally heard the name, lest I forgot to do the three prayers and incurred Allah's wrath.

A few pictures of Ayatollah Khomeini decorated our walls. One large portrait hung on our living-room wall, with those serious eyes staring, watching over us. His gaze pierced through me, making me feel defenceless, vulnerable. His name had the prefix "Imam". Not saying "Imam" before his name was not just rude, it was an unwritten sin.

Baba had made friends during his war days. He'd begun climbing up the ladder the Islamic regime had created for the most devoted: war veteran, beard, and connections were the way in.

We had moved to an apartment in a big white block of flats standing ten storeys tall. My little brother Sina was born there: probably an accident, but nevertheless the most spoiled child. I lost my precious spot as the youngest.

And then, there was the boy next door.

There is always a boy next door.

My memory of him is a blur, his face a halo, his edges soft, his voice an echo.

Being close to him was guilt free. When he hugged me, I let him. I closed my eyes and pressed my head against his chest, soft like a feather, the warmth of his embrace seeping into my belly. I got jealous if he played with Saman. I longed for his touch every day.

The corner of a frame tears through this memory.

A golden frame, the picture of Imam Khomeini sitting within.

The message is as sharp as the look, unlike the softness of the next-door boy's hug. The stern look mutes the gentle echoes in a flash.

Under the Islamic banner erected by the holy Ayatollah, there was no place for those feelings.

Punished. Executed. Hanged from a crane.

September 1996, eight years later

The tall, slim figure was about to go inside the building,

"Mr…" I called.

When he turned, his clean-shaven face wrinkled, displaying that warm smile, as always. "Oh, Majid, hello."

The chemistry teacher greeted pupils every time as if he hadn't seen us for ages. His gentle manner and soft voice only added to an endearing personality.

"Sorry to bother you; I just wanted to give you this," I said, blushing, as I handed him the neatly wrapped book.

He looked at it quizzically before saying, "Oh dear. Thank you. What is this for?"

"It's...It's nothing. I'm leaving this school, and I just...just wanted to say thank you."

I stood there, hands behind me, staring as he carefully unwrapped the gift.

He gasped when he saw the title, *Old Tehran Pictures*. "This is so sweet and kind of you. You have gone to the trouble of buying me this? Oh dear."

Overwhelmed by his reaction, I was suddenly engulfed with guilt. *The trouble I went to.*

"No, no. It was no trouble at all. The book was sitting on our bookshelf and no one read it."

Silence followed. I looked side to side for an escape. He kept his eyes on the cover for a while, then cleared his throat.

"Oh, OK. Well, thank you. It is beautiful, I'm sure. I...I need to go to the office, now. Well, good luck, wherever you go." He whispered another "oh dear" as he walked away.

I kept the grin on, ears hot, cheeks red. He was the only good memory I was going to keep—his kindness.

As he disappeared into the building, I noticed someone standing at the entrance: the school principal. His raven-black beard was neatly cut to show the corners of that angular jaw, and his eyes, deep like a bottomless well, serious and sharp, stared at me. His face was rigid, as if he'd seen Medusa. I held his gaze for a second. The look could no longer burn into my head, not like before.

No more fear. Damage done, I was leaving.

I knew then that I would never forget him, an unrelenting shadow cast over my life, one that would take years to shake off.

I was fifteen.

After what I had been through, a new phase of my life was beginning. I was planning to bury it all, as if the last year had never happened.

Two weeks later, in my new school, I found my seat at a shared desk. As I shuffled myself on to the wooden bench, I did not look at the boy next to me, until a hand came into my vision.

"Hi, I'm Ali."

I turned my head, shaking his hand, hesitant. My first thought: A kind smile. "Hi!"

1988, back to childhood

I was growing up in the heavy shadow of the sharia.

Maman taught us Islam's principles, the sins, halals, and harams. The sins were age appropriate: lying, stealing, wasting food, or touching the Quran without a *vodhu*. At seven, I learned not to get on Allah's angry side. You'd have to be out of your mind not to fear him. The sin I particularly feared was wasting salt.

"If you waste salt, in the afterlife you will be made to pick up each grain with your eye lashes."

I tried to imagine it: on all fours, face stuck to the floor, blinking methodically to try to pick up a grain of salt. It was frightening. I still don't know why Allah is fascinated with salt in particular. As I got older, the list became longer, and the retributions more ominous.

I mirrored Maman when she prayed. I'd put a chador on, to feel what she felt: that intimate warmth of faith. I'd fold the cloth on the sides of my cheeks, the way she did, and check myself in the mirror. No hair visible. Perfect.

She would tut and laugh. Then she would sit me down next to her on the prayer mat as she read the holy book, still sorrowful, still with a tissue scrunched up in her hand. I wondered what the words meant. I was jealous. I *wanted* to learn.

Baba would often have friends over, sitting in a separate room on the floor, chatting. One had a calloused forehead, a thicker beard than Baba, and smelt as if he showered with rose water. He always patted mine and Saman's heads, saying, "*Masha'Allah*, you are growing fast." I'd blush and Saman would pull away. I could tell he was an important person.

Later, I would go to our building's common grounds and play with the next-door boy, trying to ditch Saman so I could have him to myself. He was only a few years older than me. His mum wore her scarf loose, showing her golden dyed hair, and she wore red lipsticks. In their flat, there were no pictures of Imam Khomeini, but instead they had paintings and decorative ornaments. It even smelt different—unfamiliar, sweet, wrong. It defined him: the boy next door, from an alien life, evoking an alien feeling within. The sparks of an unholy battle to come were beginning to flicker.

We did not stay in that flat for long. When I turned eight, we moved again, into a newly built apartment where I spent the next twenty years.

What a twenty years it would be.

The Good Muslim

1988

Our new flat in Tehran was perfect. I fondly remember every corner of it. Baba and his rose-water-smelling friend from the war partnered up to build the place. He was to become our upstairs neighbour.

Located in a quiet, narrow street, it had a quirky and charming feel to it. The long yellow brick building stretched along the street, bending with its curves, giving the illusion that it was bigger than its actual size. We owned the first floor. Once inside our apartment, to the left were eight white marble steps up, leading to a living room, and to the right, through another door, was the rest: kitchen, TV room, and three bedrooms. The separate living room proved useful on many occasions later. We had a small communal backyard with a flower bed in the middle. Saman, being the eldest and entitled to independence, as he put it, got a bedroom to himself, and I shared with Sina. Our bedroom overlooked the backyard, away from the street.

Pictures of the Ayatollah went up on a few walls, Quran verses printed and framed on others. In the TV room, a big bookshelf dedicated to religious books—including a few Qurans, in various sizes, fonts, and colours—filled one wall. Our old TV sat on a table, showing state TV's two channels: the source of our entertainment. There were no chairs or sofas, but large kilim cushions with a traditional carpet design on them leaned up against the walls. The stone floor was covered with big carpets, wall to wall. Food was served on a *sofreh* on the floor, and we sat around it. Most of life happened in that room.

Our local mosque was about ten minutes' walk from home. Prayer calls, the *azaan*, could be heard three times a day, and every so often we offered prayers there. Inside, the sour smell of socks and feet, mixed with a rose-water scent, was our welcome to Allah's house; the eye-watering combination was a hallmark of any religious gathering or speech.

June 1989, around six a.m.

This memory began with a ring.

Ring, ring, ring

It took me a while to realize I was not still dreaming.

Whispers in the TV room. I kept still and held my breath to make out the voices. It was impossible. I needed to see.

Sina was still in a deep sleep. I tiptoed past him and peeked through the ajar bedroom door.

A night light was plugged in, and in its faint glow I could see Maman sitting on a prayer mat surrounded by shadows that made the room look distorted. And there was that noise. A hiss—uninterrupted, loud, ominous. I stepped out.

She was in her prayer chador, a tissue crumpled in her hand. There was no Quran open in front of her. Instead, the phone receiver was next to her on the floor, screaming that dead tone.

She cried quietly.

I had not seen her cry before, ever. Not like this. Occasional tears here and there at a religious mourning ceremony, perhaps—but this was a different cry altogether. It reeked of sorrow and pain. As if my stomach had expanded into my chest, my breath struggled to get out.

She looked up. Whether it was the low light or the long limbs of shadows embracing her, I could not read that look. Suddenly rediscovering her surroundings, she patted the floor for the source of the constant beep, found the receiver with a trembling hand, and put it back on the base. She looked at me again and gave a quivering smile.

I stared down at my toes, ashamed that I had seen her like that.

"Majid, come."

Her voice came through broken vocal cords. I sat quietly by her side on the prayer mat and looked at her face again.

"Imam Khomeini has died," she said, putting her hand on my head.

The Grand Ayatollah, dead.

My chest heaved.

"Where...where is Baba?"

"At the mosque with the upstairs neighbour." She sniffed and swallowed. "He called. They announced it after the morning prayer there." She broke into sobs again.

I watched her, bewildered and distraught. How I wished she would stop crying. I wished Baba was home and not at the mosque.

I sat with her as she prayed. The shadows danced around her as she moved, taunting her with their long legs until the light of day pushed through and Baba was back.

"Go to bed, Majid. It's OK," she said, composing herself.

I rubbed my eyes. "But I want to stay," I said, with a yawn.

She patted my back. "Bed, now; schools will be closed today."

I looked at my father, who was sitting on a chair at our kitchen counter, bent, elbows on knees and head down. The authoritative man I knew looked vulnerable and broken.

I climbed back into bed. I could hear incomprehensible whispers from my parents' bedroom: words of comfort. I stared at the ceiling, tears streaming down my cheeks. The death of the Ayatollah was truly like losing a father.

The funeral was one to be remembered. Allah himself would have taken tips for Judgement Day. We and our neighbour attended for a short period; then, before hell broke loose, came home and followed the rest on TV.

Millions of mourners wearing black crammed together. The sun whipped the crowd with its midday blaze, lash after lash. Dust rose to the sky as they marched. Many had mud smeared on their faces. They hit their heads with both hands and thumped their chests. Their screams and wails merged into a loud incomprehensible shriek. The crowd moved as one entity, a turbulent sea of black, with random waves pushing and pulling. Huge water pumps sprayed the crowd, the water evaporating instantly.

When the coffin was taken to be buried, it was swallowed by the sea of grief-possessed mourners. We gasped as we saw Khomeini's body, wrapped in a white cloth, falling out of the coffin, his dead face bare. It was eventually recovered again by the Revolutionary Guard and taken away by helicopter. A few people died in the stampede.

The burial was deferred by three days and his body put in a glass box on a raised stand, on display. The enormous mourning crowd surrounding it did not shrink at any point.

I was genuinely upset at the death of the father of the revolution. That some people were celebrating his death would have never crossed my mind, not for a second.

The Ayatollah's pictures in our home were adorned with a black band from then on. His death made him holier. His grave turned into a shrine, a pilgrimage site, with a huge golden dome and four minarets surrounding it. Yet another divine spot where prayers and foot odour mingled.

If memories had colours, this one would be grey. It pours in from the corners of my vision to coat everything. It was everywhere I turned my head.

I poked my finger through the hole in my trousers, torn when I fell a few minutes earlier. Still grey. No blood. Just a scratch. Phew, I thought. I can still pray.

I looked around the grey asphalt school grounds from where I sat in a corner; students were coming out of the school building towards the shared basin, where a long line of steel taps twinkled in the bright sun.

I had rushed to be the first for *vodhu* and had tripped just before getting there. The caretaker, in his usual worn-out grey suit, had been sitting on the upturned bucket he was supposed to use to mop, his favourite spot. He'd seen me trip and only watched. His smirk pushed up the corners of his bushy moustache, which was home to an ecosystem of crumbs and whatnot. The creases on his forehead were so deep, I wondered what was hidden in them.

The final "*Allahu Akbar*," Allah is the greatest, echoed out in a muffled nasal tone from the grey cone-shaped speaker. Time to move. *Azaan* was finished and I was going to be late for the prayer.

It was compulsory to attend midday group prayers at school.

I took my shoes and socks off and shoved the socks in my pockets, one in each. The back of my shoe poked into my heel as I slipped it back on and tiptoed awkwardly towards the taps, trying my best to avoid any further eye contact with the caretaker.

The prayer room was on the top floor. Water still dripping from my arms, I rushed up the grey stone stairs, pushed the shoes off, and walked in on the soft carpet barefoot, pockets bulging with balled-up socks. I found myself a spot at the end of a row and sat. Then I breathed. I was on time.

Our Islam teacher was leading the prayer. I could see the back of his head in front of the neat rows of students and teachers. The only person facing us was the guide, another student, who had the coveted job of reciting Arabic instructions, like a conductor. He was intently looking at the lead's lips. It was only when he recited a specific line that we were allowed to join in the group prayer. The speakers hissed with a distorted deafening beep as the overenthusiastic student tried his best singing voice. We all stood up.

With an Arabic phrase for each move, along the lines of "Allah is great, blessings," we bent and repeated prayers. As I got on my knees to put my forehead on the prayer stone, the graze on my knee scraped on the carpet and I flinched, but was careful not to turn my head or I would have broken my prayer. The squished spot at the end of the row meant, every time I prostrated, my hair was caressed by the toes of the person in front me. At the same time, my nostrils were assaulted by the sharpness of their smell. To endure it was another test by Allah, I kept telling myself. Focus on the prayer.

When it was my turn to be the guide, I was both nervous and thrilled. The responsibility of all the pupils' prayers rested on my shoulders. Were I to mispronounce an instruction, or—God forbid—forget one, all of their prayers would be ruined. I would have to ask for a lot of forgiveness. Our old caretaker, with his crumbs and creases, joined us that day. When I finished successfully, even he gave me a nod of approval. Maman will be so proud, I thought.

My grey-tinted memory is not just that one day, but many of them, blended together, one after the other. Cleanse, pray, conduct, repeat. My faith was becoming my identity. The sharia lessons continued after school as our way of life.

Full immersion.

Oh, and there were lessons, too: maths, geography, history, and Quran. The holy book didn't only have a class, it had its own competition, which I entered aged nine.

To be in with a chance of winning, I had to memorize the thirtieth chapter of the Quran, and I worked harder for that competition than I had for any other lesson. Maman beamed with pride. She sat with me for hours, correcting my pronunciations, helping me to practise my memorized verses. When Baba's friend saw me practising one day, he even nodded and whispered another "*Masha'Allah*," God has willed it.

But we needed a divine guarantee. I needed to pray for my success in the holiest of places. The city of Qom is home to one of the most important mausoleums in Iran—second only to Mashhad, where the Prophet's great-great-grandson was buried. We generally made annual trips to one or the other, but this time we made an unplanned trip to Qom just for me. Praying close to this heavenly source would not be ignored by Allah, and I needed his attention for my competition.

In Qom, I entered the main building of the shrine—someone related to a Shia Imam; I was not sure of the connection, and that was irrelevant, anyway—and I was overwhelmed with its grandeur, its holiness, and the condensed air. The doors were so tall, it felt like I was about to enter a giant's house.

I put my palms on the polished surface of the door. The coolness of it tingled my hands. I looked at my reflection as my breath misted the surface: big glasses, blushed cheeks, and black hair, which I had meticulously combed that morning, spending too much time in front of the mirror. I liked to imagine my hair was as long as Maman's and brush the pretend hair all the way down to my shoulders. It made me giggle.

A shove, and I came back to reality. A man gave me an angry look as he passed.

OK, here we go. Like everyone else, I kissed the ornamented door before walking in.

The vaulted ceiling inside the golden dome was decorated with mirrors and colourful tiles, all reflecting light from an enormous chandelier in the middle. And there it was: directly below the chandelier, the silver cage-like structure of the *zarih*, surrounding the grave. I was certain I could see light emanating from inside. The murmurs of worshippers bounced back from the walls.

Maman had gone to the women's side with Sina, who was young enough to be allowed in with her. I found Baba a few steps ahead and ran to hold his hand. Saman was sitting in the courtyard outside, on the ledge next to the water fountain where men cleansed themselves before they entered. At fifteen, disinterest in almost everything was becoming his thing.

I got myself to the *zarih* in the centre and clung tightly to the shiny lattice structure. Through the holes, I could see a deep green drape covering the tombstone, and a smaller chandelier with dimmed green lights was lit above it. I closed my eyes and whispered an Arabic prayer, and then, in Farsi, I begged Allah to help me win the Quran competition. I kissed the cold metal and joined Baba to offer prayers.

Winning the prize, another Quran in a shiny cover, was my greatest achievement to date. Prayers had worked. Maman was right. I knew then that, if I wanted anything, I had to go to Qom or Mashhad.

My mother told me the real prize would be given in the afterlife.

I wanted the *real prize*.

To cry, to mourn, and to grieve was promoted in the sharia I learned growing up. During my childhood, any happy event or party, even if it was for a religious reason, was associated with an inherent sense of guilt. Shia Islam's mournful history did not leave much room for celebrations.

The biggest and by far the most important example of this history is the tragedy of Ashura: the story of the Prophet's grandson. It falls on the tenth day of Muharram, first of the Islamic months. The Islamic calendar overlaps with the Persian one, dotting it with religious events, the purpose of which is higher than any date display. It helped us navigate our way to heaven. The religious events—Ramadan, Muharram, Haj, birth or death of this or that Shia Imam—always took precedence over the Persian events. Sharia always won.

In Muharram, no weddings are held or allowed for two months, and music is banned. TV channels become dominated by gloomy religious talks about the event.

1990, Ashura mourning day

My brothers argued over space next to me on the back seat. Maman, in her black chador, sat in front, tutting. My nose stuck to our car window; I felt it vibrate with each drum stroke.

BOOM. BOOM. BOOM.

I had started the day grumpy. I was nine.

"Get up." Baba's stern voice had left no room for argument.

Annoyed, my sleepy eyes had found the clock: six a.m.

"What? Why?" I'd said, with a moany voice.

"You know why. No time for games. Get your black shirt… Hurry up."

Ashura: the one holiday on which we were not allowed to sleep in or enjoy ourselves. Like a religious pub crawl, we were going to go from one mourning ceremony and speech to another, wearing black. This routine was repeated yearly, devotedly. The first *majlis* kicked off at seven a.m. and served breakfast. A *majlis* could be held anywhere—a mosque or someone's house. The itinerary was always the same: a religious preacher, followed by recitals of the tragedy and chest thumping. This one was at a big house belonging to another wartime acquaintance of Baba, now a minister.

BOOM. BOOM. BOOM.

I ignored Saman's elbow poking into my back as my brothers continued to wrestle. I was transfixed by the mourning carnival. They took place all around the city, closing the main roads. The one we were passing was large, with huge drums, and speakers playing loud musical recitations of the event.

Following the drums and cymbals, men of all ages were self-flagellating synchronously, flicking bunches of short chains against their shoulders, and behind them walked a long trail of mourners, thumping their chests together in time with the drums. It was like a dramatic mourning dance. I had done it before, but not in a procession as big as that one. It even distracted my brothers, who began imitating the chest thumps as they watched.

When we arrived at the first *majlis*, Maman went to the women's section, setting a time to meet us outside for the next one.

Breakfast was being served in the front yard. A long thin plastic sheet was spread on the floor and people were sitting around it, deep in conversation. A man walked the length of the plastic sheet, carrying a huge copper teapot in one hand and plastic cups in the other. When he stopped in front of us, I noticed his feet first, the hole in his sock, over his big toe. The sour smell of foot odour was mixed with the sweet tea aroma. I took a cup from him, and he poured the drink, the thin plastic offering little protection against the scalding liquid. Next, a barefoot boy served assorted cheese and bread on a plastic plate. I placed the plate and my cup where he had stood a second ago and ate my bread and cheese with tea. A moment later, Baba got to his feet, signalling that time was up. We followed him inside.

We passed the mourners one by one, careful not to stumble over them. Some looked up with bloodshot eyes, others had their faces buried in their hands, crying or asleep, it was hard to tell. The air was heavy with the familiar smell of rose-water spray and feet. We found a corner and sat on the floor. I gave an apologetic smile to the sweaty man next to me who I had accidentally kicked. He grunted like a walrus disturbed while sunbathing and looked away.

The story of the martyrs of Ashura was being retold by the preacher behind the microphone, as it was every year. The gory tale was meant to move us, make us cry, and the tears shed to open the gates of heaven. I should have known the story by heart by then, but somehow every year a new detail, a new anecdote, and a new tragedy was added.

I concentrated hard on the speech, desperate to get a tear out. I tried my best to imagine the scene: thirsty men in the desert, a newborn shot in the throat, heads on spikes, men with both arms and both legs chopped off, but still fighting (was that even possible?). I had to make it happen. The man next to me was now shouting, sobbing, and hitting himself in the head. The walrus had awoken. Perhaps he really did feel the pain and agony of what happened on that day a thousand years ago, even after the millionth time of hearing it. He was going to make it to heaven, and I did not want to be left behind. I was beginning to fear I was not pure enough.

Cry, damn it—cry!

When a drop finally formed in the corner of my eye, I had to try hard to disguise my joy. I was going to make those tear ducts work harder.

A *majlis* usually ended with the mullah reciting prayers into the microphone and the crowd shouting back, "Amen." We begged Allah for the "triumph of Muslims over heretics," the "reappearance of our saviour and deliverance by Mahdi: the twelfth Shia Imam, the saviour in hiding," the "downfall of America and Israel," and a few other chants. By then, the angels had descended and were mourning with us, purity being at its maximum. Prayers *would* be answered.

After my last loud "Amen," I followed Baba out. Everyone was now chatty and smiling, as if a show was over, heaven tickets booked and guaranteed. We were going to the next one for more tears.

I was going to be a good Muslim.

Did I know that, some fifteen years from then, my Ashura would look as different as it did?

Those memories will come.

Love Letter to the Sharia

1996

"What time will you come over, then?" Ali puffed into the phone.

"I'll offer my prayers and head over—say, twenty minutes?" I imagined him rolling his eyes.

"Fine, I'll do the same."

I hung up and quickly splashed my face and arms with water and wiped my head from crown to hairline—*vodhu*, ready for prayer. Becoming fifteen meant I could not skip prayers anymore. I couldn't do a lot of things. If I saw a glimpse of our upstairs neighbour's hair, an inherent feeling of remorse would descend on me. The punishment she was destined for was worse; women who didn't cover their hair in front of men would be hung from their hair in hell for eternity. No more looking, no more touching: all haram.

Ali had a religious upbringing too, although his family was more liberal than mine. I finished praying in Arabic as quickly as possible, got dressed, and went into Maman's bedroom. She was brushing her hair, sitting on her bed. The constant pressure of a cloth on her big hair had flattened the Afro over the years. A prayer mat was open on the floor next to the bed, like always; I suppose there was no point folding it and putting it away. She looked at me inquisitively. My mother's eyes always said more than her lips. Since last year, whenever she saw me going out, I could tell there was a tension, a strain in her look. She *had* to be careful.

"Where are you off to?"

"Ali's. I've told you."

The eyes softened instantly. "Oh, yes. Say hi to his mother," she said with a smile.

Ali's dad had known my father for over ten years. They were safe. Six months in. New school. New beginning.

A chance to change.

Later that night, after we finished the film, Ali lay on his bed, looking at the ceiling. "You know, you don't talk much about last year. Why *did* you change school?" he asked. His voice was soft, like his personality.

I leaned back on his computer wheelie chair and stretched my neck to relieve the uncomfortable tingle creeping up under my skin. "Does it matter? It was a shit school, anyway."

"No, it doesn't. It's just…don't you miss your old friends?"

Friends, I thought. Unintentionally, I gritted my teeth. "Nah, didn't get that close to anyone."

"Really? A whole year, without a friend?"

My eyes began to sting. A memory flashed before them, of *him*. I closed my eyes and breathed out. "That's right. I told you, it was shit."

Ali held his hands up, now sitting on the bed. "OK, OK. Whatever."

Ali was gentle, docile, and he had principles. Everything he did was scripted. He always looked out for others, earning the nickname "holy father" at school, which he secretly enjoyed. His round face, permanently blushed cheeks and chubby physique complemented his personality: a cuddly bear one would feel safe with.

I regretted my harsh tone instantly. "Sorry. I know how you and Saam have been friends for years. It just didn't happen for me."

Saam was my other new friend. Together, we formed a trio I felt happy, innocent, and safe within.

Ali smiled. "Which reminds me, you should stop laughing when Saam's teasing and tormenting others. He loves it when he has an audience."

"I know. But it *was* funny, last time." I grinned at the memory. "Even you were laughing, *holy father*."

Ali's lips trembled as he fought back his giggles.

Saam was a large boy with a plump face and a wicked sense of humour—not an entirely appropriate one, but nonetheless funny.

His eyes had this twinkle when he was up to no good. He laughed at his own jokes till his face was red and his eyes wet. He was loud: the opposite of Ali. The holy father was in a constant battle to stop Saam teasing other kids at school, tutting at every outrageous comment he made.

"My brother found a new girlfriend—the third one this year," huffed Ali. We were sitting in the school playground during break the next day.

"Another one? Have you met her? Is she sexy?" said Saam, taking another bite of his sandwich, a piece of tomato bobbing up and down at the corner of his mouth as he chewed.

"No, he rarely brings them home. Someone is always home."

"I can bring girls home. My mum doesn't mind."

"Sure you can, Saam. *If* you ever find one," said Ali, laughing.

"I'm not surprised about your brother, to be honest; he has the looks," I said.

Saam stopped chewing. I realized both were looking at me, Ali frowning and Saam with his mouth open, the half-chewed sandwich visible.

"What?" I said. "You know what I mean…his style." My face had become hot.

Ali gave a small cough. "I need to learn his tricks, one day," he said, his eyes still on me.

"Porn," said Saam, inflating his second chin somehow.

"He does not learn how to find girls from porn, Saam. Also, I hate it, anyway—it's too much."

Glad for the change of subject, I asked Saam, "Seen any new ones?" I was empowering the new me.

"Oh, yeah, do you want to see it? There is this girl with huge tits—"

"OK, OK. No, thank you," I said, with my hand held up and facing away. "Sounds amazing," I added. There was a temptation to watch porn, but my religious beliefs were stronger. I obeyed sharia, heart and soul.

Relationships were taboo in my household, and sex even more so. We wouldn't even mutter the word. I barely knew what it meant to have sex. The only subject which included girls or women was marriage.

A feeling of envy towards my friends was building up inside me. A pang.

I couldn't help thinking, Am I missing out?

1990, six years earlier

A purple-coloured memory, like the hyacinth on the *Haft Sin*,* tasting of salty nuts and smelling like the sea. It belongs to Nowruz** and to the south of Iran. This memory is like spring itself, a trigger for change.

I rolled down the window an inch. The hot and humid wind hit my face and beads of condensed water formed on my glasses.

"Roll it up, Majidee, or the A.C. won't work properly," said my uncle, driving. Adding a prefix or a suffix to everyone's name was his specialty.

He'd picked us up from the airport. Atoosa, my cousin, who was two years younger than me, was sitting next to me in the back, along with my brothers and Maman. Baba was in the passenger seat next to his brother.

Muharram and its tears over, we were spending another Nowruz at my uncle's in the south. I was glad the mournful month had not fallen on Nowruz. The Persian new year's celebration was one of the rare events for which no forced crying was needed. But the clash with Muharram would happen next year. There would be no trips to the south then. No celebrations.

Maman held the tail of her scarf up to her nose as we passed the fish market, another one of my uncle's favourite tricks.

"Breathe it in!" He laughed. "It's good for your lungs."

---

* *Haft Sin*—"Seven S"—is a spread with seven symbolic items, all starting with the letter *S*, each representing an aspect of life. It is a New Year's Persian tradition.
** Nowruz is the first day of the Iranian new year, usually 20 or 21 March.

I rolled the window up to avoid the stench. Too late. All of us kids made noises of disgust, and screamed, fuelling my uncle's mirth.

Atoosa, still too young to need to wear a hijab outside, had her dark brown hair tied in bunches, with a fluffy pink band on each.

She saw me admiring it and said, "Do you want to run your fingers through it? It feels nice."

I nodded.

She pulled off the hairband and handed it to me. I ran my fingers through her loose hair. The silkiness was like water.

"It…it feels so soft."

"You can brush my hair when we get home."

My excitement was difficult to hide, and Maman's tut difficult to ignore. She did not say anything, but I already knew I was getting close to the realm of harams.

Boys are religiously mature at fifteen, and not to obey the sharia from that age onwards meant burning in hell. I still had time.

At their place, not only did I brush Atoosa's hair, but she also let me play with her collection of Barbie dolls.

I sat on the floor, cross-legged, next to her. We dressed up a few, but the special ones were only hers to touch. She made up love stories between Barbie and Ken, and put their faces next to each other, as if kissing. I watched with my mouth open. Instinctively, I looked towards the door, making sure Maman was not watching.

Later, lying on my mattress on the floor, I took Ken and Barbie and looked at their permanently smiling faces. I replicated what Atoosa had done, a kiss on the lips. The buzz in my ears warned me how wrong it was. I pushed them away, shut my eyes, and smiled.

The next day, while the parents were out shopping, Atoosa called me to the TV room. She was flicking through the channels. They received Dubai TV, which was a world away from our two-channel state TV.

"Our favourite show," she said, her eyes on the screen.

I followed her gaze. It was an American soap with storylines of scandalous relationships between pretty women in revealing dresses and handsome men. Atoosa briefed me on all the characters and their various dramas. I gasped as the man on TV embraced his lover. Atoosa laughed.

My uncle's wife and daughters did not wear headscarves in front of us or anyone else indoors. They lived in a dream where men and women sat together at parties, women wore make-up, and on TV they touched each other and spoke in English. I knew it was all wrong, but it was also compelling. Satan was good at seduction. I *wanted* to stay there.

Back at home, we would return to our religious routines, abiding by sharia law. Islam was still very present, being carved into my life, shaping me.

"Why?" was a rare question in my childhood, and, if ever asked, the answer would be left to Allah's infinite wisdom.

1991, Ramadan

This memory tickles my nostrils with a warm cardamom smell and fills my ears with the soft hiss of the wall-mounted gas lamp. It is intimate, like an embrace from Allah himself as the calls to prayer reverberate. But it is a memory with a dark corner that taunts me.

I was ten.

That evening, Maman had made my favourite meal for iftar, for breaking our fast. Her *tahchin*—with that to-die-for golden brown crust on top, *tahdeeg*—had been tickling my nostrils and daring my faith all day. At the *sofreh*, Baba sat in his usual spot at the top, cross-legged, tapping on his knees. I could hear the grumbling orchestra of Saman's belly next to me, louder than my own. Dates, tea, bread, and cheese were already on the spread, teasing us.

"*Allahu Akbar...*" God is great.

The sound of the *azaan* from the TV was both melancholic and sweet. The golden dome of a mausoleum was on display on screen.

I broke my fast with a date, whispering Allah's name before putting it in my mouth. Maman, now an expert in Iranian dishes, skilfully turned the pan upside down to reveal the perfectly crusted rice. This masterpiece sat in the middle of the *sofreh*. My stomach acid was now burning my throat, eager to digest the food.

And then, total darkness.

"Again? This is the third one today," Baba huffed.

The power cut was yet another test sent by Allah. I heard Baba grunt as he got up to find the matches. The gas lamp provided not only the dimmed light, but also the constant background noise, like the whispering sound of praying angels.

I put the first spoonful of *tahchin* in my mouth. Finally.

The crunching of the *tahdeeg* released the flavours of saffron and turmeric. Before finishing my first serving, the room was filled with light again. The TV turned itself on, showing a bearded old cleric, in mullah gear, standing in front of a group offering prayer. A dull reality show.

"*Allah humma sallé alaa Mohammed va aalé Mohammed.*"

All of us recited the Arabic prayer out loud, sending our blessings to the Prophet and his family. I wondered if the Prophet Mohammed, sitting on his throne in heaven, receiving our prayer, was thinking, What is electricity?

Maman smiled and turned to Baba. "Let's hope we won't get as many power cuts tomorrow evening," she said.

"*Insha'Allah,*" replied Baba—if God wills it.

Maman repeated this under her breath.

Tomorrow was a big day: our annual iftar party.

We'd been preparing all week and, when the day came, our home was a beehive: Baba popping out to the shops every ten minutes, as something or other had been forgotten; Maman shouting orders left, right, and centre to us three and our maid.

I was not fasting that day, as still too young to need to. Plus, I was able to pick on the food beforehand and test Maman's cardamom rice pudding while still hot. I was proud of how I had arranged the *sofreh* in our living room, creating enough space for forty-odd guests to sit next to each other on the floor. Portions of dates, bread, and cheese were neatly placed on the spread.

As I ran up the steps to the living room, I heard my mother's shout behind me: "Majid, you haven't taken your shoes off! They are *najis*."

"They're not, Maman. I just went downstairs to grab the shopping."

"That is exactly why you should leave them outside."

Najis: the Arabic word which I feared.

Poo, piss, ejaculate, dogs, alcohol, non-Muslims, and many more things—all were *najis*. Touching any of them required cleansing afterwards. If, Allah forbid, I touched a dog, I had to wash my hands seven times with water and clean soil, whatever that meant, to cleanse them.

I took off my shoes, placed the bread on the *sofreh*, and rushed back out.

In the communal hallway, our upstairs neighbour's son was sitting on the stairs, hugging his knees. Three years older than me, we used to play on his Atari games console or in the backyard. He looked up and said, "Hi."

I quickly said hi back and walked past, knowing Baba was waiting for me downstairs.

I liked him. He had rosy cheeks and a sporty figure, and he wore large glasses. His mousy hair was parted at the side and a soft down had begun to show above his lips and on his cheeks. During our games downstairs, I sometimes hid his toys or didn't hand him the ball when he asked for it, just to get into a playful wrestle with him. There was no time for any of that today; the sun was setting, and hungry guests would start arriving soon.

Ten minutes before the *azaan*, almost everyone was there, sitting next to each other on the carpet. The air in the living room was heavy with stale breath, chatter, and laughter. A few of the women had gone to the kitchen to help Maman. She'd tied the hanging tails of her scarf behind her head, beads of sweat on her forehead. She was in her element, happy, excited. Some guests were washing their hands and faces to prepare for prayer before breaking their fasts, and children in our bedroom rummaged through our toy box.

The pile of shoes at the front door had become unmanageable. I knew guests would end up wearing each other's shoes on their way home, and I wanted to find my own to make sure no one walked off in them. Suddenly, I felt a push and almost lost balance. I looked up and saw the upstairs neighbour's son smiling down on me, mischievously. I straightened up and poked him back, then ran out into the corridor and up the stairs towards his flat, barefoot and giggling. He followed me. I kept running till I got to the roof. While trying to open the bolted door to our rooftop, I felt him against me, all of him, pushing and giggling.

I could have opened the door and kept the chase game going. But I stopped and turned around, and continued prodding him. Before I knew it, I was lying on the floor, face down, and he was on top of me, tickling.

Then it stopped.

We were both quiet, his rapid breath on the back of my neck.

His weight on top of me, pinning me to the dusty floor.

His hands gripping mine.

"*Allahu Akbar, Allahu Akbar.*"

The sound of the *azaan* coming from downstairs meant the feast had begun. Maman would be looking for me. I was supposed to be carrying the tea tray for guests. I didn't want to leave, and laughed between grunts to muffle the deafening sound of the prayer call. It was too late. He got up, shook his clothes, and, without saying a word, ran downstairs. I looked at my own T-shirt, thinking, Now, this is definitely *najis*, then followed him downstairs to the clink-clanking of plates and cutlery in our flat.

I washed my face in the bathroom, but could not wash off the guilt. Why am I feeling ashamed? I thought. Something was not right about our game, but I had wanted it to continue.

Maman called me shortly after and handed me the tea tray. I avoided eye contact. She will know, I thought. She will see it. I walked into the living room to the expectant guests. I gave a shy smile and held the tray in front of them, one by one. The thud of my heartbeat did not ease.

I saw him later that evening. I tried to resume our game by poking him in his stomach. He was not amused. He pushed my hand back and turned away. I stood still, wondering what I had done, beginning to believe I had unknowingly committed a haram.

There were many harams in the Islam I practised, and I mean *many*: seeing a woman's hair; eating certain meats, like pig; drinking alcohol; having sex before marriage; sodomy and masturbation; as well as lying, rape, and murder. All were haram.

The upstairs boy was approaching fifteen, that milestone of religious maturity. Perhaps what *he* had felt in that moment was a haram. He was at the age when his harams and halals would count.

Our games were not the same after that night—*he* was not the same. A switch flicked off.

Seeds of Doubt

1997

Damn, what time is it? Just ignore it, this time.

I pulled the duvet over my head, pretending nothing had happened. I screwed my eyes tight, but it was like the images were burned into my eyelids, flashing by in front of me. Put your hand between your underwear and pyjamas, I whispered to myself, worried my pyjamas would become *najis*.

You won't be able to pray like this; get up and sort it out. GET UP!

The voice in my head was too loud to ignore and the guilt had built up so much it was making me nauseous. I opened my eyes, stared through the dark at the ceiling, and took a deep breath. The images of my dream began to invade the black void again, dancing in front of me.

Sina's heavy breathing from the bottom bunk made me jealous; he was sleeping deeply, blissfully unaware of the disgusting thoughts floating above him.

I pushed away the duvet, the hair on my arms standing up as the steel chill swept over me. I shuffled quietly to the small ladder, making sure my brother's sleep and innocent dreams remained uninterrupted. My eyes adjusted to the dark as I made my way to the door, keeping my hand in my pyjamas, creating that most important barrier between my damp underwear and my pyjama bottoms.

Damn. That golden strip of light under the bedroom door meant only one thing: Maman was awake. Shaking off the temptation to go back to bed, I opened the door and stepped out of my bedroom. There she was, on her prayer mat in the middle of the TV room, in her chador, most of her face silhouetted by the small night light behind her. She looked up, still muttering prayers, and our eyes met for a split second. It was more than enough.

She knows.

She didn't break her prayer, looked back to the Quran open in front of her, and continued. There it was: shame, again, like an alarm sounding in my head, getting louder. I glanced at the clock on the wall: three a.m.

In the bathroom, I locked the door and quickly undressed, trying my best not to let my pants touch anything else. I dropped them in the sink and got into the tub, teeth chattering. I recited the well-rehearsed prayer: "I'm attempting to cleanse myself of this sin, to get closer to Allah." First, I rinsed my head and neck, then the left side of my body, and finally the right side, all while praying for forgiveness. Sleep was like a distant memory, but I yearned to get back into bed. Almost done.

Once dried and with my pyjamas on again, commando style, I tiptoed past my mother, who was still deep in prayer. I could feel her eyes following me as I got closer, making each step slower with an invisible force, as if I were walking in a swamp. I avoided her eyes and closed the bedroom door gently behind me, releasing a sigh of relief. Sina's quiet snores were an unexpected comfort to me. I tried to go back to sleep, hoping against hope that the dream would not return.

I knew the dreams were wrong. I knew they encouraged an evil sin.

Once the adrenaline rush settled, my eyelids got heavy, drifting me away to the quiet rhythm of night.

What now? How is this possible?

A real mess. Washing pyjamas was way more tedious. The duvet was damp, too. I clenched my teeth to keep the shout imprisoned in my throat. There was a bit of light, my bedroom clock showing five a.m. I had to creep to the bathroom again. Sina was still asleep, his mouth open, dried saliva on the corner of his lips.

At least I could offer my morning prayers straight after.

So another day began, one of many more to come. The dreams, which I had looked forward to just a few years back, were nightmares at sixteen. I had begun to have a sense of how wrong they were, although I didn't yet understand why or know where they came from. In my previous school, I had learned how to cleanse myself after one. If I forgot or felt too lazy to shower, I would not be able to offer prayers, which in turn made me fearful about Allah's punishment. The fire.

I hoped Maman prayed for me each time she saw my walk of shame towards the shower.

On more than one occasion, I cried as I asked for forgiveness from Allah. One drop of pre-cum and I was back in the shower. Five or six rounds of the cleansing ritual in a short period of time meant that, when I finally pulled the duvet over my sleepy head, it was with wrinkly fingertips. All of it for Allah to be happy with me again and allow me to pray in Arabic.

Maman always said that, when offering prayers, all attention should be diverted to Allah, every word meant sincerely. I barely knew the meaning of those words, but I tried. There were times when I put proper effort into it, taking my time, and feeling a sense of achievement afterwards.

A gradual shift in my religious practices was becoming apparent. More often than not, I offered prayers just to tick a box and get the job done, keeping the hellfire at bay. I was guilty of a few sins here and there, but was always quick to repent—I made sure my bit of heaven was secure. I made sure not to repeat my mistake.

The mistake.

1991, six years earlier

Three nights in Ramadan are super holy. It is believed, during one of these nights—Lailat al-Qadr, the Night of Power—the Quran was wholly spoken to Prophet Mohammed, and every year on that night angels descend to earth. Devout Muslims stay awake all night, praying. I was taught one prayer on that night equals a hundred at any other time.

The rituals were countless and, the more one did, the purer one got. Many other books of prayer were read in addition to the Quran itself. They came with their separate sets of instructions: during parts of the readings we stood, and for other parts we prostrated with our foreheads on the prayer stone. A Quran would be held on the top of our heads during the prayer. It was a religious dance, done in mosques; the music was an Arabic prayer, and the reward was heaven, with rivers of honey and milk and eternal youth.

Maman used to say, "Whatever you wish for on this night, as long as it is from the bottom of your heart, you will receive it." This was a promise the ten-year-old me held on to.

I finished the book of prayer. I read the Quran. I pressed my forehead on the prayer stone so hard it left a mark in the middle: God's words, carved on the stone, were imprinted backwards on my forehead. I squeezed my eyes tight, held my breath, and concentrated, begging and begging. I felt the words coming up from my belly, as my heart beat faster than ever. This was a prayer Allah would hear.

Maman sat by me later, her fingertips caressing the red print on my forehead. "What did you pray for?"

She hoped for something like "the good of the Muslims" or "good health," "a decent education" or "heaven".

Her forehead creased in an expression of amused concern as my answer came: "I prayed to Allah to turn me into a wizard."

It was my ultimate wish. Magical powers. To be able to do anything: fly, shapeshift, teleport, you name it. And, when I finally slept, I knew I really had nailed it. I do not think anyone in the history of mankind has prayed more sincerely than I did that night.

When, to my immense disappointment, I was not a wizard the next morning, my first thought was that maybe I had done it on the wrong night. So, I repeated all the rituals again on the other two possible nights, with great conviction and from the bottom of my heart. Still, nothing the next day, or the day after, or at any time since. That was when the first seeds of doubt were planted in my belief.

Sunni Muslims believe a different night to be the night when angels embrace us in their wings as we beg for blessings. I would be fuming if I ever found out Harry Potter was a Sunni Muslim who had prayed on the right night.

1992, last Friday of Ramadan

A memory pulsates my insides like the chants vibrating my eardrums, as intense as my small, clenched fist.

"Majid, hurry up, wear something warm…not that one…yes, that's better. Now, go get Saman."

On a mission, determination sparkled in my mother's eyes.

No excuses accepted. This was important.

I was eleven. Maman wanted to instil an ideology in our immature brains to instigate a passion mirroring hers.

Imam Khomeini had renamed the last Friday of the holy month Quds Day, "Jerusalem Day". We were going to the annual rally in support of Palestine and had to be there before the Friday prayer at midday. It was a pilgrimage we were not allowed to miss.

I pushed open the door to my eldest brother's bedroom. "Come, we're leaving."

An angry look and he pushed the door closed in my face. Saman was turning out to be a grumpy teenager, his behaviours more erratic and his attitude withdrawn. I did not like stepping on his toes. We never spoke that much about anything, and, as we got older, the gap only seemed to widen. I ran back to the front door, where Maman stood impatiently.

"Can we take two mats, this time?" I asked. Last year, the upstairs neighbour and his son had bumped into us at the event, unprepared. They had taken most of the space on our mat, and I ended up sitting on a newspaper on the wet asphalt.

"Take what you want, but we're leaving—now. Where's Saman?" she said.

I shrugged. "In his room. I don't think he's coming."

Maman shot an angry look towards his bedroom door and told me to wait in the car with Baba and Sina. Minutes later, Saman shoved himself next to me in the back seat and slammed the door. I knew he wouldn't win, not on Quds Day.

Once close to Tehran University, where the Friday prayer was held every week, Baba parked on a side street. A big mural of the Ayatollah smiled down from the wall next to us.

It was time to join the procession. Young and old marched purposefully together, some carrying flags, some banners. Some had headbands with religious chants written on them, as if going to war. On these special Fridays, all the streets leading to the university were closed for the march. As soon as we joined the crowd, the chanting began, led by a guy with a megaphone.

"*Allahu Akbar!*"

"Death to America!"

"Death to Israel!"

"Free Quds!"

I shouted with the others, my fist clenched, punching an invisible Uncle Sam in the air. Sina chanted too, but Saman just walked with his hands in his pockets. Maman looked proud. She shouted with us at first, but eventually left us to go to the women's section. After all, the last thing we men wanted during a prayer was the devil tempting us to look at women covered head to toe in chadors. I longed to find out what happened in that section where we were not allowed, that pool of sin.

After the march, during which we had walked over the Israeli and American flags, we attended the prayer led by one of the regime clerics. He gave a speech immediately afterwards, which went on for an hour and was mostly a rant about the miserable state of the world, all because of the great Satan, America, as famously named by Ayatollah Khomeini.

I sort of understood the idea of an "occupied Palestine," but a hate was being embedded in my mind, firmly aimed at America and Israel.

So Ramadans and Muharrams came and went, but so too did trips to the south, and to Turkey to visit Maman's family. With these trips came more doubts, seeping in through the chinks in a tight sharia armour.

A touch of the Western world was influencing me in ways I did not realize at the time.

1997, five years later

At sixteen, I was still following religious routines, though too liberally for my parents' liking. I saw more of my cousins when they came to Tehran, listened to Western music, and paid less attention when offering prayers. But drinking alcohol was such a huge sin that I did not dare entertain it.

Ali, now my best friend, shared my beliefs, and I was happy to have him by my side. Over the years, my faith had lifted me to a moral high ground from which I looked down on the weak and sinful—an elevated position which made me feel safe. I automatically despised people who drank. I was above them in Allah's embrace, although it no longer felt as warm as it used to. The moral high ground was becoming wobbly as my horizons broadened and temptations became wilder.

Thanks to Atoosa, my cousin, I now had a selection of Western pop songs recorded on a cassette. Inevitably, with any unruly behaviour came a nagging feeling of guilt, like an itch on my back I could not reach. I had begun to ignore it, perhaps even enjoy it a little. My mum and dad did not approve. Listening to provocative music about un-Islamic relationships between men and women was haram.

"Get Down" by the Backstreet Boys became a favourite. Under my duvet, lying in bed, I played it repeatedly on the small cassette player. Bedroom door shut, I would lose myself in the sensual lyrics, letting the lust drown me, blunting the crawling guilt under my skin. If my parents walked in on me, I'd immediately stop the music and hide the player.

It was all about to change. The religion, the innocence, were about to take a hit. I was about to reopen a door I had closed shut two years ago.

Same year, Ankara

That look. Those lips. Those eyes. A memory with an unforgettable face, both a nightmare and a dream.

Another annual summer trip to see my mum's side of family. It was a different trip, this time—only us children and Maman.

Baba was in Mecca for haj. His name had been on a waiting list for two years and finally his turn had come—or, as Maman said, "He's been called." It was the ultimate Islamic ritual to visit the Kaaba, literally Allah's house. Haj was not a holiday one just booked, but a duty, a must.

And so, it was only us in Ankara—Maman's solution to dampen her envy.

It was mid-afternoon. The grown-ups were having a siesta, and I was enjoying the variety of TV channels, flicking up and down.

On MTV, I stopped—a second too long.

My finger on the remote control paralysed, my eyes became hypnotized by his. Piercing blue eyes and an innocent but cheeky smile. The way he looked seductively at me and showed his tongue lustfully as he said "love".

I felt my pulse bang in my ears.

Heat filled my chest. Who is he?

I read the title of the song before the end of the video: *"Love Sensation by 911"*. Another look at him and he was gone. I waited, hoping it would play again. It didn't. I must record it, next time.

From then on, I made excuses to stay home, and skipped family reunions. I sat by the TV, waiting, prepared to capture him on a VHS tape, and, when I finally did, he was mine.

Now, I knew his name: Lee. I lost count of the number of times I watched the video, rewinding and playing it again, pausing the screen at the right moment, when he was looking up at the camera, looking at me, and I'd stare back.

Could I ever meet him?

I didn't know what to do. I had a desperate urge to be close to him. A TV screen in Ankara was as close as I could get, and time was against me.

Counting the days I had left with him before we went back to Iran turned into an excruciating torture. I had to ingrain his face into my memory, somewhere safe. When our last day arrived, I ran to the TV room to see the music video one final time. My heartbeat fluttered on my temples and behind my eyes. I could hear Maman's chatter with her sister at the door, both laughing. I entered the room, only to find my uncle on the sofa, his feet up, watching the news on TV.

He glanced at me and smiled. "I'll be coming in a second. Just checking the football results."

I shuffled from one leg to the other, staring at the video cassette on top of the VCR player. Please, please, please, let me see you once more.

I took a step forward, standing next to him now, looking blankly at the TV. The reporter was looking back, speaking in Turkish.

"Majid, come on! The driver is here," called Maman.

No, no, no. Please.

With a grunt, my uncle pulled himself up, grabbed the remote, and switched off the TV. I gasped a half breath and took another step towards the screen, but his huge body blocked my view, and then he was hugging me, tapping me on the back.

"Come on, young man; your mother is waiting."

I looked over his shoulder at the tape, where I was leaving Lee. My eyes filled with tears.

My uncle, holding me by the arms, was evidently touched. "Ah, we are not going anywhere. Stop with these tears, Majid. You are a strong man. A strong man does not cry. *Masha'Allah!*" And he gave me two hard taps on the shoulders.

I made an incomprehensible sound, imitating laughter, and walked out with him.

When we returned to Tehran, I became withdrawn, as if I had suffered a true loss. I missed that sting of desire, of being close to his 2D face. The joy, the excitement, the guilty pleasure. The new feeling was like a fog expanding in my head, numbing my senses, obscuring logic and sanity.

A week later, I was awoken by an unmistakable squeal. At first, I thought I had dreamed the loud *Baaaa*. It ripped through yet another dream of Lee, where he was sitting in our living room, singing.

"*Baaaa.*"

I looked out of our bedroom window. A flocculent sheep was tied to the railing in the backyard, looking as confused as I.

"They brought it an hour ago," said Sina from behind me.

I kept my nose stuck to the window. "For Baba," I whispered, as Sina joined me. Baba was coming home from haj that day.

"What'll happen to it?" he said.

I looked at his round face and sleepy eyes; he was still in his pyjamas. I slid my index finger across my throat and stuck my tongue out from the corner of my mouth.

Sina winced and looked back to the animal.

"Sacrificing an animal for a haji is tradition," I said, feeling guilty. In Iran, religion justified it.

"Can we go down to feed it?"

Knowing sleep—and, with it, Lee—had long gone, I agreed. We took some lettuce from the kitchen and went into the backyard.

As I fed the animal and watched her jaws grind together, I whispered to her: "You know, you ruined my dream. Lee, the boy I love, was here." The thrill of saying the words hit me like a high I had not felt before.

Her gaze locked with mine and, for a second, she stopped chewing. Big black eyes. The hairs on my neck stood on end. Then, a swallow and another loud "*Baa.*" I shook my head and smiled to myself, passing the lettuce to Sina as I got up.

Back inside, Maman was fixing her scarf in front of the mirror.

"Going out?"

"Yes; I need to kill some time and that animal won't let me sleep. Just for a walk in the park," she said.

I could tell it was not the noise that kept her awake. Her eyes were beaming, her fingers fidgety. She was excited.

"Can I come, Maman?"

"Yes, yes—be quick, though. We don't have much time."

I returned to my bedroom for a change of clothes, smiling to myself. Today is a happy day.

It was unusual for the two of us to go for a walk together, but Maman had perhaps sensed my despondence. As we left, we looked up at Baba's welcome banner erected in our street, gently dancing in the wind. Maman smiled and hooked her arm in mine as we walked. We chatted about unrelated, trivial matters, even cracking a joke now and then. She told me how our upstairs neighbour had sorted out delivery of the sheep, and she laughed as she described the hassle of moving the animal into the backyard. There was an intimacy between us that I had not felt for years, since back when I used to bury my face in her chador to breathe in her scent.

Gentle winds rustled leaves on big old plane trees, as if they were in a heated conversation among themselves, muffling the sounds of cars honking on the streets nearby. I looked at my mother. Her eyes were soft, with only a few extra smile wrinkles at the corners. The scene was set.

I told her about the music video, sounding casual, using the same tone she had used when talking about the sheep, hands in my pockets and head down, kicking a pebble.

"…I really like the video."

She stiffened, just a bit, but was still calm. "Oh, that's OK. Well, you can see it again next time, maybe."

I was not sure if she meant it. Was she deliberately being liberal? The welcoming and warm nature of her response burst my flimsy casual bubble and my emotions poured forth. "Maman, I love him!"

It had slipped out of nowhere. I'd let my guard down and opened the door of the closet a crack. The seal broken, the monster smelt freedom. It grabbed the opportunity like a rabid animal and spoke for me. Hell, it shouted for me. I wanted the world to know. It had convinced me love is love and I could love anyone, without any dirty thoughts—right?

Wrong, actually.

My mother was silent, which on its own merit was a rarity. Her faith had transformed her into a vocal woman, her voice always rising above others to make a point—her point. But now she was silent out of shock, wires having short-circuited in her brain.

With her silence, everything else seemed to go silent for a moment, too. I could imagine sparrows and ravens turning their heads to see if they had heard right. The wind stopped blowing and the trees stopped their whispers. All of a sudden, the world seemed to close in on me. I shivered with fear.

Maman pulled away her hand. I wanted to grab it again, as if I were falling into a bottomless pit. Maybe my feelings were wrong. But how could that be? I had been so sure of how pure they were, or rather *it* was sure.

I composed myself, almost pleading for an affirmation as I said, "It's OK to love anyone, right? Not anything bad or dirty, just…just love, like a friend, or…or family."

But it wasn't like a friend or family member. I knew it wasn't, and she did too.

"You shouldn't be thinking like that about men, or say those words about a boy," she said, her voice serious, her eyes worried. "It is not right. People will think differently, and you need to be careful about how you express your feelings, even if it feels like a friend."

Of course I was wrong. I should have followed my gut when it warned me that something about my feelings for Lee did not fit. And now I had let Maman know. I had let her down, let myself down, opening that bloody door. I had to forget the stupid video.

"OK, OK. It's just a silly video, anyway," I said, blushing with embarrassment.

She sighed and looked away. "Don't ever say anything like that again, do you understand?"

I only nodded, biting my tongue. I wanted to ask what she was thinking or try to rectify the damage, but it was already too late.

I had said the *L* word, about a boy.

Now, I had ruined a memory. If memories had colours, hers would have been white, serene. Not anymore. I had violated it with an ugly stain.

For the walk back, she didn't hold my arm. Her smile wrinkles disappeared and the warmth in her eyes was replaced with worry. She whispered one last word under hear breath, in Arabic: "*Astaghfirullah.*" I seek forgiveness from Allah.

I had underestimated the impact of confessing to that feeling. What I perceived as an innocent love was in fact dirty and shameful. The stony look was the worst. It reminded me of something. It had a meaning. Concern, disappointment. I could not put my finger on it, at the time. I had seen that look before, but not on her.

A few hours later, Baba arrived.

On the street, I stood behind family and neighbours, only seeing Maman's back, in her floral chador. I inhaled deeply, hoping for a bit of that smell to warm my nostrils and ease the ache in my chest.

Nothing.

The only person facing me, on the other side of the street, was the butcher, in a stained apron, sharpening his knife. Next to him was the clueless sheep, still straining her vocal cords as if preparing for an opera. If only she knew these *baa*s were her last.

The sheep's final calls were muffled by the cheers, *Allahu Akbar*s, and the clapping as my shaved-headed baba stepped out of the car, wrapped in the typical haj attire of a white robe. The knife struck her throat and a crimson river flowed on the asphalt. People cheered again and I stared into the big black eyes as life left them—the eyes that had not judged me when I confessed to her.

Her faithful hoofs continued to kick, still trying to get her away from danger. It was too late.

That night, the familiar look I had not been able to place came back to me. How that dream was different from the night before.

His face appeared, penetrating through the cloak of black. The look, a reminder of shame.

I had promised it wouldn't hurt me again: the head teacher's face, within inches of mine, in bed, his eyes beaming fire, unblinking. I shook my head to get rid of the image. The shrieks of a dying sheep surrounded me. I tried to push him away. I kicked and kicked. But, like those of the headless sheep, my kicks were futile. He was there to stay. Lee was truly gone.

A Stir Within

1995, first year of high school
A year hard to forget.

"It is white." Dramatic pause. Stroking his messy beard, he continued, "You may feel pleasure when it comes out, or it may only wake you up in the middle of the night."

I could tell from the despair in his voice that he only experienced the latter. Our Islam ethics teacher was a young, bearded, bony figure, with a white, long-sleeved shirt, which he wore untucked and buttoned all the way up to his neck. Cool. The class had been gathered for that extra lesson at school. I sat next to Milad, giggling.

The hip Islamic ambassador carried on: "It is *najis*, and to do anything to facilitate it coming out is unnatural and haram."

Ah, the message: another *najis*, another haram, another sin Allah would be testing me with. I had no idea what he meant by "facilitate".

"If it happens in your sleep, this is how you must cleanse yourself…"

And he taught us what I would become an expert of: the midnight showers. I was only half listening, at the time; I was busy drawing a new cartoon for Milad.

1998, three years later
I was nearly seventeen when Saman's behaviours made an unpredicted shift. His tantrums, his angry rebellious attitude— all took a dramatic turn. From listening to Madonna cassettes on repeat to *that*.

A new school friend introduced Saman to his mentor, a sharia guru who looked like a textbook Islam teacher from school: young and slim, with a messy beard and a prayer-stone mark on his forehead. He spoke in a calm tone, a godly one. He was on a different level, his path purely a religious one. Having been taught Shia Islam in Qom,* his recruits—young men like himself—circled him like moths in awe of his halo. I struggled to understand what the appeal was. I wanted to rummage through my brother's head to find answers; something in him had changed.

Something had been killed.

Saman was slipping away, being drawn into this dark hole. He became a recluse and grew a beard. A *Tasbih*—an Islamic rosary bead—replaced his cassette player, and the words of Allah replaced Madonna's lyrics.

The change was welcomed by our mother. I, on the other hand, was slipping into a different black hole. The religion's grip was tightening around one son and loosening on the other.

Technology, a potential threat to one's faith, was always a struggle to get hold of in our household. It took energy and time to convince Baba to get a VHS player, and later a computer. A pinhole was being opened to the outside world, but not only for me.

Iran was changing. Those of my generation were called the "children of the revolution." We were desperately trying to get up to speed with the rest of the world. Our new Islamic regime had to move swiftly to keep up, to adapt, and to keep everything Islamic. Dial-up internet was becoming available. Filters needed to come in, and quickly.

1995, first year of high school

I'm not done with this memory yet, and it may never be done with me.

"Can you draw me another one?"

I looked at Milad, surprised. "I just gave you one—plus, you can draw good ones yourself."

---

* The holy city of Qom is where Iran's religious clerics are made. It is not far from Tehran, in the middle of a desert.

"Not as good as you." He held up my cartoon: a girl, hair loose over her bare shoulder, big eyes and dark lips, smiling.

I *was* good. The cartoon girl's dress was minimal; Milad wanted it like that, and I enjoyed designing clothes. I had drawn a deep cleavage, open to her belly button, and one of her long slim legs was showing through an exaggerated slit in her dress. I was pleased with my creation. I was pleased that he liked my work. I was fourteen,

"OK, OK—I can do another."

A smile spread over his face, pushing up his rosy cheeks speckled with a few spots. "Can you . . . can you make the dress sexier?"

"Sexier than that?" I laughed.

"Yeah, this is good, but maybe more skin?"

I tilted my head, looking at my drawing. "Hmm, maybe. I can do something here, perhaps?" I pointed to her other leg, which was covered.

"Yes, that would look nice. So, tomorrow, maybe?"

"Sure."

Pleased, we went into class.

At fourteen, puberty was creeping in and had revealed a disobedient side to me. Milad was now my best friend and, with him, a new notion became appealing: secrets. They strengthened a bond which felt everlasting. We talked about subjects which were taboo in my household: girls, sex, porn. Well, he talked and I listened, occasionally tutting. He was from a far more liberal family than mine—one similar to that of the boy next door from years ago.

My secrets were my drawings. Girls with bare skin—who, in real life, would have been bound to burn in hell—were dangerous territory. My mum and dad would have been livid if they'd seen the pictures, but my best friend was different. Milad had begun collecting them. It was flattering.

He did something else, too.

He brought a monster to life.

1998, three years later
Sex.

A huge taboo.

A grave sin.

When we watched uncensored Western films, we fast-forwarded any sinful scenes. They included kissing scenes, nudity, and of course sex. A sex-scene rule was "stop and fast-forward." Saman was in charge of the remote control, protecting us all diligently. I didn't complain; I believed it to be the right way.

Titanic had been released. Having heard so much about the blockbuster, I was quick to borrow it from Ali, unaware that it was not a film for our household. Watching it with my family was a tense experience and I hated it. I felt there was too much sex and obscenity for a film depicting a tragic event, and I found Kate Winslet's nudity shocking and appalling, believing she would have a lot to answer for in the afterlife.

Later that night, once everyone was asleep, I crept back into the TV room. I closed the doors and sat a few inches away from the screen, which was the only light in the room, the sound on mute. I put the tape back in the VCR. I swore as the machine made that damn whirling noise swallowing the tape. I checked the doors were shut and no sound was coming from behind them.

I fast-forwarded it a few times to get to the right bit. There: Jack opening the car door for Rose, who pulls him into the back with her.

A hand appeared on the steamed window, leaving a print.

Jack was sweating. He was panting.

I watched it all with my mouth open. I pressed rewind, looking around, making sure I was still safe. I watched it again, and again.

I was now in love with Leonardo DiCaprio, but this was not the innocent love I'd had for Lee from 911. There was something very wrong with this love. I was turned on. A guilt-tainted lust. I couldn't stop.

A few days later, I saw the picture at a news stand: pursed lips, messy hair, and innocent eyes. Leo's face was on a film review magazine. The next thing I knew, there was a cut-out picture of him in the desk drawer in my bedroom, hidden under books. I looked at it every day, and my imagination ran wild. He was the first of a few to sit there. The desk drawer turned into my shrine for hot men.

I followed the 1998 World Cup closely with the rest of my family. I supported England, all because of one person: Michael Owen. Another crush.

After the tournament, I started following every Liverpool football match to see him, often recording them on a tape to look back at his best moments.

Unlike Lee, Leo, or the rest of them, I was not going to allow our TV screen to be the only way I saw him, creating that impenetrable barrier. I needed to act.

A letter, or—even better—a card, with a picture of Persepolis. How could he not be interested?

I spent hours in gift and card shops, on a mission to find the perfect picture of the historic site.

Next was the main problem: what to say?

I sat at my desk one day, pen and paper ready. I started imagining his reply to my as yet unwritten letter, then mine to him, and then the thoughts took off, creating an exhilarating whirlwind in my mind: we would exchange telephone numbers, talk on the phone, then I would invite him to my home, and he'd agree, he'd visit me, here, in my bedroom.

I stopped there.

Then what? What would I do when he was here?

I didn't know. I just wanted to be friends with him. That was all I was thinking of—friends. Wasn't it? I smiled at the thought and looked at the piece of paper in front of me.

I started, **Dear Michael**...

After practising my handwriting and writing several drafts, I was ready to transfer it to the card. I sent the letter to Liverpool

Football Club, the only address I had for him, hoping it would find its way into Michael's hands. Slipping the card into the post box, I prayed. I asked Allah to get this letter to my crush and get a reply, and then the wait began.

A few months later, my prayer was answered—sort of. Lots of colourful brochures arrived. Not exactly what I had expected, but I was still excited. I read them carefully, one by one.

And there it was: a letter, addressed to me. **Dear Majid**...

OK, it was not written by Michael himself, but someone had done so, someone who may have seen him or knew him, or at least they had signed it. I read it again and again. It was from the Liverpool FC fan club, an invitation to join. I begged my father to pay and let me join.

Among the various leaflets was a small one advertising a Michael Owen wall calendar. Next, I was begging Baba to buy that. I bet he thought, *This is sweet, he is into football*, rather than, *He's into footballers*. After another few weeks of waiting, it arrived. I put my nose to the glossy cover and breathed in. It smelt cold and foreign. It was Michael.

The best bit was it did not belong in my drawer of secrets. His picture was going to be hung on the wall.

From then on, when I offered my prayers in my bedroom, it was not the Grand Ayatollah watching me, but a topless Michael Owen.

Not quite what I imagine my father or Allah had in mind.

The Breeze of Change

1995, first year of high school
"Sissy Majid."

I turned my head to look.

I cursed myself for doing so. I had promised myself, next time they called me that, I'd ignore them. *That is not your name.*

They stood there, giggling. One held his hand near his chin, bent at the wrist, his lips in a pout.

I hated myself for the smile I brought to my lips forcefully. I was in on their joke. It *was* a joke, wasn't it?

As I turned back to join the queue, a whiff of aftershave stung my nostrils.

"Ah, Majid. Be careful," the principal said, as I almost bumped into him. His lips were smiling, eyes rigid.

I stood frozen for a second.

He was wearing his usual neatly ironed white shirt, his top button undone, unlike the ethics teacher. His smooth, silky hair was combed perfectly to one side, a few strands loose on his forehead. His tap on my shoulder broke the trance. "Your class is starting, get in the queue."

"Yes…yes, sir. Sorry I bumped into you like that…"

He'd already moved away, getting the rest of the pupils in line, like a flock herded by their sheepdog.

As I waited to go into the classroom, I was thinking hard about how I'd deal with the name-calling next time, how I would tell them to stop. Had the head teacher seen and ignored it?

Then I felt it.

A hand brushed my bottom.

I stopped, unable to move. It must have been accidental. My brain was getting good at lying to me. It can't have been an accident, though. It lasted that one second too long. I had to look.

He stood behind me, smiling. Tall, slim, wearing tinted glasses, he had greasy hair and wet lips, the corner of his bottom lip between his teeth.

Who is he? I had seen him in our class. There he was, confidently looking in my eyes. I half opened my mouth as he winked at me and walked away. My mouth remained open. I hoped Milad had not seen that. This was a secret *no one* was allowed to know.

I wanted to be angry and say something, because I did not, I should not, want that mysterious desire to be there.

Or did I?

As the queue moved into the class, I lost sight of him and sat at my desk with blushing cheeks and a troubled mind.

1998, three years later

Tehran: traffic, pollution, bling, poverty.

My city.

The rich and the poor were divided by a social and financial gap—no, an ever-growing crater. The partition was also a geographical one. Southern Tehran was home to people of lower socio-economic status and poorer education, whereas north Tehran was posh, sparkly, and with big blocks of extravagant flats, and Western-style detached houses with big gardens. There was a middle class somewhere in between; however, the majority of the population fell into either the upper or the perceived lower class.

The Iran I grew up in was a classist society. It was ingrained into our culture.

Baba had made a name for himself. He worked hard, and his wartime friends and connections had helped. We lived in north Tehran, among the more privileged minority. I did not notice it; it was the only way of life I knew. A bubble. We had a maid, an old lady who came twice a week to clean and cook, and another woman who came every two weeks to iron shirts. I knew little about how or where they lived, taking them for granted. People who I saw so often were invisible. The comfort I was used to in that bubble, however, was not replicated in my religious life.

Maman was obsessed with being seen as open-minded, progressive, liberal. She wanted to show us how Islam was in no way limiting, that Allah was open-minded and welcomed all. But her nervousness around my uncle's family, Atoosa and her sisters, was palpable. My uncle and his family had moved to Tehran a few years back and we saw more of my cousins. I noticed Maman's exaggerated laugh and how she would suddenly be busier than usual in the kitchen when they were around. But she always made her opinion known, one way or another.

"Hijab protects both women and men against the fire of hell," she used to say, followed by another artificial laugh. She was worried for her sons' afterlife.

Saman, on the other hand, limited his relationship with our cousins. He did not play the game of "pretend to be liberal" and risk a sin in doing so. He kept his eyes on the floor, avoiding their uncovered heads: the Devil's arrows, meant for his eyes.

Every time he looked at the carpet to avoid these "arrows," I felt more irritated. I could not help but remember how different he was just a few years back, laughing with our cousins, sharing secrets. What *was* that "something" that had shifted?

My cousins vented their frustration on me.

"How dare he?"

"Who does he think he is?"

"We gave him *our* Madonna record, and now this."

I had already started twisting and moulding my faith to my liking, creating a version of Islam I was comfortable with. I convinced myself that it was not Islam that was a problem, it was Saman's wrong interpretation of it.

A memory smelling of aftershave and sweat, and stamped with defiance. It brings a smile to my lips and a flutter to my chest.

"I like the pink one better," I said, leaning on the door frame, arms folded.

Atoosa was trying on the third lipstick that night. She sat cross-legged on the floor in front of a small mirror in my bedroom. A ziplock bag lay open beside her, a spectrum of colours smudged all over it, as if a miniature paintball war had happened within. A clutter of make-up brushes, pencils, powder palettes, and small bottles of nail polish encircled her.

She looked up at me and blew a kiss. "Really? I prefer the beige. Classier." She winked.

At fifteen, she was getting prettier every day. She had long black hair with big waves, brown eyes, and a petite figure with budding breasts. Atoosa was already exploring the dating scene, and I felt privileged to be in on the secret tales of her exploits. She had another one, that evening.

Although a premarital relationship was against the sharia law and haram, it did not stop boys and girls finding a way around it. If there were no clubs, bars, or social media, there was traffic—a lot of it. Certain streets of the city had become cruising grounds. Boys and girls drove up and down the same street for hours, flirting, exchanging numbers, and chasing one another. A mating dance. That's how Atoosa had snatched up a boy, and, after a few telephone calls, it was time for the real date.

I was learning the art of seduction.

"Can I come?" I whispered the words, worried about her reaction. I wanted to share the thrill in person, to at least witness someone else flirting with a boy.

She frowned, applying more blush. "No. What would he think?" There was a hint of entertaining the idea in her voice.

I sat next to her immediately, pushing aside eyebrow pencils and lipsticks. "Just say we're going somewhere else afterwards. I promise I won't talk. Promise."

Her concerned look turned into a mocking giggle. "Well, OK. I suppose it's fine, as long as you're quiet." She shrugged. "Be ready in ten minutes, and wear something nice."

I got up and walked to my wardrobe in disbelief. She agreed! I'm going on her date!

And then suddenly I remembered: "Can I offer my prayers before we lea—?"

Her fiery glare stopped me. "Forget it. You can come next time. I'm already late."

Is Allah going to rob me of this opportunity? I thought.

I looked at my small prayer mat folded in the corner, then at Michael Owen's picture on the wall, his mouth half open, leaning on one elbow, three shirt buttons undone and his chest glimmering through.

Never.

"No, no. I'll repay the prayer later. I'll get ready now."

Atoosa shoved all the make-up back in the bag and got up. "OK. Wear something nice," she repeated, and left the room.

I stood still for a minute, breath held, chest thumping.

A few hours later, I sat quietly on the back seat of his car, my hands between my thighs. It smelt of cigarettes and spicy aftershave. Atoosa's date had been doubtful when he'd seen me waiting with her, eyeing me up and down, but it seemed her pretty face and beige pout was not something he wanted to give up on. So, there I was, my cheeks hurting as I kept up a forced smile, hoping he could not hear the flapping in my chest.

I looked down at my shoes, toes touching and heels apart, like an upside-down V. Atoosa laughed at his jokes and he stretched his arm behind her seat. He had a skinny arm, his T-shirt sleeve pushed up. I could smell his deodorant mixed with something sour. He tapped his fingers behind her seat like a drumroll, hesitant to make the next move. I could see the soft hair on his arm. I wanted to touch it, to feel his skin. He gave me a sidelong glance. Can he see what I am looking at? I wondered. I bit my lower lip and resumed staring at my shoes, thinking, Please don't read my mind.

They finally said goodbye with kisses on cheeks, and he turned back to me. "Nice to meet you too, Majid." He extended his hand and I looked at it for a second before shaking it. His skin was soft and his palm sweaty, his handshake firm. That was the touch I was jealous of. That was what I wanted more of. I couldn't help wishing he would kiss my cheeks, too.

At home, having created a modern version of Islam for myself, I began a covert mission of transforming our way of life. This required patience and politics.

Each time I brought a friend home, as they entered our living room, I could see how they paused for a second, taking it all in: the Qurans and the religious Arabic books on the bookshelf, the framed verses of the holy book and the pictures—*those* pictures. On our living-room wall, there hung not one, but two pictures of Ayatollah Khomeini. As soon as my friends saw all this religious memorabilia surrounding them, a judgement was passed. Something needed to be done.

One day, a few weeks after accompanying Atoosa on her date, I stood in front of the picture, staring at Khomeini's face: those extra-long bushy eyebrows dangling over his eyes in a frown, those pursed lips surrounded by an unruly white beard, and that gaze, which seemed to be challenging me: *Don't you dare*. Looking away, I lifted the frame from its hook, keeping as much distance between myself and the picture as I could, as if worried he may bite my face off. I had not planned where I was going to put the picture. It could not go in the bin; that was a step too far. I left it in the gap between the chest of drawers and the wall. Once hidden, the empty outline on the wall where he had resided for the past nine years looked clean, new. Chuffed with myself, I glanced at the other picture. You're next, I thought—and, with a smile, I left the room feeling lighter.

The next day, I thought of something to fill the empty space on the wall. But, as I stepped back in the living room, I instantly froze.

There he was, on the wall again, as if he'd never left. I blinked twice in disbelief. His face…Was he smiling? Looking around to find an explanation, it hit me: my mother. Of course, it was never going to be easy. The ensuing anger reinvigorated me to finish my mission. I picked the picture up, this time staring straight in his eyes as he went behind the chest of drawers again. *You won't win.*

This cycle was repeated a few more times before he finally stayed down there, behind the heavy wooden drawers, his replacement being another framed verse from the Quran. At that point, Maman could not decide which was holier. A victory, still. On the day I put up the framed Quran verse, I'd looked at the other golden-framed picture of the Ayatollah. "You can stay," I sighed, and left the room.

After months of arguing, Baba agreed to buy a cheap set of second-hand sofas and chairs for the living room. Guests would no longer have to sit on the floor against the kilim cushions. We still ate on the floor, around the *sofreh*; however, guests would now use our dining table—the same dining table which had served as a shelter during bombings, years ago.

We bought a computer, and with it came games and, later, internet. The fortifications of the sin-proof household had been breached, and unwanted intruders were sneaking in.

I still attended the pro-Palestine Quds Day rally on the last Friday of Ramadan, and went to the Eid prayers with my family, but I didn't want to, and would make any excuse to get out of doing them—mostly unsuccessfully. Saman, on the other hand, did not miss any of them; he was at the door before everyone else, with his *Tasbih*. The gap was widening between us. And Sina, my younger brother, was still too young to have the curiosity to do anything different.

I also skipped a few prayers now and then, and sometimes I forgot to pay them back and repent. I no longer cleansed myself immediately after every wet dream, leaving it till the morning or even after school, which meant I was not able to pray at school either. The ensuing guilt was inevitable, but I made little effort to change my behaviour. I was starting to get fed up with religious routines.

I was first introduced to online chat by Ali, with Yahoo! Messenger. The idea of being able to chat with someone on the other side of the world was incomprehensible. Messenger had chat rooms for different continents, countries, and different interests. We could chat about computer games and other everyday hobbies with someone in America or Europe. It blew my mind.

I started checking out other chat rooms, specifically for Asia. It was surprising how the biggest continent in the world had chat-room participants that were mostly from one country: Iran. Yahoo! Messenger was a massive platform, with different rooms—like a night club with different floors for everything, from teenage pop dancing to chill-out zones—and all the participants were Iranian. That was where my imagination gave birth to my online persona.

With Atoosa, I began chatting up guys online, as a girl. She was excited about our little online adventure and didn't mind that I was more enthusiastic than she was. It was my chance to experience flirting with a guy, first hand.

Sending pictures online was a big step, and it almost never happened. Most people at that time did not have a digital camera. Our way around it, to keep our subjects interested and keep them drooling, was to use a fake picture.

With our dial-up internet, after waiting for thirty minutes and staring at a screen where a picture was being downloaded, line by line, I finally had a black and white picture of Natalie Portman. I drew a scarf on her head, for dignity. She wasn't as famous back then, and certainly not in Iran. They fell for it. Credit to Natalie, she was attractive even with a hijab on.

I played that game online for a few months, but when guys started insisting on meeting up with Natalie Portman in hijab, it had to end.

So, I stopped, or rather I moved to other chat rooms, where my eyes widened and my jaw dropped.

The Ayatollah and the Violin

1995, first year of high school

One memory which keeps resurfacing.

The queue incident was playing on my mind. I now noticed him, even from across the school playground. I saw him all the time, consciously keeping a distance from him. I buried myself in schoolwork, made sure I spent every break with Milad, and kept drawing.

I needed the distraction from him, from that wicked desire.

He had only been testing the water. A few weeks later, our queue was heading into class when it happened again.

"Hi, darling," he whispered in my ear, in a hiss. I could feel the dampness of his breath as he got closer.

It wasn't his hand this time. He was pressing his crotch against me.

I moved myself forward to create separation, my breath held, and, without looking back, I replied, "Hi."

He closed the gap, pressing harder, and I felt his breath on my ear again, the warm blow of his long exhale.

I pushed the boy in front of me in a panic and quickly found my seat, pretending to do work in order to avoid making eye contact with him. He stood still. I could see his lustful stare from the corner of my eye. I wasn't going to look up. I wasn't going to let him take this any further.

I was scared.

Not of him, of that feeling.

Did I enjoy it? Did I want it to continue? Was I attracted to him?

I was already thinking of how I would have to beg for forgiveness when I next prayed. I should not have let these sinful thoughts roam free in my brain, smashing up all my beliefs like a child having a tantrum.

1999, four years later

I changed school again for my final year of high school, the pre-university year. Unlike the first time, this was only because my high school did not have a programme for students who wanted to apply for medical school. Since that time four years back, I had not had a major slip-up. And now I had made friends who would remain friends: Ali and Saam.

The new school was not as religious as my previous one. Midday prayers were not compulsory, only recommended. I attended them mostly, occasionally taking the conductor role. At the end of that year, we had to sit the dreaded university entrance exam held nationwide. To fail that exam would bring shame upon one's family.

I was almost eighteen. I needed to do something to create a distraction from the mad exam hype.

"Baba, could you and Maman go out for my birthday, so I have the flat to myself?"

The unsettling question made him switch off the news on TV. Maman, on her way to their bedroom, stopped and took a few steps back.

"Why?" Baba's voice was gentle, his eyes scanning me.

"Well, I want to invite my friends for dinner. I want us to have the freedom to go wherever we want in the flat, nothing crazy."

"You can do that anyway; we don't need to be out. We'll stay in our room," said Maman.

My parents always kept tabs on who our friends were, but since four years back, they'd been more particular about *my* friends. I wanted to reassure Maman.

"It's different. I'll tell you who will be coming, and Ali and Saam will manage guests."

Maman was sceptical. "What do you think?" she said, looking at my dad.

After a long-drawn breath, he said, "I don't know. I don't mind. Don't do anything silly." With that, he got up and left the room.

It was all I needed. Maman stood there, looking at me. I shuffled my feet.

"Eight to ten people, maximum," I said.

"From your class, right?"

"Yes, where else?"

She took a deep breath and smiled, finally. "Fine."

I quickly went to my bedroom and sat behind my desk to write the names: friends, acquaintances, and my latest crush. He was a friend of a friend, a classmate—he *had* to be there. I had barely spoken to him, but his coy smile and the way he ran his fingers through his brown hair were seared into my brain. The list was only an excuse to write his name among invitees, right in the middle.

The day arrived. My parents got dressed up, ready to leave the flat. Maman had cooked dinner for us, so all I had to do was serve it. Baba was sitting in the TV room as I stood watching impatiently, waiting for the news to end. My guests would be arriving at any minute. As soon as it was over, I coughed to grab his attention.

Maman answered for him: "I need to offer my prayer before we leave."

Flustered, I clenched my fists and left the room, and then the bell rang.

Too late now.

Baba pretended he didn't know what the time was and looked at the intercom in surprise.

"Just stay, it doesn't matter anymore," I huffed, and pressed the buzzer.

One by one, they arrived, wearing their best shirts and aftershaves. I asked them to take off their shoes, then guided them to the living room, where they were welcomed by the stern Ayatollah and all the rest of it. I could not differentiate between a look of surprise and one of disappointment. My new friend came with his friends. A trail of aftershave and desire followed him as he walked past, tugging on my belly like a leash.

We sat in the living room in a circle. The pleasantries over, a silence was filling the room.

"Majid, where are the girls?" one of the guests finally asked.

I laughed at the obvious joke. When I saw he was still looking at me, confused, I said, "Errr, there are no girls; we are all here."

"Ah, OK—silly me," he said, and chuckled nervously.

I glanced at my crush. He exchanged a look with the other guest, shrugged his shoulders, and they both laughed. My smile disappeared. I got up and went to the computer, swearing under my breath—at the Ayatollah, at the religion. Ali came and stood next to me, put his hand on my shoulder, and squeezed. When I glanced up, he gave his usual calming nod, with a hint of a smile on his lips.

I did have plans to jazz the night up—if not with girls, then with some traditional music. I had asked one of my friends to bring his violin along, and he was pleased to oblige. He even brought a stand for his sheet music. He fiddled with his instrument for a while, tuning it, and eventually played us some traditional Iranian music. I had asked that he play something happy, but there was only so much he could do with a violin. Baba joined us for the performance. I was proud, sitting in that circle, listening to him play. Happy eighteenth birthday to me.

I lost touch with the classmate I was attracted to—or rather, he slowly distanced himself from me. Looking back, I don't blame him.

Years later, eighty gay and trans people were jumping up and down to Rihanna's "Don't Stop the Music," off their faces, in our villa outside Tehran. That memory will rectify this one.

My final year at school ended with the long anticipated and frightful university entrance exam. I cannot remember how many prayers I offered before the exam. And it worked: Allah listened, and I was accepted to medical school.

Back then, career options were dictated by social norms and family preferences. What job will make my family proud? Which one has a higher social status, or makes more money? These were the main questions, not, What am I interested in?

And so, in autumn 1999, medical school began. This was the first time I would be sharing a classroom with the opposite sex, and I would do so for the next seven years.

There Are Others

1995, first year of high school
I knew how to avoid him now. His stares, accompanied by his saliva-smeared grin, didn't stop, but they became easier to evade. I made sure Milad stood behind me in queues always, my protective bubble. He was the best friend I had always wanted, my confidant, and he continued to collect my cartoons with enthusiasm.

The change of vibe between Milad and I was unexpected, but I convinced myself it was innocent. That it was natural.

It was break-time and we were walking around the perimeter of the school playground, on the asphalt, as we usually did, when my hand brushed against his.

He held my little finger first, then I felt the stroke of his thumb over the back of my hand before he interlocked his fingers in mine, giving them a light squeeze.

No discussion. Not even a flinch. I looked at him. He was walking with his usual slight hunch and talking in his usual nasal voice, looking ahead. I did the same, smiling.

From then on, to *not* hold hands was weird.

Our chats took us to my favourite cartoon on TV: *Little Women*. Yes, the famous *Little Women*, dubbed in Farsi and the storyline changed to cut all the sinful bits. I followed it religiously. Unlike the little girl in chador, drying dishes for her mum, in the Iranian cartoon I had watched when Tehran was peppered with Iraqi bombs all those years ago, the March sisters seemed to belong to what really was the perfect family, in my opinion.

"Which one would you be?" said Milad, his palm against mine, a smile spread across his wired teeth.

I could have said, *I don't know what you mean*, or, *I don't want to be any of them*. I could have said, *I'm a boy*.

I smiled back. "Betty."

Just like that, we had created a secret, letting a part of me loose in public for everyone to see.

He kissed my shoulder and whispered, "My little Betty." The countless spots on his face—some about to pop, some already scarred—were protesting the new intruder rushing in his blood: testosterone.

Now I spent every break with him. When I handed him a new drawing, he would take my hand and kiss my thumb, his eyes droopy, staring through his eyelashes from above his glasses. "It's beautiful, like you," he'd whisper. It gave me butterflies. I had found a *boyfriend*.

The feeling did not last long, soon replaced by an unfamiliar ache.

A month later, it had somehow become more difficult to get hold of Milad alone. I often found him in animated conversations with other boys.

He was laughing with someone else again. I was across the yard and couldn't hear him, but there was a pang of jealousy within. Milad looked up. I waved, excited. He looked away, as if he had not seen me. I walked towards him.

"Hi." I gently kicked his shoe.

He looked up, surprised. "Oh, it's you. Hi. What's up?"

I winced at the cold reception and sat next to him. I put my hand on his knee, close to his, waiting for him to clasp it. He didn't.

"Is everything OK?" I said.

"Yeah, sure. Why wouldn't it be?" he said, with a fake smile. Then, as if getting back in character, he winked at me and gave me a tiny peck on my shoulder. "My little Betty. See you in class?"

He got up, my hand dropping from his knee. I watched as he walked away, hands in pockets, hunched. Something began to feel heavy in my chest. My best friend, my boyfriend, was holding back something. Had I upset him?

Deflated and annoyed, I went back to the empty classroom and sat at my desk. When he sat next to me, I didn't look up.

"Having fun?" I said, with venom in my voice.

"Why would I, darling?"

I held my breath. It wasn't Milad. I looked at him: the messy hair and tinted glasses on his grinning face. He put his hand on my thigh and squeezed.

Where is Milad? I thought.

The boy then took my palm in his and clasped it gently.

"The class will start soon," I said in a hushed, broken voice.

He didn't say a word. His fingers between mine, he moved our hands to his crotch. I felt his erection with the back of my hand, which he was now rubbing against it.

I only looked at him, thinking, Milad wouldn't want you to do this, Betty.

The sound of the bell made us both jump. I pulled my hand back and he got up. When I looked over at the classroom's door, I saw the back of our principal's head. I took a deep breath and looked at my hand.

1999, a few weeks before first day at university

When I walked into my bedroom, I was not expecting to find Saman sitting at my desk.

He was flicking through my photo albums and did not look up.

I rushed to my desk drawer in a panic, thinking, Has he seen my secret collection?

The edges of the magazine cut-outs were sticking out from under another book, still safe. The relief allowed me to breathe again. I shut the drawer.

"What are you doing?" I asked.

"Just looking at your birthday-gathering pictures." He turned another page. His tone was matter-of-fact, flat. He barely seemed to have noticed me closing my drawer or my flushed face. His *Tasbih* was on the desk.

I looked at the pictures, the night of the violin and the Ayatollah.

"Who is this?"

I followed his finger. He was pointing at my crush. In the picture, he was leaning forward, his elbows on his knees, and looking at the camera with a lopsided smile and a wink. I remembered taking the surprise picture. I remembered my fake laugh.

"Majid?"

"Oh, him…Erm, school friend—well, kind of…We were friends then." I felt I needed to find an explanation for him being there.

Saman was not listening. "He's good looking."

I coughed. *What?*

He flicked to the next page and paused on another picture, where he was laughing with others. I did not say anything. After a few moments of silence, I started tapping my fingers on the desk. It was either that or the *Tasbih* next to my fingers that brought him back. He shut the album, picked up the beads, and stood.

Something had been killed.

A memory flashed before my eyes—a name, a boy: Payam.

How could I have forgotten?

I could not breathe. Payam had been Saman's best friend. He was all Saman had talked about for a while. My brother even had a T-shirt of Payam's somewhere in his room.

Saman's drastic change had happened when his new religious friend came in as Payam went out, deleted.

As Saman was leaving my bedroom, I finally spoke: "Do you…? Do you still see…your friend…? What was his name…? P-Payam?"

He stopped, but did not turn to face me. His left hand was counting beads. "He was not a friend." And he walked out.

I stood there and looked at the closed door. I swallowed to relieve the pressure in my throat, and then put the album back in the drawer.

Something *had* been killed in my brother.

*

University: *The best years of your life.*

The words echo in my head as the memories of my university days flow in. It's what everyone said. It was a promise I was looking forward to when I stepped through the gates.

I get it. They can be one's best years. I saw how they were for others.

But my religion had planted barriers in my way that I could not overcome. It held me back from mixing with groups of friends who partied, had girlfriends, drank alcohol, and enjoyed those years.

Oppressed youths exploding with defiance let loose at underground house parties, where girls wore heavy make-up and tiny skirts, alcohol was sourced illegally through a black market, and, at the risk of being busted by the police, they leapt around to haram Western music.

I wanted to mix, but a voice inside me would make me stop and rise above the sin. The other problem was the unruly desire inside me, now louder than before. The monster in the closet. The secret which I struggled to define or understand was getting harder to contain. I did not want my peers noticing it.

University brought along some freedom and independence, and, although it was not much, it still made a difference. In a classroom where girls and boys sat separately, hormones ran wild. Guys flirted left, right, and centre. It was a new, exciting chapter in many lives. And so it was for me, just in a different way.

I noticed him on the very first day of uni.

Pouya was tall, with light brown eyes like milky tea, tanned skin, and a full head of thick black hair, neatly gelled into what were supposed to be messy spikes. He could be described as "touchy-feely," always sitting close enough so there was a point of contact, whether knees, thighs, or arms. His handshakes always lasted a second longer than necessary, and, when he withdrew his hand, it stroked mine all the way to my fingertips. A sensual tingle was associated with every touch. Is he teasing me? I wondered repeatedly. Or is this just how he is with everyone? I settled on the latter—it was easier—and so I decided to ignore him and my feelings of temptation as best as I could.

His handsome face had not gone unnoticed by the girls. It was difficult to miss how they looked and giggled as he walked past—or was it only me who secretly noticed the competition?

No, not my competition; I'm not one of them.

I had to keep focus on the main task: finding my own girlfriend.

*

This memory is a tiny light in a void of black, like the computer screen I was sitting in front of. It is like wedging a crack open in a sealed box, click after click.

It was an autumn evening.

I had been getting better at Yahoo! Messenger, and was exploring other chat rooms in the Asia section when I came across a room on the list: *Gay Asia*.

The name flickered on the screen: *Gay*.

What went on in this room?

I moved the little white arrow over it. Although sitting alone at my computer, I looked around instinctively. It was just me and the Ayatollah.

Gay Asia was only a click away.

Maybe next time. I moved the cursor away and released a sigh. I signed out and leaned back, stretching with my hands behind my head, lost in thought.

Then, in a panic, I immediately signed back in, thinking about my saved history on the webpage and on Yahoo! What if what I have done is logged somewhere? It took a few minutes before I realized how paranoid I was becoming. I turned off the computer and went to the kitchen.

Maman was adding the final touches to her famous *fesenjoon*. I stood next to her, watching the dark brown stew bubbling away, releasing that mouth-watering pomegranate and walnut aroma.

"Looks delicious," I said.

She laughed. "We'll have some tonight, but it will be even better tomorrow," she said, proudly.

Transfixed by her slow stirring, my mind was still two doors and a few steps away. I looked at her satisfied face, desperate for a distraction.

"Is there something—?" she began.

"No, nothing. Can't wait to eat that." I turned around, knowing she was still looking at me, and quickly left the room, closing the door behind me.

Sitting back at the computer, I stared at the screen as I waited for it to load, one hand in a clenched fist on my restless leg, the other sweaty on the mouse.

Yahoo! Messenger, chat rooms.

Click.

Romance. (Really?)

Click.

Gay.

I paused for a second.

Click.

There it was: *Gay Asia*. The voice in my head said, *Don't think, just do it.*

Click.

And I was in.

I could not believe my eyes. More than forty people were there—people like me, sitting in front of their computers. It was like a busy train terminal, men entering and leaving. The common chat platform was buzzing with messages. I could read and understand what was being written—it was Farsi, or rather *Penglish*.* I checked the name of the room again: *Gay Asia*.

Is everyone here from that one country in Asia? I thought. My country? Are these men closer than I think?

A question spiralled through my brain: How many of us are out there?

---

* Penglish: Writing Persian with the English alphabet.

My face was almost stuck to the monitor, reading every message carefully, when Maman's voice from down the corridor made me jump: "Food is ready!"

"Coming!" I shouted back, and signed out.

As I walked down the steps, there was a warmth in my chest. I will be back tonight, I thought.

I could not enjoy the *fesenjoon* as much as I'd hoped. I didn't care about the food anymore, or my favourite TV series that night. I kept looking at the clock, conscious of how slowly the evening was progressing.

Finally, just before midnight, when all lights were out, I returned to the computer. Logging in again, I knew other men in many households not far from mine were also in front of their screens, chatting in this wondrous virtual world.

My first private message opened a new window: **Hi, ASL?**

Excuse me?

Bye.

I had no idea what that was about. I closed the window, confused. I needed to learn the lingo, and fast. I knew I wouldn't get much sleep that night.

A part of me wanted to share the news with Ali and Saam. But I reminded myself what had happened the last time I trusted a friend. This would remain a secret.

Chatting turned into my pastime activity, day and night. Sometimes, when woken up at night by yet another unwanted dream, after showering, and if my mum was asleep, I would go online. It was not risk-free.

I learned ASL meant "Age, Sex, Location," and my answer was: 20, m, Teh. The next scripted questions came one after the other: Where in Tehran? and so on. No pictures were shared. Instead, we described ourselves in a blind interview. I asked, Height? Weight? Eye colour? Hair colour? Glasses? Beard? Moustache? and then imagined what they looked like, and they did the same for me.

I was like a child in Disneyland for the first time. The gay chats were like a drug with a high I wanted to be addicted to.

After a few months of chatting to many guys, I mustered the courage to take it a step further—to meet one of them.

We had already sent voice messages on Yahoo! a couple of times, ascertaining that we were both men, at least. When he brought it up the fifth time, I agreed to meet him. Online, we set a date. He told me what he would be wearing, head to toe, and I told him the same. My blue rucksack was what I told him to look for. I was going to see him after class.

We were all set. My first ever date.

The day arrived.

My anxiety kicked off from the moment I opened my eyes in the morning. After my morning prayer, I went online hoping he had left a message and cancelled.

He hadn't.

I could cancel.

I don't need this, I thought. What am I going to do afterwards, anyway?

I hovered the cursor over his ID and clicked, opening a window. The icon was grey: he was offline.

Salaam. I'm really sorry, but I won't be able to make it today. Hope you see this message before leaving.

I read over the drafted message. It was civilized. I'd save myself from the stress, from the sin. But the other voice in my head started speaking: *What is the harm? If you don't do it now, when will you? Stop being so scared.* I closed my eyes, took a deep breath, and closed the window. I would see this through.

I could not concentrate in the classroom for one second. My conversations with classmates were awkward, their voices only whispers playing at the back of my loud, rampant thoughts. For once, I was hoping not to run into Pouya lest his infectious charm dissolve my resolution. I could still just go home and forget it all.

Once class finished, I went to the taxi stand, where drivers stood by their cars, each shouting their destination. I still wasn't sure whether to go home or meet my date. Some taxi drivers had a few people in their cars already, waiting for it to fill up. I glanced at my watch: twenty minutes till our date. I looked up at one of the drivers with a smile.

"Vanak?" he asked.

It was near where my date was. This *was* my ride. I couldn't bring myself to say "yes," so I only nodded. He pointed to his car, three people sitting in the back already. I sat in the front seat, hugging my rucksack tight, pressing it against my chest to quieten my heartbeat. The cloud of doubt descended on me again: What am I doing? This time, it was much louder than before, and in an alarming tone.

I went for the door handle to get out, but it opened from the outside and a mammoth figure of a man shoved himself next to me, squashing me on to the driver, who got into the car at the same time. After the second attempt, the huge man banged the door closed and turned to me, smiling. Is he the Devil in human form, I wondered, blocking my escape? I gave a crooked smirk back and looked straight ahead. It was too late now.

I muttered a few Quran verses on the way in an attempt to calm myself. We were supposed to meet outside a shopping mall. Once out of the taxi, I quickly made my way to the other side of the road, opposite the mall, and sought refuge in the busy afternoon crowd. I sniffed my shirt, worried that the obese Devil in the taxi had left some of his sweat on me. Every passing person's face looked familiar, all staring. A friend, a relative, an acquaintance. What if they see me here? I thought. What am I going to tell them? Though there could be a million reasons for me to be there, I knew I would fall short of excuses. *I* knew why I was there, and I wouldn't be able to hide the shame with another lie.

I looked across the crowds, trying to make him out, scanning people walking out of the mall. Then I spotted him, standing right outside the main entrance. A slim figure with sunglasses, scruffy stubble, and...wait, is that a ponytail? It was then I realized that describing yourself online and leaving the rest to the imagination was not ideal.

There he was: a gay man, someone like me.

People were walking by without noticing him. I was the only one there who knew his secret. I could go and say hello, have a milkshake perhaps, and then leave. Easy.

Someone like me...The thought repeated itself in my head. *Am* I like him? I wondered. Do I *want* to be? It scared me.

He was looking at his watch now; I was late.

I started walking in the other direction, only a few steps, and then I turned back. I should say hello. After our many chats, all I could see now was a stranger with a ponytail, on the other side of the road. I was standing right opposite him.

He looked up. Shit.

I can't do this.

The blue rucksack. It was too obvious.

He knew he was looking at me, his date.

He crossed the road.

I turned around and started running.

I didn't know why, I didn't know where to.

I ran without looking back, bumping into a few passers-by as I went, repeatedly saying sorry.

Once a few blocks away, I stopped and cautiously turned around, panting. He hadn't followed. A sigh of relief and I hailed a taxi towards home.

I don't need this. I don't need him.

The messages left on Yahoo! Messenger afterwards were not pleasant, and I guess I deserved them.

Parallel to this online life, I carried on being straight at uni and at home. I did not lose sight of the true mission: a girlfriend. It was the thing to do at university, the rite of passage, and it was what would fix me.

I had a fling with one of Atoosa's friends at the beginning of university. My cousin hooked us up. She was pretty, had an infectious laugh with an endearing snort escaping now and then, and she was not religious. I could call her home and ask her mum to put her on the phone. Her mum would even sometimes ask how I was. I, on the other hand, had to call her from a telephone booth at the end of our ally. A premarital relationship was haram and a recipe for other sins to follow. If my parents found out, I'd get an earful, followed by, *When are you going to marry her?*

Our relationship went as far as holding hands once, for five minutes. It lasted no more than a month or so. She was smart enough to realize early on that she wouldn't gain much from a relationship with this boy, and she was more than happy to call it a day, each going our own way. Only, I didn't know where I was headed.

I could not focus on my mission until I had locked away my other thoughts and desires. It was time to deal with the monster.

Keep Hyde Hidden

1995, first year of high school
I was ashamed to say anything about my encounter in the classroom to Milad.

Not because of what had happened.

But because I had enjoyed it.

Now, every time I looked at the back of my hand, the thought of what it had been pressed against evoked an uncomfortable yet thrilling stir in my belly.

I was guilty. I had *cheated* on Milad.

Next day, while walking in a circle in the school hall with my head down and remembering the event in a loop, I felt a thud against my shoulder.

"Oh, hi. Sorry—didn't see you there." Milad's cheeks were red, and beads of sweat shined on his forehead.

"Hey, are you OK?" I said, rubbing my shoulder and smiling.

"Yeah, yeah, I'm fine. Sorry about that." He pointed to my shoulder.

"It's fine; how many times are you going to say sorry?" I said, with another laugh, poking him on his shoulder. I looked at his hand hanging limp by his side. I wanted to reach out and hold it. *I* wanted to apologize.

He saw me looking at his hand and quickly put both his hands behind him.

My heart sank. Does he know already? How?

"Listen, I need to go. Catch up soon?" he said, gleefully. The fake tone did not help.

"Oh, OK. Yes, sure. Do you want any more drawings, by the way?"

Already a few steps away, he turned. He forced his lips into a smile. The corner of his mouth was trembling. He wasn't looking at me, though, but at a point behind me. I followed his eyes. The head teacher was standing in the doorway to his office, wearing a grey suit over that white, ironed shirt. I turned and looked at Milad quizzically, wondering, Is he in trouble?

"Sure, sure. Chat later," he said, and he left, rubbing his forehead, or was it his eyes?

I turned back again and met the principal's gaze. Dark and serious. He smiled and gave a courteous nod, the unruly strands of his hair falling over his forehead. He was good looking. Something about him unsettled me, though, something made me look away, as if to avoid a needle pricking my eyes. I gave a half smile and walked away.

I was worried for Milad. I had been so obsessed with myself and my secret, I had forgotten about him. His absence. His coldness. My gut twisted.

If I lost Milad, I would lose everything.

2000, five years later

The new millennium had begun.

Iran was changing. Boys and girls my age were generating a gradual shift in culture, religion, and dogma in their favour. I, unknowingly, had become part of that movement.

I had been to a few parties with Ali where Western music was played and people danced. At some, alcohol was even served in a different room, where it was less obvious. Mixing with girls without their hijab, and dancing—although I was terrible at it—was exciting. The fact that those parties were illegal only added to the thrill.

A new gap was forming in society, one that had perhaps always been there, but was becoming more vivid. People who were devoted to Islam, or pretended to be, were benefitting from the biased system. Frustration was building up in those who felt discriminated against, the non-religious, a frustration not only with religious people and the regime, but with Islam itself.

The murals of martyrs and ayatollahs on the walls of the city were beginning to fade. The cracks in them mirrored those in the society they looked upon.

There were now daily reminders of the tight grip religion had on our lives: it was an unwritten law that men had to have a beard as a sign of devotion to Islam; those who had a connection, no matter how distant, to somebody who had been in the war—or, even better, had died a martyr in the war—gained advantage over others when applying for a job.

I often wondered how it would have affected us if Baba had used his tokens—war, beard and friends—to his advantage. How it would have affected me. He got the offers, to be head of this office or that, but he declined and kept his friends only as friends. Our upstairs neighbour was different. He had ascended the ladder and had become a deputy minister in the government, and he was not going to stop there.

In a country which was rebuilding after a horrific war, money talked. The gap between the rich and poor widened and, in the abyss, corruption grew.

Traditional values were cherished. Families lived together until children were married off. Jobs awaited only those people who finished university, and, if someone had brownie points—beard, prayer-stone mark on their forehead, and connections—they had much better job prospects than their peers, jumping the line.

Ali was the observant one of my two best friends, analysing everything around him and putting everyone in well-defined boxes. He used to say my father was like the Godfather. He looked after his family, but his words were final and to be obeyed. Maman laughed when I told her this, but didn't disagree. So, we lived under the same roof, counting on our pocket money, given weekly by the Godfather.

"If you get a proper degree, your future is guaranteed," Baba used to say.

Saman was the first in line to be sent away. He hated the idea of going to the land of harams, America. "Send me to Qom, instead," he insisted. The city in the middle of a desert. The city of mullahs, religious clerics. But he could not change the Godfather's ruling and was sent to America to do a master's.

On the evening of his departure, I went to Saman's room. He'd gone to the mosque for one last prayer in the house of God. His bedroom was a corner of our home I'd rarely visited since he was a teenager. Being in his room felt like crossing a red line. It felt wrong.

I looked around: two huge suitcases in one corner, a desk with a few Arabic books and a Quran on top, his messy single bed, and a prayer mat open in the middle of the room, just like Maman's. The curtains were drawn and the air heavy with a faint scent of rose water. The walls were bare and the wardrobe door ajar. This was unusual; my brother normally kept it locked.

I looked inside. It was almost empty—just a few shirts hung from the rack, light blue to beige. I was about to close it when I noticed the white sleeve of a T-shirt poking out at the back. Saman had stopped wearing T-shirts several years ago, saying, "It is more Islamic for men to cover their arms," or something like that.

I pushed the shirts aside.

There it was: a white, neatly ironed polo T-shirt hung there. I felt the fabric.

"Payam."

The *friend*. No longer one.

The memory had been killed, *almost*.

As if touching a hot iron, I pulled my hand away and closed the wardrobe door. I looked around, worried someone else might have seen it. I felt it was a secret that *had* to be kept like that, at the back of a wardrobe. I left the bedroom before he came back and avoided eye contact when he got home.

A few hours later, he was gone. His bedroom remained the same, minus the suitcases and the prayer mat.

With Saman gone, life became a little less intense at home. No more constant reminders of religious occasions, no more telling

Maman if a strand of hair dropped out of her scarf, no jumping at the remote control in panic, and no loud praying. He had been the guardian of sharia law we did not need. The quiet was welcome.

Gradually, with the internet, with parties with Ali and Saam, and in university, I was getting a glimpse of the Western world and endorsing it.

Online, I didn't leave everything to the imagination any longer. I dared to share a picture of my face on Yahoo! Messenger a couple of times, and it was reciprocated by others.

Another step forward: I had mustered the courage to meet up with a few guys for tea or a drive. It was not as bad as I had feared. They appeared normal, with ordinary lives. I had never let a date progress to a second one, or anything else. Not even a kiss.

Going online, chatting, and meeting up was not guilt free, but I persuaded myself that it was just a phase. I wanted to get it over and done with. I needed to draw this lingering chapter to a close.

Atoosa was the first to show me the video.

Red latex suit, long hair swept back off her face, and lips glimmering while singing in her typical nasal voice, Britney Spears had me glued to the TV screen. She brushed her tongue on her upper lip as she sang, just as Lee from 911 had. But, whereas I had wanted to be *with* Lee, I wanted to *be* Britney. At the time, though, I felt the difference was negligible.

I borrowed Atoosa's tape and secretly watched the "Oops! I Did It Again" video at home on repeat. If Maman had found out, I would have had another lecture and potentially the VCR taken away. But, with Saman gone, I was getting bolder. So, until that moment came, I was going to watch it again, and again.

The video offered a flicker of hope: if I liked Britney, perhaps I would like other girls too. Perhaps I could end the phase.

Living a double life, one pulling towards Britney and redemption, and the other tempted with virtual escapades and dates with men, was becoming my normal.

At university, sitting next to Pouya in the classroom when our knees or shoulders touched and neither pulled away was like a drug I could not get enough of. The warmth of his skin trickled through me and travelled all the way to my chest. Despite all the distractions I planted in front of me, despite Britney, the urge in my head was getting stronger.

But my solution, a girlfriend, was not OK with my family. The rule that a premarital relationship between a boy and a girl was haram hung over my head. I was in a sticky situation I had to deal with alone.

1995, five years earlier

This is it: a memory I wish I didn't have.

That room, with no air or escape.

It is a memory like molten tar, seeping in slowly, swallowing everything in its blackness and settling in as it solidifies. It cannot be wiped.

I was drawing. It was a good picture. The woman had curly hair tied in a bun above her head, her breasts were barely covered by the loose, silky fabric of her dress, and her long slim legs were both bare. She might as well have been naked. Milad will like this one, I thought.

I did not notice Baba at my bedroom door until he coughed. I immediately closed the notebook. His face was serious and his voice calm. Baba never got involved with trivial everyday matters, fights or quarrels—those were my mum's territory.

This can't be good…What have I done?

I kept my hand on the notebook, pressing down.

"We are taking you to see a counsellor today, for career advice and to help you decide what to study at university," he said finally.

Though I was relieved he did not care about the sinful drawing, what he was suggesting sounded strange to me. But maybe Saman had been through the same. Maybe this is how it's done, I thought.

"Isn't it too soon for that?" I said.

"No, it is important to know what you want to do early on."

I already knew the decision had been made. I could not delay the inevitable, another speech about my future and career. I moaned and got up.

As he left, he called out to my mum, "I'm going downstairs; be down in ten."

Maman is coming too? I poked my head out of the bedroom. She was fixing her headscarf. A tiny clip held it in place just below her chin.

She turned to me, smiling. "Hurry up. See you downstairs."

In the car, I did not notice the unusual silence, my mind elsewhere. I had already decided how I'd finish the cartoon and was imagining how Milad would be pleased. I was thinking how I wouldn't wait for him to hold my hand; I would hold his. I was going to get my friend back, my confidant, my boyfriend. The thoughts brought a smile to my face.

Once there, Maman and Baba sat outside in the waiting room.

I looked at the sign on the door and, among the credentials, a word stuck to my brain like glue: **PSYCHOLOGIST**.

Sceptical, I walked into the room. I closed the door and took in the well-decorated office. An uneasy feeling began creeping up my spine like insects marching.

Furnished with dark mahogany furniture, it was spacious and lit by evening sun rays shining through large windows. It could almost have been romantic; however, it felt as if the air had been sucked out by a giant hoover. Religion was dominant everywhere: lots of books, mostly Arabic, were arranged in a wall-to-wall bookshelf; framed pictures of the late Ayatollah and the current supreme leader sat on a huge desk. Behind it was a smiling man with bad stubble and a prayer-stone mark on his forehead, wearing a brown suit.

"You must be Majid. Hello. Please, have a seat."

Fiddling with my thumbs, I sat opposite him on the edge of the chair, making little eye contact.

There was a bit about career advice, none of which I remember, but the change was swift when he opened his desk drawer and took out a bunch of papers, laying them meticulously on the desk in front of me, saying, as he put them there, one after the other, "Should...we...talk...about these now?"

His voice was calm, almost soothing. The question was anything but. A rhetorical question, one I wished I could answer with, *No*. My eyes scanned the desk, bulging in disbelief as I saw my cartoon drawings of women staring back at me, with their big eyes and dark lips.

It was Milad's collection, all of it.

I felt dizzy. My heart started banging on my ribcage like a caged rabbit witnessing a wolf's approach. My ears became hot.

"Wh-what...? H-How did you...?"

He put his elbows on the desk and his hands in a prayer pose in front of pursed lips. Eyebrows raised, he was allowing me to take it all in. Was that pleasure I could see in his smug face? He said nothing, his smile smaller now as he looked at me.

"Errr, they're just drawings which I gave to my friend." I swallowed, quickly adding, "They don't mean anything—just drawings I did when I was bored."

I was trying hard to connect the dots, desperate to comprehend the spectacle unfolding before me. They weren't decent or Islamic, true, but a reassuring thought came into my head: He can't do anything about it; it is none of his business. My anger was directed towards Milad, who had betrayed me.

He was never in trouble. *I* was. All that enthusiasm, his and mine, was for this.

I wanted to get out of there, but the counsellor was just getting started. The worst was yet to come. What followed made me forget about the drawings.

He took another piece of paper from his drawer. "What concerns your principal, and me too..." he said, looking at the note.

The principal? I thought. How deep does this conspiracy go? That smile, that nod. He had been on to me. How naïve had I been?

The counsellor carried on reading from that piece of paper, as if he didn't already know what it said, the cunt: "…He likes to hold hands with other boys in school, interested in the same sex. He gives himself girls' names: *Betty*…"

That name, I thought, the hair on the back of my neck standing on end.

My sacred secret with Milad. I was hearing it from this man's lips.

It sounded filthy.

He is disgusted, I thought. I am naked, exposed. I wish I could die. I wish, when I'd asked Allah to turn me into a wizard, he'd bloody listened. I wish I could vanish.

I was unable to complete a coherent sentence. Scenarios were uncontrollably being played in my mind. None pleasant. None bearable. It all came back to one nauseating thought: Do my parents know about this? FUCK! FUCK! FUCK!

"It's just…Just a game, nothing else."

"I'm sorry, I didn't catch that."

"Just a game, it's nothing," I said louder, clearing my throat.

"Do you *want* to be a girl?" he said, after a pause.

I chuckled unintentionally, looking to the floor, hoping it would open up and swallow me.

Milad, why did you do this?

His face was now a concerned one.

"What? No, of course not. Like I said, it's *just* a game." I was close to tears. I only wanted the interrogation to finish. "I…I'm sorry…I didn't realize what I'm doing is not right…It was just a silly game."

I looked up. I saw a big Quran behind him on the bookshelf, among all the other religious books. I saw the Ayatollahs on his desk, still smiling. The room suddenly felt smaller, walls closing in. Where was this going to go from here? What would Maman and Baba do? I needed to get out of there.

"Can I go, please?" I said, sheepishly.

I would like to think his humane side kicked in at that point and he took pity on this boy in front of him, shaking like a beaten dog, or perhaps he was simply saturated with the joy of achievement.

"You can come back, and we will talk about this at our next appointment." And he asked me to leave the room so he could talk to my parents.

Next appointment? I thought, and stumbled out. Without looking up, I walked past my mum and dad and sat down as he invited them inside. After a short while, they came out and, without a word, we left.

On our way home, I sat quietly on the back seat, staring out of the window, my eyes stinging, my cheeks wet.

I had been betrayed, by everyone: friends and family. Left bare. To be humiliated. To be punished. Milad—I wished I had never known him. I was alone.

My mother was quiet in the front of the car, my father driving. Baba suggested I go back and see the counsellor again.

"I am not crazy," I said, my anger taking over and giving me a courage I did not know I possessed. "I will not go back *ever* again." My voice broke on these last words, which were met by silence initially, my parents taken aback by the abrupt answer.

"Of course you aren't crazy," my mum said softly. "That is not why we wanted you to see him."

I did not want to hear any of it. "No, Maman. I will not go back there…If you think I'm mad, put me in a hospital."

She turned her head and looked at me for a second. Her eyes seemed tired. It was enough. She turned back and said one word: "OK."

I noticed the side glance Maman and Baba exchanged, before Maman turned towards the window.

We were all losers.

We drove home in silence.

I heard them whisper in their bedroom that night. I could tell Maman's voice broke a few times. It reminded me of their whispers on the night the Ayatollah had died. Was this worse?

I closed my bedroom door and leaned against it. I wished the pain of my heaving chest would stop. I wanted to tell Maman how sorry I was to make her cry.

She prayed all night, that night.

I never went back, and my parents never brought it up again, nor did they ever say anything about what they had been told.

But one thing had become clear to me: I had to fend for myself.

I had to become better at keeping secrets. Betty was the innocent face of something ugly. A ghoul stirring within me, a monster with foul breath and ugly teeth, desperate to show his face. The seed of a new me was planted that day. The me who would be the perfect boy, parallel to the distorted one. My Dr. Jekyll to Mr. Hyde, fitting in within our religious society.

I made sure Maman's prayers were answered.

Tug of War

2002

Pouya's arm rested on my shoulder as he spoke with another classmate on his other side. I was conscious of every inch of the touch, the weight and the heat, like a hot rod melting into my flesh.

Then I heard it: laughter.

High pitched, but not loud. It was a laugh that turned heads, one that had a fading ripple at the end. The source was two rows behind.

The giggles were distracting me from my shoulder. From Pouya.

Her name was Leila.

Pale-skinned and slim, her hijab was slightly pulled back, showing side-parted brown hair. She had a bright pink lipstick on, and, unlike other girls in our class, that was the only make-up she wore. Her eyes were grey and, when they met mine, her gaze intense, flirtatious. Her nose had a tiny hump and her eyebrows sat wide apart, as if being pulled from the ends, making her forehead appear stretched and shiny.

She whispered something to the girl next to her. When she looked too, I turned away. Pouya's arm had disappeared and so had the warmth. He had noticed.

"She's caught your eye, hasn't she?" he whispered, poking my side with his elbow. His breath tingled my earlobe.

"Hah, don't be silly," I snorted. My mind did not stop whirling. A flicker of hope was lit.

Here was someone I could talk about with my friends: with Ali, Saam, and Atoosa, even my parents.

No, not my parents. They'll want me to marry her.

Although, at twenty-one, I was not able to support a family, it was not a problem from my parents' point of view. In his

Godfather role, my dad would have been more than happy to provide for and support us.

The thoughts of having a girlfriend, even a wife, had taken off after only a look. I could not, no, I did want to stop them. It was nice to feel normal.

Later that week, I told Ali about her. I did my best imitation of him and Saam when they talked about girls: casual but keen.

"She looks like Britney Spears, actually," I said, thinking of my only other girl-crush.

Ali's eyes narrowed. "Really? Then you must be in love."

OK, maybe that was going bit too far, I thought, but only shrugged and pretended to laugh.

"Well, when you do ask her out, *if* you ever dare, watch for the *basijis*." Ali was always thinking of the next step—or, as he would have perceived it, the next hurdle.

He was not wrong. There *was* a bigger problem with having a girlfriend: the so-called "morality police."

This division of police was an amalgam of a branch of the official police force and over-enthusiastic and brainwashed volunteers. It was a product of the Islamic regime, responsible for upholding the sharia law. And members were otherwise known as the *basijis*, the militia.

The morality police knew who to recruit: young men and boys from lower socio-economic backgrounds. Geographically, the majority were from south Tehran or other cities—the underprivileged and the unluckiest of a society which was drowning in corruption. They were given a new identity, a new power. With rifles in their hands and badges on their shoulders, they suddenly had godlike power over everyone else—especially over those they viewed as the true enemy: the rich, the privileged, or anyone who would otherwise look down on them, mostly living in north Tehran. The regime had managed to use the divide in society to its own benefit.

Basiji men were not always in uniform. Regardless, they were easy to spot as they had the *look*. Beige, long-sleeved, loose shirts, never tucked in their trousers, and they were never wearing jeans. They had serious and intimidating faces, with varying degrees of beard length, and a prayer-stone mark on their foreheads. They all smelt of that unmissable aroma: rose water, as if they were the embodiment of a walking, talking mosque. The *look* was practised, an effort put into it.

Police vans with the iconic green band around them, emblazoned *Morality Police*, were parked on streets in north Tehran, usually next to a newly built, flashy mall or restaurant. The officers wore a dark green uniform from top to toe, with stubble on their faces, and they too had the calloused forehead and the strict, menacing look. They stood by the vans, vigilantly keeping an eye on us, ready to fill the cargo. They had female personnel too, as it is haram for men to touch women should force be required to implement the sharia. These female members were nicknamed the Commando Fatimahs.

I had heard terrifying stories of boys and girls caught together by the morality police. Stories of girls being subjected to a forensic examination, and, if their hymen was broken, they would have to be married to the boy. Punishments for girls always seemed more severe than for boys, as if to emphasize a message that "they should know better" and "they should not tempt men." Not that men got away without any consequences: there were also tales of boys having their heads shaved or receiving lashes. If I was going out with a boy, no one cared. This system inadvertently made being gay easier.

In my quest to defeat my inner demons, I did not want an encounter with the *basijis*.

The prospect of being normal and having a girlfriend seemed real in my head, but the truth of my temptations always came back with a vengeance. I needed distance from my monster. It felt like I had an elastic leash tied around my neck, connecting me to the monster. Each step further away became harder, tugging on my windpipe, making me long for the leash to snap.

I found myself back at the computer, at the gateway to the virtual gay underworld.

When I was twenty-one, the family went on a pilgrimage to Mashhad.* I could not face another trip to the holy city, so I made an excuse of having to study for a fictional exam.

This was a rare opportunity to be home alone for one night.

Something had taken me over, like a cloak stuck to my skin, extending through my insides, blurring my vision, numbing my consciousness. All the barriers I had put up had been dissipated by this animalistic urge. I was not going to sit home and chill.

As I bid everyone goodbye, holding a Quran for them to pass under one by one, kissing the book, I worried that Maman would see the wild look in my eyes, hear the thud in my chest.

Once they were out, I logged on to Yahoo! One of the guys in my favourites list was online. No time to waste.

Hi, what are you doing this afternoon? I clicked *send*.

I stared at the screen, swearing at the internet speed.

Just at work, finishing around five. Why?

Do you want to meet? My hands were trembling as I typed.

He was typing, then deleting, then typing again. I bit my lip.

Eventually, a message appeared: **Yes, where?**

I blew out my held breath.

We set a time and place.

After a short walk, we sat on a park bench not far from my home. He had short brown hair, was clean shaven, and was wearing a white shirt and blue jeans. He was handsome.

An awkward silence ensued for a while. I side-glanced at him leaning forward on the bench, hands under my thighs.

"If there was no one at mine, I'd ask you to come over," he finally said, stretching. A whiff of his aftershave tingled my nostrils

---

* Mashhad is a holy city north-east of Iran. The eighth Shia imam is buried there.

and pulled on my stomach. I knew where this was going; I had already told him I was home alone.

My reply was hesitant, almost in a whisper: "Well, there's no one at mine."

That was all he needed. "Should we go to yours, then?"

"Could do…" My voice was shaking, coming through saliva-engulfed vocal cords.

"OK, let's go."

His assertiveness got me up on my feet immediately, stopping me from conjuring an excuse. I was more than happy to pass on the decision-making to him in a vain attempt to blame him in my mind for what was coming. A disturbing urge within was shouting that I should go for it. Each step closer to home was accompanied by a beat rise in my pulse. I made no conversation on our way to mine, scared that my voice would give away my fear and the increasing build-up of nausea. *I'm about to commit the unspeakable haram*, I thought to myself. *The one punishable by death.*

I was expecting an invisible force to somehow stop us. People passed by on the street. *Why are they all staring?* I needed to get away from their judgemental, poisonous looks. Our yellow bricks came into view. Home—almost there.

We sat in the TV room on the only chairs there—he on the seat in the corner and I on a small camel seat next to him. I did not know the next step. The darkest of my desires had won. I kept up a forced smile, but was still unable to say anything.

He broke the silence, yet again: "Do you want to have sex?"

He put his foot on mine and stroked it with his; my impulse was to pull back, but I didn't. I liked it, and I became even more nervous.

"Could do," was all that came out of my mouth.

"Should we go to your room?" he said, his foot still on mine. The warmth of his foot was making my face hot.

"Sure."

My bedroom was only five footsteps away. I was too conscious of how I was walking in front of him, and kept telling myself, *Not too stiff, not too camp, breathe.* After what felt like a hike up Everest, we sat on my single bed.

"Are you really a virgin?"

"Y-yeah..." Surprised by his surprise, I added, "Is that a bad thing?"

"No, no...just follow my lead."

With a tiny chuckle, I hid my sweaty hands under me. Did part of me wish that he'd say, *Yes, it is a bad thing, and I don't want to have sex with you?*

I let him take the lead, out of brain power to initiate anything. I allowed the cloak to spread over my brain and the numbness to take over.

He kissed me.

My first kiss. This was it.

Everybody wants their first kiss to be cherished and special. Mine was with a guy I met less than an hour before.

A *guy*.

His lips were soft and his kiss gentle. His subtle aftershave filled my nostrils again, like a cool breeze. He put his hand on my face, saying, "Relax, it's OK."

And I did, as he gently pushed me back on to the bed, his lips on mine. His tongue brushed the inside of my upper lip. The strange alien wetness tasted sweet. The tremor in my body halted as I felt his body heat on top of me, his weight pushing me back into the mattress. The rest followed on from there. I did what he told me to do, one thing after the other.

Far away, Maman was clinging on to the ornate gilded *zarih* around the holy shrine, crying, praying—perhaps for me.

As soon as I closed the door behind him, I said out loud, "There! It's done! It was terrible, and now you know. Happy?" I took a deep breath, giving a sigh of relief, but I didn't feel relieved. His smell stuck to my skin like slime. I wanted it off.

A few minutes later, I was standing in the shower to cleanse myself: head and neck first, left side and then right side of my body. I bent my neck under the shower and closed my eyes. I whispered in Arabic, "Allah, I beg for your mercy, and I come back to you." As the stream of water gushed on my neck and dripped down from my face, it was joined by tears, flowing uncontrollably. My body began to shake, the sob no longer contained. I scrubbed till my skin was raw and red. I promised Allah that it had been the first and last time.

I tried, but the leash did not snap. Instead, it pulled me back with a dizzying force, back into the arms of the monster. It dug its claws into my flesh and held me tight, like it would never let go again.

For days and weeks after, I didn't go online, keeping my head down; a sickening guilt was bubbling up inside me. At the same time, a little malicious voice kept repeating, *Do it again*; it had had a taste of freedom, and now was more difficult to restrain. The exciting sense of adventure associated with doing something so taboo and sinful was hard to ignore.

I did not want that feeling.

I already knew what my prayer to God would be in the holy Ramadan nights:

Allah! Please make me straight, make me normal.

His Kiss, Her Kiss

2002

Reading Leila was difficult. Every time I inched close to the subject of a date, she steered the conversation towards something else. I'd created a new Yahoo! ID in the hope of starting a new life, and we exchanged details. I knew I had to delete my old ID, but kept delaying. The tug of war between my two lives had no clear winner yet.

Seducing a girl was unfamiliar territory. The person who I turned to for advice was none other than Pouya.

We chatted on a bench in the uni grounds. He sat close, too close, like always. He held my hand between his, talking about Leila confidently, not noticing how distracted I was by his proximity as he continued giving me tips—tips I was not hearing. The softness of his skin touching mine and the moisture on my hand between his made it impossible to focus on Leila.

I had to pull my hand away. I *had* to keep focus.

"Thanks, I'll give it a go," I said, not knowing what I was going to give a go.

"Good luck." He stroked my arm and winked.

The hair on my arms stood up.

Walking away, I rubbed my hand and looked back. He was fiddling with his bag. I smelt my hand, hoping for his scent.

He does that to everyone, forget it, I told myself. I needed to impress *her*.

I knew an ulterior motive had drawn me to Pouya. A hiss behind a rattling corner of my head, locked away.

Leila eventually agreed to a date. I jumped up and down in joy as I told Atoosa the news. We were going to the cinema.

A day before our date, she left me a message on Yahoo! to say she was bringing her best friend with her. Not asking if it was OK—she had already invited her.

I turned to Ali for his analytical view.

"That is slightly weird," he conceded, when I told him, "but maybe she'll feel less awkward if her friend is there."

"Yeah, should be fine." I knew Ali had probably read my mind and expected the inevitable question: "Can you come with me?"

Being the most conservative person whom I knew, all of Ali's decisions, moves, and actions were measured and thought through. He hated surprises and never did anything spontaneously. My request would have disturbed his perfect equilibrium. He was not keen on the blind-date scenario, but after going through pros and cons and every possible outcome, he agreed to come.

We got there early. I don't know if it was the cold or just nerves, but I could not stop the tremble in my legs, not even when Ali attempted to make casual conversation or obviously faked a yawn; he was nervous too. I looked towards where Leila was going to make an appearance, half listening to him. "Shit, there she is."

He stopped talking and tried to make out which of the many people walking in our direction was Leila, his reference being Britney Spears. When she was close to us, I made eye contact and smiled. Ali was still searching.

Then, my eyes widened. The stress creeping up under my skin was more for Ali's sake.

I could see Leila and her friend, but there was someone else with them: a tall figure, walking behind them.

"Oh my God, she's brought her father," I told Ali in a panic.

His face turned white. "Are you joking?"

"No, no…That…that is her father, behind her."

Ali pinched me and gritted his teeth as he squealed. It was too late to do a runner.

Leila greeted us with wide smile. "Hi! Sorry we're late—traffic was awful."

"No problem; you're just on time," I said.

I turned to her father, but, before I could say anything, she jumped in: "I told Dad about the film. I knew he'd like it too, so asked him to come along."

I shook her dad's hand, with sweaty palms and my mouth half open. Then I introduced a very pale and angry Ali.

So, we watched the film, Leila's father sitting between me and her. I could hear Leila's giggles with her friend, but did not dare to look. Ali, on my other side, remained fidgety throughout.

Once we had said our goodbyes, I sat in Ali's car, in a daze.

"Was this a dream?" he started.

I began to laugh hysterically.

"Which one was Leila?"

I had to look at him to check if it was another joke. It wasn't. "What do you mean? The one in the red scarf, obviously."

His eyes widened. "Are you kidding me? *That* was the girl you think looks like Britney?"

"Yeah, she does, doesn't she?" I said, with a proud grin.

"Are you blind? The other girl looked more like Britney than Leila. Her *dad* looked more like Britney!"

"Don't be silly. The resemblance is obvious."

"You are an idiot and need an eye check," he said, shaking his head while pinching the bridge of his nose.

I insisted I was right—though, years later, I would see his point. She didn't look anything like Britney Spears.

The unpromising first date put my mission on hold for a while, but I kept in touch with her via Yahoo! Our interactions had only just begun.

November 2002

Marriage is embedded within the fabrics of a religious and traditional family. That holy rite of passage to procreate is always an arranged one. After returning from the US, my eldest brother, Saman, was introduced to a girl via family friends. The first of three sons.

A memory smelling of rose water, meant to be holy, but it is one blemished with a lustrous red, as deep as lipstick.

My attempts at finding a girlfriend were proving fruitless, and soon boredom had put me in front of a computer screen again, exploring the secret world of Iranian gays. I ignored the conflict within me to keep sane.

I was deep in a chat with Babak on Yahoo! After a few weeks of talking online, I was tempted by his third invitation to meet up. About to agree, I heard the apartment door and Maman and Baba talking as they walked in. I quickly said goodbye to a disappointed Babak and opened the living-room door.

"So, how was it?"

My mother, taking off her colourful headscarf, looked up. "It was good, very nice family."

"I meant, what was Maryam like?" I was annoyed with her obvious answer. "Did Saman like her?"

"He didn't see Maryam," she said, laughing.

"What? Why? Wasn't this *the* introduction meeting you've been planning for ever?"

"Yes, yes. I was surprised, too, when he asked us in the car what she looked like."

She did not sound surprised. Was that a hint of pride I heard in her tone?

"What does that even mean? They're going to get married."

I knew the answer, but needed to make a point.

"If he believes it is not right, then it isn't. It could be haram," she said, shrugging and then giving another laugh.

The Devil's arrow: he truly made no exception. Perhaps this would be a consolation to my cousins: *He did not look at his potential future wife, even though she was in a chador.*

Maman could see how extreme my brother's behaviour had become, but she was encouraging it. I clenched my teeth.

"So, what? You described her for him?"

I remembered my own blind dates on Yahoo! before the age of pictures.

"It is their choice, and her family approve," she said, in a tone that showed she did not find it amusing. "You can choose how you want to get married, too."

There it was again, her liberal side.

I wanted to shout, *My choice has a dick!* But all I did was roll my eyes and go back to sit in front of the computer. I was going to arrange a date with Babak.

Maryam was from an extremely religious background and perfectly suited for Saman. Her father was a businessman and her mother a dentist; they were well off. When I met Maryam's mother, it was hard to imagine her in a white coat, hard to imagine her reciting anything but the Quran, let alone medical terms. She held her black chador over her mouth, creating an upside-down triangle on her face, limiting the amount of skin visible to the bare minimum. The appearance, typical of women with a strong faith, was practised and mastered. She held the chador in place with her teeth, if she needed something from her Louis Vuitton bag. Was it me, or did everyone always try harder to imagine women in chador naked? At work, she only saw women; her practice was sin-proof too.

The decision to marry was not made by either the bride or the groom, nor by their families, but by Allah, or rather a mullah in Qom. *Istikhara,** Islamic fortune telling, had always been a paramount ritual for my mother in all important life choices, and Saman was an even stronger believer than she was. And so, a mullah in Qom was asked if something carried a good or bad omen. He opened the Quran at a random page and provided an interpretation without knowing what that something was, to remove bias. Allah sanctified their marriage.

A couple of months later, the wedding day arrived. Saman, who by then had changed his name to Mohammad, branding himself more Islamic, would finally see the face of his wife.

---

* *Istikhara* literally means "to seek that which is good."

I ran my fingers on the silky fabric, feeling the texture of the tiny embroidered patterns, thinking how the deep maroon colour would complement my black suit. I had borrowed the tie from Ali the night before.

"Won't your dad mind? Or Saman...sorry, Mohammad?" he'd said. Ali, yet again, was thinking about all eventualities.

"I don't think so. I've made up my mind. I *want* to wear a tie," I said, as if begging for Ali's assurance.

It was not even Ali's—it was his brother's, and *he* had already tied the knot for me.

I put the loose tie around my neck and looked in the mirror. I had not told Maman or Baba I would be wearing it to Saman's wedding. It was too late now, and the tie was beginning to feel heavier each second. Maman had already been criticizing "Western influences" (as she put it) on my behaviour. Was a tie a step too far? I was about to find out.

I pushed the knot close to my Adam's apple, worried that I might strangle myself. I touched the cut on my neck and winced. I had begun clean-shaving as well—another tut-inducer. Shaving with a blade was frowned upon in our sharia, as it made men look like women, those lesser beings.

My younger brother, Sina, walked past and side-glanced at my attire. He stopped for a second, about to say something. Then he moved on. Typical, his thoughts were his and his alone. On that occasion, I was grateful for it.

I opened my desk drawer. In the corner was a used lipstick of Atoosa's. I'd found it months ago, behind my bed. Something had stopped me from giving it back to her. She doesn't like red, anyway, I'd thought, always beige, and I'd put it in my drawer.

I picked it up and rolled the red waxy appendage out. I looked in the mirror again and tried to imitate Atoosa, half-opening my mouth to stretch out my lips. I put the flat surface of the sharp diagonal tip of the lipstick on my upper lip and pressed, slowly moving from the middle to the corner. The change of the colour was so intense and dramatic, I almost squealed. I smacked my lips together like she used to, and then I heard Maman.

"Everybody go down—Baba is getting impatient."

I looked at my face again. *She'll kill you.*

I wiped the colour with the back of my hand, but, when I looked up again, it was still there: deep red lips on a face which was now also blushing in panic. I ran out towards the bathroom, hand on my mouth, past my mother, who was clipping her scarf in place.

"Majid, where are you go—? Is that a tie?"

I did not stop. "Yes, yes…I'll be down in a second," I said, voice muffled.

In the bathroom, I rubbed my lips with soap and water to get the colour out. When I looked in the mirror, it was like I had peeled a layer of skin off my lips—they were raw, with a few blood spots, but no artificial colour at least. I shook my head and sighed.

By the time we got to the venue, a restaurant, the "tie conversation" was over. Baba had said it was OK to wear one for the wedding, and Maman eventually said it out loud: "You look handsome, Majid." It was more than I had hoped for. I did not care what anyone else said after that, not even Saman.

Maman separated from us at the entrance, heading towards the women's section. I stood watching, jealous of her, of all of them. Indistinguishable black figures, women in chadors, greeted each other with nods, the click-clacks of what I imagined to be high heels echoing on the marble floor. Occasionally, when one of them adjusted their chador or got something from their sparkly bag, the veil parted and revealed for a second a heavily made-up face, a Western dress underneath. I looked away instantly, only to slowly look back from the corner of my eye. The jealousy burned like acid.

"This is going to be fun." Atoosa had suddenly appeared next to me, making me jump with her sarcastic comment. Her bright yellow silky scarf was loose on her hair, her make-up heavy.

"Oh, hi. You look pretty," I said, eyeing her up and down, adding, "Trust me, it'll be more fun on your side."

She laughed. "Nice tie. How did you get that past your—? Wait, are you wearing lipstick?" She seemed more amused than horrified.

"N-no, of course not!" I touched my sore lips with the back of my hand.

She raised an eyebrow. "I gotta go, anyway. Enjoy the fabulous party! Don't forget to dance with Saman." And she walked towards the entrance to that mysterious hall where women were free to show off their hair and their dresses.

I headed into the men's hall with Sina. Baba was already greeting guests, wearing his usual mismatching oversized brown blazer and grey trousers. I felt special, being one of the very few men who had a tie on, exchanging knowing looks with the distant relatives: *I'm on your team. I'm open-minded.*

It was a truly Islamic wedding. The music was the constant clinks and rattles of cutlery and plates, the speeches were, well, non-existent, and the dancing only in my head.

Saman, or Mohammad, had at least trimmed his beard slightly, and he wore a collarless white shirt buttoned all the way up, under a grey suit. He threw a fiery look at my tie, at one point, before being distracted by other guests. I held my head high and straightened the knot. I needed everyone to see I was not like him. When he disappeared, I thought for a split second that he might have run away, and chuckled to myself at the image.

The image vanished when I heard a loud, "*Ya Allah, ya Allah,*" from the women's section: the warning that lustful eyes were headed their way, so they'd better cover up. It was followed by high-pitched ululations, which meant only one thing: Saman was there.

What?!

I could not believe I felt envious of him. How is he even allowed? I thought. Surely he would stumble, as he wouldn't be able to look up.

Atoosa filled me in on the details later. Even though the women had all covered their heads to allow him to sit next to his wife for a bit, his focus remained on the carpet. What a missed opportunity, I thought.

Regardless, I was proud of my achievements. Shaving, wearing a tie—with these small rebellious protests, I was digging an escape shaft out of the prison around me, which was the sharia itself.

2003

The face of Iranian politics began to change in 2003, when Mahmoud Ahmadinejad became mayor of Tehran. He was a religious hardliner with a "revolutionary spirit" and a "fuck you" attitude towards everyone, both within the country and abroad. Two years later, Mohammad Khatami, the reformist moderate president, would give his seat to Ahmadinejad, consolidating the latter's grip on power.

At the time, my life was not impacted much. Gays in Iran did not own a space in the community. Whether a moderate mullah or a hardliner was the mayor or the president, a haram remained a haram. Eight years of Ahmadinejad in the presidential suite and the indirect consequences of this, however, did influence my determination to leave Iran.

Sharia law now landed harder on Tehran, like a heavy fog, as if the smog over the city was infused with rose water. There were more morality-police checkpoints and more Commando Fatimahs, more busting mixed parties and more confiscating satellite dishes.

For me, my personal struggles took precedence. My beliefs may not have been as strong as they used to be, but I was still terrified of Allah and his vengeance.

My prayers unanswered, the compelling desire I continued to feel drove me to meet more guys. After my first transgression, I had promised myself and Allah that it would also be my last, but I had sex again, and with each slip my fear of it waned. In moments of reflection, another disturbing thought started burrowing its way into my head: this may just be who I am—I like men.

By the time I was twenty-three, I had started dating Babak, and was glad to have done so. He was my age, with light and kind eyes, glowing with sincerity. I liked how he ran his fingers through his curly, dark brown hair, with no worries of messing it up. It was a stark contrast to my perfectly gelled and parted hair, a tsunami-wave of a quiff at the front.

With him, I was comfortable. I didn't spend hours finding a T-shirt that matched my jeans before seeing him, didn't check my hair in every car and shop window, and yet he made me feel special. His scent was his. It was the warm smell of his skin, his hair, his sweat, but no aftershave. I inhaled it to keep it locked in my head like a treasure.

Our dates were usually in a café, or we'd go for walks. I loved it when he interlocked his long fingers in mine, pressing our palms together. I held his hand as if my life depended on it. I had not felt like this ever before. Leila, even Pouya, seemed so insignificant at the time.

We sometimes found a quiet dark corner on the empty streets of Tehran, late at night. I'd rest my head on his shoulder, close my eyes, and breathe him in, and he would stroke my neck and talk. We'd then kiss, hidden from sight, under the cloak of the night. The adrenaline rush was fun and the secret that I only shared with him sacred.

But secret kisses were not enough. I had to take the risk.

I dared to ask him to come to my home when my family were out. The window of opportunity was a narrow one, but the urge to be with Babak was overwhelming.

He wasted no time coming over, arriving ten minutes after my parents had left, every second of which I paced around the room. We exchanged no words; I took his hand and led him to my bedroom.

We lay in bed, legs entangled, some twenty minutes later. My head was on his chest and my hand rested on his tummy. The steady rise and fall of his breathing and the drum of his heartbeat was soothing. He was talking about his plans to move out, get his own place and start a business. I was making knowing *hmm* noises, eyes closed, thinking, maybe I should move out too, when I heard it.

A clunk, followed by a louder thud.

I opened my eyes and looked at Babak. He was still painting a picture of his future self. Trying not to scare him, I got out of bed slowly, nervously, and walked into the TV room. He stopped talking and followed me with his eyes.

Peering around the curtain, my eyes confirmed what my ears had suspected: only Maman would shut the car door that hard. A chill dug into me at the sight of her, turning my shout into a screech. She was walking to the main door of the building, Baba checking something on the tyres. I ran back to the bedroom and gave instructions in the shortest way my brain could conjure: "Parents are coming in, wear clothes."

He saw the panic in my eyes, no room for games. No pretence of calm. The colour left his face and his pupils welcomed the adrenaline. I got my trousers on, trying hard not to trip while hopping with one leg in. He did too, not saying a word. With every tick of the clock, my mother was another step closer to the building entrance, to the sin. There was no time to wash my face or do something about my messy hair. We ran to the apartment door, flew down the few steps to the main door, and opened it.

I stood, face to face with Maman, already breathless.

Startled, she looked at me, and I looked back in a brief staring contest. I put on a fake grin, swallowing my saliva and struggling to breathe normally. I saw her eyes moving from my face to my shoulder, seeing who was standing behind me. The surprise in her eyes turned into concern. I could imagine the wheels in her head turning, piecing evidence together. I had to stop it.

"Oh! Hi, Maman!" I said, thinking of every possible question she would ask and quickly adding, "This is Babak; I know him from the gym; he's here to borrow a film."

Thinking this was a good time for him to speak, Babak came forward. "Hi! Nice to meet you."

Nice to meet you? Really? I'd had it under control.

She looked at me and him, a forced smile forming on her lips, her eyebrows still in a frown. "Hello," she said, a hint of a question in the way she said it.

I heard the car beeping as it was locked. Baba was coming.

That was it, we had to get out and leave.

Maman opened her mouth to say something, but I interrupted: "OK, I'm just going to the end of street with him. I'll be back in five. Bye!"

And we walked past as fast as we could, without looking back. No eye contact with Baba. The whole encounter was less than ten seconds, but it had felt much longer.

Once I'd said goodbye to Babak, I walked home slowly, thinking of every possible scenario, of what she might ask and what I must say.

I moved straight to my bedroom to avoid questions and to make sure the "crime scene" was clear. It didn't take long before my mother was standing at the door with a serious face.

"How do you know him again? Why was he here?"

I was not entirely sure she truly wanted to know the answers to those questions. She was making a point: she knew something was not right, but her fear of finding out what it was exactly made her hesitant. Hence, when I gave the same answers, pretending to be annoyed, she dropped the subject. She was not happy, nor convinced. She looked concerned, and that scared me. The thought of Baba getting on board terrified me.

Once they'd gone to bed, I had a quick religious shower and asked for Allah's forgiveness, like a broken record, while thinking of how I wanted to do it again.

With Babak, I was happy for a month or two. Nonetheless, every once in a while, reality slapped me in the face hard, leaving a mark that burned. It was the guilt burden. I knew I should not lose sight of putting an end to the phase which had lasted much longer than I'd anticipated already. I didn't want that distraction, Babak, to stop me from my main goal: finding a girlfriend and moving on.

I must let him know that this is not permanent, I thought.

We argued. "This is just a phase" and "Once I find a girlfriend and become normal again, it has to end" became lines I repeated more often than I dare to admit. Frustrated with my logic, his answers were the same: "You won't be able to change; stop fighting it. It's not a bloody phase. It is who we are." It annoyed me how he had resigned himself to accepting that lifestyle, calling it *normal*—a word no one in my life had used to describe that heinous sin. I didn't want to be like him. "No, not me. I will get over it."

I knew I would eventually find what I found in him, in a girl: the right sex.

This memory feels like the healing of a wound: desperate for a scratch, but delicate, and painful when touched.

I was having an overnight stay in hospital after a minor operation. Babak and I had not met up or talked for a week, following a recent argument over the usual.

When Maman and Baba left, a sudden hospital-induced loneliness sank heavily on my chest. I flipped open my mum's mobile phone, left with me for the night, and typed in a text: Hi, just wanted to let you know I'm in hospital.

I looked at it for a second. It was a cruel way to fish for sympathy. I closed the phone and laid my head on the pillow, shutting my eyes, still clenching the phone.

Nope, definitely not able to sleep.

I looked at the green screen again, the only light in my room. I typed again: Hello, how are you? You know the pain I had the other day? It needed a small operation and now staying in Sadr Hospital for the night. Thought you might want to know.

Much better. I pressed *send* and folded the mobile closed immediately. I turned to face the ceiling, holding it close to my chest, taking deep breaths, waiting. The silence, occasionally interrupted by a phone ringing outside, gave me the creeps.

Five minutes.

Ten minutes.

Half an hour.

Nothing.

Anger began to seep in.

How dare he not answer my text? I thought. He does not deserve me.

I felt the bandage over the op site, still numb. I was about to lift the blanket to have a peek at it when I heard it: a knock at the door.

Light switch. I squinted as the lights blinked with a buzzing static.

It was Babak, standing with a bunch of red and pink flowers, a few of them bent with broken stalks. I inhaled sharply, my eyes stinging.

"Hi." His voice was shy and hesitant. "I wasn't sure if I should come." He held out the flowers. "I can just leave these and go, if you think it's too risky. Sorry, not the best bunch. Last-minute buy."

I continued to stare.

He shuffled on his feet and cleared his throat.

I pointed to the chair next to my bed. "You came," was all I could say.

With a wide grin, he closed the door, walked to my bed, and, before I could object, kissed me. Instinctively, I pulled my head back with eyes open, looking towards the door, and groaned.

"It's OK," he whispered, as he brushed his lower lip on mine, the familiar tingle.

I wanted him more than I implied. I put my hand on his soft, clean-shaven face. He parted his lips from mine, forming a small gap. His breath warm on my mouth, his smell filled my nostrils.

He leaned his forehead on mine. "I missed this." He breathed out.

I smiled back. As much as I hated admitting it, I had too. I said nothing, looking again at the door. He turned his head towards it. Looking back at me, his grin widened, his eyes gleaming. I knew what he was thinking.

In a blink, he was at the door, turning the lock. I only shook my head. I *was* scared, but did nothing to stop what came next. He lay next to me on the hospital bed. The heat from his body next to mine relieved the building tension in my muscles. Careful not to touch the bandage over the stitches, he gently caressed my body with his hand. I drowned myself in the moment. The pain, the fear, and the panic melted away. I was floating.

When Maman asked me the next day who the flowers were from, I automatically said, "Ali," smiling at the thought of Babak.

The break from our arguments was temporary. It was only a matter of time before they took over again in full force.

Around the same time, Allah opened a door, only a slight opening. I had waited and prayed for it, but when the chance came, I was hesitant. Had I let the monster have its way for too long? Was I getting used to the buzz it gave me, to the ringing in my head? I needed to prove to myself I was stronger than it.

A message had been left on my Yahoo! Messenger.

Hello. It has been some time. How are you? My sister and I are going on a hike. Do you want to come?

It was Leila.

As simple as that, and as carefree as she always was. No dates or times were given, as if she had typed it in a rush, among other daily activities. Had it been me, I would have drafted and redrafted, and would have run it past Ali, Saam, and Atoosa a billion times before sending.

Well, I did go to Ali to analyse every aspect and possibility before replying. I needed to make sure my reply sounded equally casual.

She gave me her number soon after, and, just like that, I was on a date with her, and her sister. I kept Babak in the dark. He would have created doubt in my mind, injecting it in my head like an opiate, giving me an addictive high with ensuing regret.

I did not mention it to Pouya either. Was a part of me worried—no, *hoping*—he would be upset? Perhaps.

The date with Leila was the moment I had been waiting for. It was filled with laughter, accidental touches of our hands, with that familiar tickle and the locking of eyes in silence. Her intense look was like a force that pushed my thoughts about Babak into a dark corner of my brain and chained them there. His scent, his touch, his lips, all giving way to a new entity: her.

That date quickly progressed to another and then another, and, soon enough, sooner than I had imagined, I had a girlfriend.

Having a girlfriend was not OK with my family or my religion, but it definitely was the lesser of two evils. I had created a secret in my "straight life" too.

And so, I broke up with Babak. The prospect of a normal life ahead stuck to my brain like cling film. I did not allow a hug, or a kiss. His smell had to be kept away, so as not to falter my resolve. He was already like a distant memory, and the phase was a nightmare already over.

I was cured.

His tears remain fresh in my memories, though. I allow them to stay as a reminder of the first victim of my conflict.

Leila had my home telephone number, but was not allowed to call it unless I had instructed her exactly when to call so I could be waiting by the phone. Our main mode of communication was email, sometimes very long ones. We started going out as a couple with my friends and their girlfriends. I swelled with a pride unknown to my friends when I introduced her as "my girlfriend."

Apart from her loose headscarf and pink lipstick, Leila made sure her manteau* was always tight enough to show the outline

---

* From the French for "coat", a manteau is the long coat Muslim women have to wear outside to cover their arms and down to their knees, if not in chador.

of her big breasts and slim waist. But she was not just pretty. She was opinionated and strong-willed, a self-made girl from a working-class background, studying medicine in one of Tehran's top universities. She was not religious and was very clear on her stance on Islam. We often argued about it, specifically about me not abiding by all the sharia rules.

"You either accept a religion as a whole, obeying *all* its rules, or you don't," she'd tell me. "You can't pick and choose what you like doing and what not."

I would still pick and choose, though; I had to, or I shouldn't have even touched her hand.

A few times, she invited me over to hers when she was home alone. I made excuses each time. I wasn't mentally ready for the next step. Unlike my first sex with a guy, there was no excitement, no anxiety, and no build up, only the stress of what felt like a chore.

A memory doused in pink, but retaining no colour. The *ding* of the lift door opening is the most prominent part of it. It is like resurfacing after a deep dive, gasping for air.

I rolled the window up as the taxi started to speed along the highway. The smell of smoke and dust was only mildly better than the driver's sweat mixed with Leila's strong perfume. It had been a bad idea to sit directly behind him. Each time he put his elbow on his windowsill, a whiff struck the back of my throat like a mustard kick. Leila was in a different zone, eyes droopy, long mascaraed eye lashes flapping, and lips wet. I was intentionally avoiding her looks.

The date had gone OK, like it always did: find coffee shop, act casual, change the subject from a future together, apologize, talk about anything but, *anything*, pay, leave. She was not angry this time, at least. Her eyes wanted something else. Oh God.

I was used to dropping her off after dates and getting another taxi home. That ride, though, was one I wanted to end as soon as possible. For once, I was less anxious about the high-speed zigzagging of our driver through traffic. It was like yo-yoing between life and death and having to high-five death every few seconds.

Leila inched a little closer to me and rested her head on my shoulder. She locked her bony fingers in mine and started to stroke my arm with her other hand. It was impossible not to compare it with how Babak's hand swallowed mine. I only hoped she wouldn't pick up on my tense demeanour; I took deep breaths and pretended to be interested in something outside, on the highway.

Then, I noticed it: an angry glance from our driver in the rear-view mirror, followed by grunts and head shakes.

He doesn't approve.

My one chance to unglue her was our malodorous driver. I needed to provoke him just a bit more. At the risk of our high-five with death turning into an embrace, I shifted myself closer to her, giving our driver a full view in the mirror.

She interpreted it differently.

The hair on the back of my neck stood straight up immediately as her lips touched my neck. My eyes widened and a nervous cough escaped my throat. It was enough for the driver to look again in the mirror.

"Can you sit apart please?" he said, his voice angry and menacing.

Leila, oblivious to all until then, quickly composed herself, shot a death stare at the mirror, and sat straight, saying nothing. She glanced at me in anger. *How dare he?* she mouthed.

"I know," I said, looking back at her, voicing my own fury. I shook my head, tutting, and turned to look outside again.

Once we got to her building, she insisted I accompany her to her floor. Having let the taxi go already, I fell short of excuses.

"I don't have much time. I'll just ride up in the lift," was all I managed to say, hands in pockets, shoulders tense.

She rolled her eyes. "OK, OK…Let's go."

As soon as the sliding doors shut, her ravenous lips were on mine, pushing against my teeth. She swung her arms around my neck and I felt her body press against mine. I reached an arm behind me, finding the wall to keep my balance.

I tried to keep my eyes shut and concentrate on one thing: enjoying the kiss, with a girl. Her lipstick tasted rubbery. I opened one eye and saw her face, magnified, her eyes closed as she tried to squeeze her tongue between my lips. I peeked over her shoulder at the numbers on the panel, lighting up one after the other.

One more floor.

Once the doors opened, she detached, looking seductive and out of breath. She asked if I wanted to go to her flat.

My abrupt "No!" took her aback. I was quick to recover. "It's getting late, and I have to go home; my mother will get suspicious. Next time, perhaps."

"OK, next time, then…Bye," she said, chewing the inside of her cheek. As soon as the lift doors closed again, I wiped my lips and stared at the mirror.

Next time. The words landed like a punch in my gut.

It was not a normal relationship, even by straight standards. Four months in, Leila's feelings took an obsessive turn.

"Your mother loves Saman's wife…what's her name? Maryam…more than me," she said. She was clear that she did not like my brother, and it annoyed her that he'd changed his name. Referring to him by his old name was to make a point.

"You mean her actual daughter-in-law," I said.

She flinched.

I knew where this was heading. "My mum doesn't even know you exist, Leila." I exhaled.

"Because you are too embarrassed to tell her about me," she said, her voice rising a notch.

She was not wrong. I was sure Maman wouldn't approve of Leila's liberal lifestyle—not praying or covering her head, her views on religion.

"I don't want to be your *girlfriend* any longer," she continued, emphasizing *girlfriend*.

Is she saying what I think she is? I wondered.

"If it's this thing that you're worried about," she said, pointing to her silky headscarf, almost slipping off her head, "I'll wear it, for her."

There was no more avoiding the subject, the inevitable had arrived. Part of me wished she was breaking up with me. Not wanting to be my girlfriend could mean either, I reasoned. But, no, she wanted us to marry, and was prepared to embrace sharia for it. The irony was not lost on me.

The push was like everything else she had achieved in life: *Keep the pressure on and you will succeed* was her motto. I, on the other hand, had always been quick to change tactics when I faced opposition. As I delved deeper into my secret life, the risk of a slip-up became graver. It was the fear of revealing what I had kept hidden which made me timid.

I was lost again. Our relationship may have been haram, but it was the acceptance stamp into the straight life I sorely desired. It was still miles better than being a "same-sex player"—the sharia's derogatory term for gay men.

I imagined our wedding. I would be welcomed to the women's section with their ululations. I could even sneak a glance at what they wore, judge their dresses and make-up.

No, stop—not the dresses. I must not care about what they wear!

But the wrong reasons for wanting a wedding were not going to stop me.

So, I told my parents about her. I had to show them I valued their opinion.

The perfect son.

No secrets.

"You can't go on seeing her unless you want to get married; it is not fair to her," was Maman's predictable comment, though she said it with a sparkle in her eyes. I had almost forgotten she could exude such softness, and it warmed my insides. Her main concern was not fairness to Leila, but for my afterlife, committing a haram.

Leila wanted to get married. My parents wanted me to get married.

The only obstacle was a flimsy one: me.

Marriage.

Just go with it, get married, you'll be fine, I told myself. I had to repeat it again and again to muffle the rattling of the locked closet, a voice within hissing, *Is this what you really want?*

Was marriage the seal on the closet I was looking for, never to be opened again?

I agreed to our families meeting. I was going to let them have their way. It *was* the right way. I knew, once I'd crossed that bridge with Leila, she would be there always. Always.

I needed more time.

I spoke with Ali about the meeting the night before.

"Are you sure you're ready to get married?" he said. "I certainly am not."

If this does not make sense in a straight world, I thought, there must be a way to delay.

"For the tenth time, Maman, it is not a *khastegari*," I insisted. The ceremonial meeting where a boy asked for the blessing of a girl's family to marry her was what I could not bring myself to agree to yet.

Maman was not impressed. "Then what is it? Who is going to be there?"

"Just...just an introduction. An unofficial meet and greet." I smiled.

The creases on her forehead deepened. "A meet and greet? What about flowers? Or chocolates," she said, tutting. She did not stop getting ready, though. She had already picked her colourful floral scarf, and, judging by the number of manteaus laid on her bed, she was making an effort to impress. Her thinly veiled excitement or nerves unsettled me.

I shuffled my feet. "Maman, it is only a preliminary meeting, probably just Leila and her parents. And no to flowers, or chocolate. It is *not* a *khastegari*," I emphasized, more to myself than her.

"What do you want me to say, there?" Baba asked in the car ride towards Leila's, sensing my apprehension. He was wearing what he'd worn to Saman's wedding: the mismatching blazer and trousers. Maman had picked it for him. He had trimmed his beard, which now had two white patches on each lip corner.

"Say we want to get to know each other a bit more before making it official. Under our families' supervision," I said. The words rolled out of my mouth as if rehearsed a million times.

He looked at me in the rear-view mirror. My eyes fixed on Baba's for only a few seconds before I looked away. He must not see me.

"OK," was all he said.

He *had* seen me.

Seen it.

Leila opened the door, with a smile so wide I was worried her cheeks were being deprived of oxygen, squeezed up. As we walked in, the disparity between my version of that "meet and greet" and hers became blindingly evident. When my brain had finished registering all the people present, I dared not look at Maman or Baba. Leila's sisters, aunts, and uncles, all with their spouses, stood up, smartly dressed. A few kids ran between the chairs that had been neatly organized in a circle. Even they were wearing mini tuxedos and dresses.

Their eyes drifted to our hands, our empty hands.

No flowers. No chocolates. Nothing.

This is not a *khastegari*, was my only thought, mocked by all the disappointed looks. I wanted to say it out loud, but feared I might get stabbed by Leila if I did. Instead, I focused on my shoes, the familiar refuge.

Despite the initial bemused reaction, smiles and pleasantries ensued. Leila's dad shook my hand firmly and we touched our cheeks—three times, to be precise. Perhaps I had made an impression in the cinema when I met him first, those few years back. The women only stood and nodded to me and my dad. No touching. Leila had prepped them well. Although not religious, they all wore headscarves—well, loose pieces of fabric on their heads, held in place by a knot under their chins—an attempt to impress my parents. Their sparkly dresses and heavy make-up gave them away. Maman, on the other hand, had her scarf held tightly in place with a clip. Her cheeks protruded, as the edges of the cloth dug into her face: *that* was a proper hijab. Not a single strand of hair was allowed out. Make-up on her face would have seemed out of place, comical.

I sat on a chair in a corner, Maman next to me. Leila's family eyed me, judging every possible angle. I avoided eye contact. I knew I was about to ruin their preparation and anticipation. Well, my father was.

Leila brought out the tea tray. At that, a small squeal escaped my throat, and I exchanged side glances with Maman. It is only at a *khastegari* that a bride-to-be brings out the tea. Maman took a cup and a sugar cube with a rigid face.

Leila despised what she called "stupid sexist traditions." She was only making a point. I was losing.

I should start imagining the wedding and the dresses again, I thought. Maybe it will be fine.

My hopeless look found Baba, who then put down his plate and cleared his throat. He had the attention of the room. Silence.

He spoke with a calm and authoritative voice: "From my understanding, these two have not yet made up their minds and need some time to think—"

"I have made up my mind. It is Majid who is having doubts, it seems," Leila interrupted.

Eyes and heads turned towards me. I smiled, a pathetic smile, wishing I could throw something at her. I held my breath, scanning the room, fidgeting with the corner of my chair. As painful as it was, she was right.

Baba continued with a sigh. He proposed the solution I had suggested.

Leila's father's face became more and more distorted, and all smiles faded slowly as Leila's family sat listening. Her aunts began looking around their chairs, as if they'd lost something—perhaps a hatch to get out of that room. I was now sure that they had expected a *khastegari*.

After a painful two hours, we left, or maybe it had only been half an hour. Leila did not say goodbye to me, and her dad's farewell handshake was limp, like a cold sausage.

Maman held my arm on the way out and whispered in my ear, "It will be fine, darling."

I looked into her eyes. Will it? I thought. Will I ever be fine? And then I looked away so she wouldn't see the tears bubbling.

The plan was set: to stop all communication for a month, and, if after that we decided to see each other still, it would be for one purpose only—to get married. The families were to be involved throughout: a semi-arranged marriage. A scolding from Leila was inevitable, or rather an angry email, but it did not dampen my sense of relief. She did not seem to care for the rules from the get-go. It did not matter. I had managed to buy some time.

A countdown timer had started ticking, a deadline set.

The Full Force
of a Hurricane

March 2004

Compulsory military service was a beast ominously crouching behind a corner, ready to consume two years of my life and give nothing back. It was the one hurdle I was told about, before any other.

But it was a corrupt beast, nonetheless. Saman had bought his way out of service. The law which allowed those who could afford it to pay off their military service was yet another hammering on the wedge separating the poor and the rich.

To leave the country legally prior to completing the service was not impossible. It required money and paperwork—lots of both. Baba left a deposit at the recruitment office to guarantee my return. In exchange I got a stamp in my passport allowing me to leave for a fixed period.

That Nowruz, I was going to London with Baba.

The foreignness, the people—they created a mental distance between me and Leila, greater than the physical one.

The girl whose flirtatious glances had crept under my skin back in our class at uni had turned into the opposite of what I had hoped for. She was a saviour who would not abandon her mission—a mission which became more hers than mine. What I had imagined to be a sweet love had only left a bitter taste.

After the family meeting Leila had set up a few weeks previously, she insisted we meet up as if nothing had changed. I, however, was not going to let this opportunity slip by. I stopped seeing her, but compromised by keeping in touch via email.

Once in London, I felt untouchable. It fuelled my courage to put an end to it. I sent her a long email and finished it with,

It has been great knowing you and I wish you happiness. Perfect, I thought, as I clicked *send*.

Her reply was quick, short, and civilized. She thanked me for the time I'd spent with her and said that I would not hear from her again.

It was nearly midnight. I leaned back on the chair and stretched my hands behind my head. The audible sigh and wide grin relieved the tension that had built up in every single fibre of my body over those weeks. Baba's snores from the corner remained uninterrupted.

I had unburdened myself of what felt like a ton of bricks.

I ventured into central London the next day. It was alien but blissful. I imagined every white, blond-haired woman in chador, and giggled to myself. Daydreaming, I walked into Soho. Colourful rainbow flags danced in the breeze over bars and shops.

I came to a halt in front of one, staring.

There were gay men inside.

I tried to make out their faces through the window, but I did not dare enter. A face turned towards me. Eye contact. I held my breath.

Quick, move, or they will know.

I was too exposed. I had looked for far too long.

I glanced around. Men held hands as they walked. A couple were kissing in a corner, in daylight, as passers-by took little notice.

A pang of jealousy pushed against my ribcage. I suddenly missed Babak, missed Pouya's touch. I missed everything I had kept hidden so long it felt like they were lost. But the memories came like a tidal wave.

Head down, I tried to outpace my thoughts, avoiding them. I did not want the memories and the reminders. It was not till a few blocks away that I raised my head again. Safe now. I breathed.

The sunny day offered peace like a silk sheet against the skin—one which could be lifted with the slightest of draughts, let alone the gust that was brewing.

When I got back and loaded my email, **1 new** had appeared next to the word **Inbox**.

> I can't believe you did this to our Leila—you ruined her Nowruz. I hope you enjoy your holiday.

It was from her sister. She's just blowing off some steam, it's all good, I told myself, silencing the crawling itch at the base of my skull. I signed off and went to bed. The rumble had begun, though.

A week later, back from London, I was still buzzed. Ali and Saam looked at my numerous pictures and listened to the stories with open mouths.

Even though my relationship with Leila hadn't given me the best or most thorough experience, I did now have an insight into heterosexual life. I struggled with it, but a positive belief persuaded me it was doable. I convinced myself that, next time I kissed a girl, I would concentrate more, forget the taste of her lipstick, open my mouth perhaps, and I *would* enjoy it.

Then, the phone rang.

Slightly surprised to hear her voice, and anxious that she had called without letting me know beforehand, I took a deep breath.

Leila's voice was little and shaky: "I know I'm not supposed to call, but I...I missed you, and—"

I could not hear the rest. "I'm fine, thanks. How are you?" I interrupted, awkwardly, thinking, Don't ask too much, or you'll be inviting trouble.

"I'm...OK...I guess. H-How was your trip?"

She had given me a way out of asking how she *really* was: my trip.

"Ah, it was great. It is a beautiful place, and the weather was good, too," I said, ignoring her hint and the prickling sensation of the hair on my arms standing on end, one by one.

"Nice." She wasn't listening. My little diversion from the main topic was over. "I *have* missed you," she repeated.

Anxiety and acid began making their way up through my chest like two friends holding hands, skipping. "We aren't supposed to talk anymore...And we said everything over email, right?" My abrupt answer had come out sharper than I intended.

"I don't think I can do it." Her voice was breaking.

Am I losing control of the situation? I thought. I needed to be assertive. "I'm sure it will be fine, time to move on. We've already said all we need to." And we had, reams of emails back and forth, long ones. I tried to produce a chuckle, lightening the mood. It did not help.

"I don't think I can live without you in my life." She gave a deep sigh.

My throat was dry and burning, not wanting to hear the inevitable.

"I just have to end it," she said. "You'll be rid of me for good."

I saw the delicate shell of reason I was so desperately trying to build crumble in front of my eyes. My heart began racing.

End it?

Yes, she had a fiery and unpredictable side, but *suicide?* Because of me? Could she? My bubble was burst with a shotgun.

You'll be rid of me for good.

Even her suicide would have been an act of selflessness, of martyrdom.

"Don't be silly...Over this?" It was all I could say back. It was enough to tip her into full hysteria.

"You think I'm joking? I will do it...I will do it right now!" She was sobbing.

OK, no more pretending to be cool.

"Don't do this, please. Let's talk, OK?" I pleaded.

The walls closing in on me, I needed an escape. I closed my eyes and stared into the blackness. London was there somewhere.

Found it.

Colours poured in from the corners and brought it to life. I saw myself standing in front of that gay bar in Soho again, mid-afternoon, watching people floating in and out, their outlines blurry and smudged. I made eye contact with the man inside again, superimposed on my reflection in the window. I needed to go in and stay in. Take shelter under the rainbow flag. How long ago was that? It felt like a distant memory or a dream. Had I really been there? He looked away. Colours faded into grey and then black. I opened my eyes. The crying on the phone, which had been muffled for a second, pierced through my eardrums.

The next ten or twenty minutes of our conversation is hazy; I explored every avenue I could think of, which wasn't many, to talk her out of it.

She did not back off, insisting suicide *was* the only way.

Resigned and defeated, I thought of one final brilliant idea to delay her suicide: therapy. I remembered Ali mentioning he used to go to a therapist for stress management during his uni exams. Typical, having a plan for stress, his worst adversary. My suggestion worked with Leila. I asked her to wait for my call back, to not kill herself while I got the details.

I called Ali immediately. Hearing the urgency in my voice, he wasted no time giving me all the information I needed. Ali was my lifeline yet again.

Leila agreed that we could go to a therapist together.

That evening, I sat alone in our living room, lost in thought. I leaned back on the wheelie chair, staring at the ceiling lamp and rotating. The slow circular movement made the light seem like a halo.

I saw Leila's face, happy, made up. She was in a wedding gown, dancing. I closed my eyes, screwing them till I felt the pressure in my cheeks. She was still there, her veil floating in the air behind her head.

I turned towards the monitor. On the flickering screen, a yellow smiley next to a Y and an exclamation mark looked back. It had been nearly five months since I had logged into the *other* ID. I could still see Leila's face in front of it, now laughing loudly, her head tilted back. I gritted my teeth as I moved the mouse cursor.

Go away, please.

I pulled the chair closer to the desk.

Click.

May 2004

Our couples sessions with a psychologist began behind my parents backs, to "uncouple" us.

Baba kept a briefcase under his bed. It contained important documents, from insurance to our education certificates, to property documents. But also money. The ever-renewing set of notes was meant to be emergency cash. I paid for the therapy with money I stole from the supposedly hidden stash. I considered it to be a genuine emergency.

Keeping the unnecessary secret was stressful. I imagined boys and girls my age making excuses at their homes to escape and get drunk, smoke weed, fuck, or party. I made excuses to sit with Leila in front of a shrink, while she cried and I came up with creative explanations for why I wanted to end our relationship. I wish I could have just pointed to the elephant in the room and shouted, *I'm gay!* If only *I* had believed it.

Back at my computer desk, I opened Yahoo! again. That day's therapy had been draining. It was the fifth session, and I was not sure how much longer I could carry on. Leila's angry shouts still rang in my ears.

A few windows popped open, left over from my unsuccessful chats the previous night. I started closing them one by one, eyes half open. The numbness they offered was becoming more difficult to achieve.

Clicking on the small *x* at the corner of each offline message, my finger came to a halt a millimetre above the mouse button. My eyes widened and my chest heaved as I read the message, again and again.

A message I had left four weeks before had a reply.

Hi. Sorry it took me so long to reply. Needed to think. Yes, let's meet ☺

It was Babak.

All the senses returned. My palm became wet as if held against his, my nostrils tingled as if his stubble was next to them, and my lips tickled as if brushed on his. How desperately I needed these sensations to be real again.

I replied.

Weekly, under the radar, the therapy sessions with Leila continued. I thought we were making progress. She gradually became calmer. After every session, we resumed the discussions over long emails. I had taken control of a grim situation and was managing to turn a corner.

But the hay walls of confidence I had built around me were about to be blown away by a hurricane.

I was ready to move on and be with Babak. We picked up where we'd left off. I told him all about Leila and my dip in the straight world. His eyes said, *I told you so*, but I was grateful he did not speak the words aloud, letting my hand take in every inch of his, the nerve endings carrying that feeling to my chest.

I met him the night before my last therapy session with Leila. We sat in his car, in a spot we often visited on a hill overlooking the twinkling lights of Tehran.

"Would you want to meet tomorrow night, then? To celebrate?" He winked.

"Don't say that." Though, it was a relief to know the end to an ordeal was close. "It was my fault. I led her on."

He looked away. "I know that feeling well," he said, with a sigh.

"Oi, you said you wouldn't make me feel any worse."

He smiled—how I'd missed that smile—and gave a peck on my lips. "You thought I'd let you off that easily?"

Before I could protest, he put his lips on mine again. The old trick always worked.

"Let's meet tomorrow night…to celebrate," I said finally.

Our session was around four in the afternoon. I sat in the waiting room, slightly early. When Leila appeared at the doorway, she was carrying a bunch of roses and wearing a bright red scarf that matched the flowers. It was slightly disconcerting, but not entirely out of character. I said hi and offered a handshake. She looked at my hand for a second before shaking it, giving a slight puff of disapproval.

"These are for you," she said, handing me the flowers. I took the bunch and whispered a thank you under my breath, then sat down again on the edge of the seat. We were called in after a minute.

From the therapist's point of view, we had come to a conclusion. She had said all she needed to say. Leila was not going to end her life. Time to move on. The session went well, up until the final moments before the end.

"I have been coming to these sessions to see you, as it's my only opportunity," Leila said. "My feelings have not changed."

It was true that we never saw each other anywhere else. To avoid more contact with her, I had been skipping classes at uni, which meant I also saw less of Pouya. I missed him, too. It made me mad at Leila, and then *that*.

The kick in the balls was harsh and hard. I had spent a lot of money and time, believing I was doing something right. I looked at Leila, mouth open. Meeting the therapist's eyes, I only hoped she was annoyed too, behind that fake professional smile. As we left the room, I looked at her again with pleading eyes and got a nod, which I interpreted as a middle finger.

"I'm not going to leave you, I can't," said Leila, once we were out on the street.

I was tired. "What do you mean?"

"I'm not going to leave you; I'll just follow you wherever you go."

There was conviction in those grey eyes. I could see a twitch in her jaw, one which only appeared when logic had left the building. The decision had been made, no room for argument. A part of me wanted to go back in the clinic and ask for help. I did not have the power to fight.

"Well, I'm going home. Do what you like," I said.

"OK, I'm coming with you."

I sighed in resignation, thinking, If I go home, she will have to leave at some point. Whatever the act was, it was bound to finish once I closed the door. I was going to see Babak later, to celebrate.

So, we started the silent journey back to my home, bunch of roses held dangling by my side, appearing as distraught as I was. We went to find a taxi. The smell of gasoline, the loud noise of traffic, and the heat of the sun overtook the moment. What if I escape? I thought. Or lose her in the mad rush-hour traffic? But my brain was merely trying to obscure the reality: she was not going anywhere.

We were within two minutes' walk of home, and I was angry.

Angry at myself for starting that relationship.

Angry at her for wasting so much time and money on therapy.

And angry at the bunch of roses I was still carrying.

She broke the silence: "I just want to know why you don't want me anymore. What is the *main* reason? Have you met another girl? Just tell me, I'll understand."

The main reason, I thought.

I couldn't believe it when I actually considered the unthinkable: Should I tell her the truth? What if she *does* understand? What if it all falls into place for her and then she leaves me alone?

Was this it? Was the first person I would ever come out to… her?

"Trust me, there is a very good reason, but I can't tell you," I started.

"I will understand, just say it. Is it someone else?"

"No."

"Then what?"

My head was about to explode. A wave of nausea made me stutter.

Did that man passing by just shake his head in disapproval?

Another voice shouted in my head: *Don't do it! She'll tell everyone!*

And then another: *Babak.*

It fuelled my paranoia. She could ruin my life with that information.

"I can't. Sorry, forget it. It doesn't matter. This has to end, and you need to stop. What you're doing will only push me away."

She had stopped listening after the word *can't*.

We were next to my building. I was still holding the damn roses and she stood in front of me.

I tried a kind tone: "Please go home, this isn't going anywhere. I'm going to go upstairs, now."

"I'll follow you."

"You can't. I'm going to close the door. Please, stop!"

If my parents were home, it would be a disaster. The secret revealed. Panic started digging through my gut.

She saw it. She sat on the kerb in front of our entrance.

My eyes bulged in disbelief. "What are you *doing*?"

"I'm not leaving. I'll sit here till someone comes."

What have I done to deserve this? What is happening?

I put the key in and opened the door to call her bluff.

She went for the buzzer, eyes looking wild. "I *will* ring your buzzer if you leave me here," she growled through her teeth.

She knew my weakness well and it worked. I was out again. She sat on the kerb again. I looked at her, glad I had stopped myself moments ago from telling her the truth. What had I been thinking even contemplating it?

It was getting dark, and Maman would have started wondering where I was. And Babak. I was not going to stand him up. I needed a plan.

Ali.

Poor Ali, he was the first person that came to my mind. I asked Leila to get up and walk with me to the phone booth so I could call home to say I was with Ali and would be late. She refused. I took her hand and tried pulling her up.

"I can't, I'm too weak," she mumbled with a sigh, and lay on the street as if her knees were not strong enough to stand.

I didn't know whether to laugh or cry. I wondered if I should be looking for cameras, hoping that it was all a funny show, filming my reaction to a breakdown. I was about to have one myself. Eventually, she managed to summon the strength to sit and be pulled to a standing position, but was not strong enough to walk properly and needed my arm to support herself. Smooth.

We walked to the telephone booth. First, I called home and let my mother know I was going out with Ali for dinner. Then I called Ali and briefly explained what had happened. He must have heard the desperation in my voice, as he agreed I could go to his to figure something out. And so we did.

Babak, I'm sorry.

Fifteen minutes later, we were standing in front of his house. Ali's older sister came down to the rescue with her brother, and Leila threw herself in her arms, crying. Ali's sister gave a small squeal initially, worried she was being attacked. My sympathy for Leila, at that point, was over. I looked at Ali, who seemed to be thinking the same. His face was confused. He had not anticipated the situation to be so bad. I was not sure Ali would have appreciated me falling into his arms and crying. His eyes said, *Don't you fucking dare.*

We went upstairs. Leila got comfortable, taking off her scarf and manteau. I told Ali the whole story. His expression was either of disbelief or despair—I couldn't tell the difference. Ali's dad was religious, like Baba. He was not home, but Ali wanted the situation sorted before he came back. I had literally made *my* problem, *his* problem. His sister offered to get Leila a taxi. I was eternally grateful, seeing the end of the ordeal. But Leila's answer was another slap to an already battered face.

"No, I'm not leaving. I'll go where he goes." She looked at me, jaw twitching.

Babak, I'm sorry.

Speechless, Ali's sister looked at us with eyebrows raised, mouthing, *What the hell?* She had only met Leila once before. Their mum was next to step in. She took Leila into the kitchen and talked for a while. I have no idea what went on in there, but I'd like to imagine she told her, *Get the fuck out of my house!* Ten minutes later, Leila was in a taxi and on her way home. That was the last time I saw her.

I thanked Ali and his family a billion times and went home around midnight.

I logged in on Yahoo! and read the message from Babak: **I guess I'm not seeing you tonight. Hope you enjoyed your time with your girlfriend.**

The bitterness of it made my face twist.

Babak, I'm sorry. But my apology remained only a thought. I closed the window and went to my bedroom.

The cat was out of the bag. I told my parents what had happened the next day: the suicide message, the therapy, and the breakdown. Baba called Leila's father and explained everything. It was now out of my hands, thankfully.

Adults took over. Maman instructed Leila to call her if she felt the urge to talk to me, hoping that she wouldn't. Well, she was wrong, and Leila called her from time to time. I was to blame, as far as Maman was concerned. "You played with this poor girl's heart," she said. "If you didn't want to marry her, you shouldn't have started it," and so on. I took it all, it was fine. I did deserve some of it.

There was one good—in fact, great—outcome from the whole Leila episode for me: for a very long time afterwards, I used it as an excuse for why I did not want to get married or have a girlfriend. I was, after all, traumatized.

Once the dust following Leila's breakdown had settled, I started seeing more of Babak again. Though, something in our relationship had shifted, too—a ripple effect from everything that had happened with Leila. Something was out of place. My insecurity had become palpable to him, my doubts worn on my face. He was being cautious for his own sake, not wanting to be pricked by the same thorn twice.

And he was right.

I found myself sitting in front of the therapist, two or three weeks later, on my own. She was surprised to see me. I told a brief version of what had happened with Leila, and she sympathized.

"So, *why* are you here today?" she asked finally, tapping her pen on the desk.

My mouth became dry, as if even my saliva did not want to be present for my answer. I looked at her for a moment, hoping she could read me and spare me the words I was about to mutter.

"Erm, because…Because, even before I completely finished with Leila, I had started a new relationship," I said at last, fiddling with my thumbs.

"Oh, OK. So, a new girl is in your life?"

"Not a girl."

"A boy?"

I nodded, breath held, saturated with guilt. I never imagined the first person I would come out to would be a therapist. I looked to the floor and reminded myself, *This is different.* You have not been forced to come here. There is no conspiracy.

I avoided eye contact.

"Right, have you told her?" she said.

"Of course not. No one can know."

"Of course, I won't write anything in your records. What do you want to do?" she said, putting her pen down.

I could see the veins and wrinkles on the back of her hands, resting on her desk. I wanted to reach and hold them when I said the words, "Can I be straight? N-normal?"

How I wish she would have said, *You* are *normal. Goodbye!*

"I'm not a sex therapist, but I can recommend a few I know of. Or, if you want to see me, I can help you."

"I would like to stick with you."

I had told Babak about my plan the night before. He had not been impressed, but was not surprised.

"You just had a relationship with a girl. Isn't that enough?" he'd said.

"She was mad. If I could be with someone not as intense, things would be different." I believed my relationship with Leila would not have been normal, even if I was straight. Though, I was missing the point: *if* I was straight.

And so began my own therapy sessions with a qualified psychologist.

I was going to become straight.

The Script and the Sparrow

2004

In 1973, eight years before I was born, homosexuality was removed from the DSM*—the criteria which, some thirty years later, in 2003–4, were used for our psychiatry module at medical school. I am now confident we were taught the sharia modified criteria, which kept homosexuality as a mental disorder on the list.

It was difficult to argue with a scientific fact when studying medicine. If a list of "abnormalities of the mind," written by smart people, included homosexuality, then it *was* abnormal—and that was if I took religion out of the equation, which at the time I could not.

When I finally opened up to my therapist and let the secret out, a heavy pressure was lifted off my chest. My failure in managing Leila and the shame that ensued had tipped me over the edge. I could not manage anything on my own. Not her, and not the monster rattling inside me, wilder than ever. The moment I spoke the words that day in the clinic, I passed on the responsibility of fixing myself to a professional. I could hold her hand to find my way out of the dark tunnel I had been lost in for so long. But that meant one thing: I had to let go of Babak's hand. Another break-up loomed.

I could not face talking about it to him. He had sensed it already. Despite his guards, he *was* going to be stung again.

"Wh-what about...you know...Babak?" I said at the end of our first session.

---

* The Diagnostic and Statistical Manual of Mental Disorders: the American classification of mental disorders.

"Is that the boy you said you have been…seeing?"

I looked down. A small nod, not meeting her eyes. I fixed my gaze on a small crack on the wooden floor, which was becoming blurred. I worried about him, and I didn't want to. I wanted the crack in me to be mended for good.

"Well, if you *do* want to commit, you shouldn't be seeing him anymore, right?"

Her voice was still calm and, when I looked up, the caring smile still sat on her lips.

I wiped my eyes and flashed a confident smile back. "Yes, right."

And so the fate of that relationship was sealed. I did not see Babak again, after that. How I wish I could hold him and say sorry.

The first step was to be around girls more often. Not particularly to become their boyfriend, but to start enjoying their company and appreciating them. Once I had more interactions with the opposite sex, the switch would eventually flick, and I would forget the desire for boys. The fire of appropriate sexual attraction would alight within. The only problem was that this would not be accepted by my family. My parents were already traumatized by the Leila experience and made it clear that the next one would be my wife. I did not have much room to manoeuvre.

"My mum won't let it be easy; she still blames me for what happened."

"I can help with that. Ask her to come with you, next time."

Sweat beads invaded my forehead in a flash. "Here? To see you?"

"Yes. Relax—your secret is safe with me. I have not written anything down and I will not tell her about your other desires."

"OK," I said, hesitant. "She can be difficult."

"Leave that with me." Her smile was reassuring.

I was glad I had come back for her help. I was going to let her make every decision.

*

It is true that gay men can make girl friends effortlessly. I started going out with a few girls from my class several nights a week, to the ever-increasing number of fast-food restaurants in the city. Saam and Ali tagged along. The more people there were around, the more distraction there was from the men I didn't want to be looking at.

Maman reacted as expected: disapproving and worried I was creating another disaster. I had already foreseen that and had a plan.

She was more open than I had anticipated to seeing my therapist. I sat outside while they had a talk. There was a sense of déjà vu: me sitting outside yet another therapist's office and my mother discussing me, only this time it was my choice, my way of making things right. I hoped my therapist would wave a wand over Maman, making her beliefs less of an obstacle in my path to redemption.

Leila and I ran into each other less and less at uni. As much as I hated it, I told Pouya about my relationship with Leila. With every detail I gave him, I hammered a nail into the coffin in which I had buried my desires for him. He listened and compassionately rubbed my shoulder. I was sure then that he was like that with everyone, including me, another straight boy with girlfriend problems. His soft brown eyes and warm hands continued to torment me, but I had a plan for that desire too.

I was going to kill it.

A hot summer in Tehran meant more and more men in tight T-shirts showing off their tanned skin and buffed figures. My next therapy session was to learn how to fend them off. Bringing up the sinful, diseased urge was entangled with a sense of shame every time. I delayed it with other words.

"When I'm out with my friends, girls or boys, it *is* fun, but…" I swallowed.

She nodded.

I looked down again. "But that doesn't stop my head turning when I see an attractive guy walking by." I winced at my choice of word: *attractive*. It was another failure to even use it for a man. I cleared my throat, continuing, "Also, I still fancy—" another wince— "I mean, *look at* men on TV, and have these dreams. I want them to stop."

I tried to make my questions sound casual, matter of fact. Clinical. As if I was sitting in class and only wanting to find out more. The emotion is not real, I told myself. It's fake. It's evil.

"Counting numbers in your head would help."

"Really?"

She adjusted her headscarf and put her palms on the desk in front of her. "These thoughts about men are a form of obsession. Making your mind do something else which has an order to it would stop other thoughts taking over."

Interesting. Her nod, her voice, and her smile made her words irrefutable.

So, I started counting numbers in my head. I counted and counted. The numbers danced in front of my eyes constantly, but they were not the only figures in my visual field.

One, two, three...Twenty-one, twenty-two, twenty-three...Oh, he's sexy. No, stop looking, keep counting...Twenty-four, twenty-five...The veins on his arms— Stop, stop...Twenty-six, twenty-seven...

It was impossible. I was failing her. I was failing myself.

She had other recommendations too, but, after that particularly absurd one, I decided to stop seeing her. I had spent too much time and money on therapy.

On a summer afternoon a few months after the disastrous day with Leila, I found myself at a different psychology clinic: Leila's. I had received a call the day before. Her therapist wanted to talk to me and get my side of the story. I agreed to see her without Leila being there.

I got there early. Sitting on the edge of my seat in the waiting room, I glanced at the secretary. She wore a full hijab, no hair showing. She seemed annoyed. For a moment, I imagined that she knew all about what had happened with Leila and that she was on Leila's side. Or perhaps she was just annoyed with my nervous foot tapping on the marble floor. I looked at the small picture of the Ayatollahs on the wall behind her, always making an appearance when I was in trouble. The sound of the door echoing in the bare waiting room made me jump. Leila's therapist, in a black chador, stood in the doorway.

"Majid?"

I sprung up to my feet like a guilty child caught, smiling. "Hi! Yes."

She smiled at me and looked over my shoulder. "Leila…?"

The smile on my face vanished. I stared at the woman. If I turned around, Leila would be standing there. Had she been hiding under the desk? I convinced myself it was the Ayatollahs' doing, their miracle. The therapist, realizing my face colour was resembling her office floor, mirrored my shock initially, her mouth remaining half open. Then, she laughed.

Really? Is she pulling a prank on me?

"Oh, I'm sorry! My secretary's name is Leila. I was just about to ask her…Are you OK?"

It took a second to register. My first thought was that Leila had *become* her secretary. She had not been on Leila's side, she *was* Leila.

I heard the therapist again: "Are you OK? I'm so sorry, I didn't mean to scare you. It just happens that they have the same name."

"Of course, no, no, don't worry. Can I go in?" I said finally, wiping my hands on my jeans.

"Sure, I'll be with you in a second."

I was glad she needed to sort something out with her secretary, Leila. I sank into the couch in front of her desk, letting my heartbeat settle down. Moments later, she joined me.

Having done it once already, it was easier to come out to her. In fact, I was intrigued how she would react to the big reveal, and I enjoyed the transient shock on her face, which she managed to cover up quickly. Coming out to therapists was turning into a pastime of mine.

It was a short consultation; she didn't have much to argue with and could not even use that information to help Leila.

I then told her how I was trying to get help and that my quest to become straight had not been successful yet. Seeing my despair, she offered to help.

Could it be? I thought. Could she, a symbol of religion and science merged, be the solution?

I was blind not to have seen it in the first place.

"Sure. I need help and I am disappointed with my own therapist," I said.

She had a better solution: given my problem was a medical condition, after all, she suggested I see her colleague next door, a psychiatrist with a special interest in sex therapy. It sounded promising and I agreed immediately.

Leila, the secretary with the stone face, was quick to open the diary and found an appointment for me there and then—another sign from Allah. My father's money was being spent on the right cause, for once. My pocket a bit lighter now, I saw the psychiatrist.

The doctor had a kind demeanour. He wore a crushed shirt with rolled-up sleeves, which gave him a more hands-on, I-fix-anything appearance. Nevertheless, what he said was unnerving. He agreed with my now ex-therapist that fantasizing about men was a form of obsession, and he took it a step further.

"It is a form of obsessive-compulsive disorder. You have obsessive thoughts about men, and this draws you to the compulsion of wanting to meet them and have sex with them."

He was confident, words floating out of his mouth as if practised and said a thousand times before, to a thousand confused souls before me. It made sense. Maybe he was right. But then again, with that definition, wasn't every human behaviour a form of OCD? Didn't my obsessive thoughts about food, also known as hunger, draw me to the compulsion of eating?

I did not argue and didn't even think twice. I had asked for help and it was being offered to me. The decision was being made by people who "knew better." He prescribed me antidepressants, which at a lower dose were given for OCD. The fifteen-minute appointment was wrapped up quickly and he offered to see me again in one month. I could not say no to any of it.

I walked out into the scorching sun, dazed, script in hand. I looked around as crowds of people walked past, unfazed by my insignificant presence among them. The loud ringing in my head muffled the honks and the traffic. My throat burned as I inhaled the thick engine fumes. I tried to think back over the last few hours: I had walked in to offer help in Leila's therapy and walked out with a prescription in my hand and a stamp on my forehead which read *DISORDER*.

It had happened too quickly. That thought, and the smells and sounds of a suffocating city made me dizzy. I heard his words being whispered in my ear in a malicious tone: *Obsessive compulsive disorder*. I wanted to scream.

I looked up.

On a tree across the street, I saw a small sparrow fiddling with twigs, hopping on a branch as if dancing. I was suddenly envious. The tiny bird did not care one bit about the sea of people walking by; she was doing her own thing, dancing to her own tune. I wanted to be her, I wanted to stop caring about what others thought of me.

A moment of reflection, a glimpse of clarity.

Looking around, I saw the green metal public bin. I glanced again at the script in my hand.

Fuck you.

I tore up the piece of paper and threw it in the bin. I gave a loud sigh, as if unloading a ton of rock off my back. I looked across the street again. The sparrow had gone. I smiled to myself and whispered a "thank you" to the unlikely small saviour. I knew I was going to be fine. I had to be.

Being labelled with a psychiatric diagnosis was a step too far and made me feel sick. Hence, my obsession with not being sick led to the compulsion to throw the bloody script in the bin.

I had given up on psychology. I had to try to strike a balance between Allah and homosexuality.

My beliefs were already milder. I missed prayers often and was far less bothered about offering them three times a day. I didn't fast every day in Ramadan. I skipped going to speeches and mourning ceremonies during Muharram (mourning month in Shia Islam), and stopped going to the end of Ramadan rally. My brothers still went, mostly. Maman was not happy with my declining commitments, but there was not much she could do about it.

Although therapy did not work and had proved to be a disappointment, it had not completely deterred me from my goal. I still tried to find a girlfriend, though with less conviction.

At university, life began to gain shape. I got closer to Pouya as a friend. He now told me about his dates with girls, and *I* offered advice. I held his hand when he needed support, knowing it would not be perceived as anything else. I wanted the smell of his skin on mine, though. Win, win.

On the other front, I had become a pro at Yahoo! chats, and had many sleepless nights sitting in front of the computer. From one window to the next, I juggled several chats at once.

In one of the many opened chat windows, I began chatting with Kian; he was smart and his cheeky chat style was entertaining. The seed of something new was planted, something I had not felt or known before, and was unaware of when I closed the chat box that night.

He was going to be my first love.

He Wins

2005

The year 2005 was one of change—a delayed adulthood of sorts. I started a medical internship, seeing patients in hospital rotations. Lectures and sterile classroom flirts were put behind me.

I had survived Leila and my brush with marriage and suicide, I had survived therapy, and I had survived the constant nag of committing a haram.

My new online love interest, Kian, put the task of finding a girlfriend on hold.

A chilling thought had begun fogging my brain: Am I really beginning to accept myself as I am?

I was twenty-four, Kian five years older. I had risked giving him my home number and he had given me his. He lived on his own, in a different city, Sari, in the north, close to the Caspian Sea. A picture with sunglasses was all I had seen of him.

What pulled me to him was his charm, and he *was* charming. Well spoken, well educated, smart, and confident. He'd lived most of his life in Canada. He told me he had been to forty-odd countries, that he worked for the UN and was now based at the UN office in Sari. He was fluent in English and French, and he was funny. To me, he was the definition of "been there, done that." He was also bisexual. I, a naïve boy who was just coming to terms with his sexuality, saw being bi as fascinating, sexy, and another accomplishment. The idea that his pool of picks included girls as well, and yet I was chosen, was flattering.

I listened to him for hours talking about his life, and he didn't disappoint. He talked in his deep, manly voice about places he had been and things he'd done, giving timely chuckles at his own mishaps. I only listened, with my mind imagining his life, imagining me beside him. We—mostly him—talked every day. I got a jolt of excitement even when I heard his answer phone, the recording in Farsi, then English, and then French.

Sometimes, I wondered whether achieving as much as he claimed he had was even possible by the age of thirty. He also joked about the sharia and the rituals I followed religiously. It didn't offend me. I wanted to be like him; his confidence was alluring. He even had a dog with a French name—Coco—and she was the other subject of most of our conversations.

I missed him on days we didn't speak, and got anxious. The withdrawal from his voice was painful and the recorded voicemail was only a temporary fix. I stopped going on Yahoo! Messenger—or, if I did, it was just to chat with him. I could not wait to meet him.

When I finally did, about two months later, I was already head over heels in love.

I told Ali and Saam about him—well, only the parts of the story which did not include anything about my feelings. Ali raised an eyebrow and stroked his imaginary beard again, but did not say anything. Ever since Leila, something had shifted in him. The holy father could sniff lies better than anyone else, and I could tell he was on to me. I avoided eye contact when telling him about Kian.

Saam was more suspicious of Kian himself.

"I have a feeling, if the UN had an office in Iran, it would be in Tehran, don't you think?" said Saam, followed by, "Don't you find his stories about his family and how he ended up in Canada elaborate and hard to believe?"

I laughed at Saam's conspiracy theories. To me, Kian was a charismatic man with a godlike confidence. I never found out whether he was a spy, which was the point, I suppose.

One of the signs of being in love is the fear of saying the words and not hearing "me too" in return. I did not dare say it, but he knew. He could pull my strings. I was the one chasing. I needed to see him.

Sina, my youngest brother, was truly privileged. He got away with a lot more than I did. If he came home after eleven p.m., our dad's curfew time, Baba was much softer on him. If he asked Baba to give him money to travel to a different city with one or two of his friends from school, his wish was granted before he'd finished asking.

Maybe I should try it, I thought. If I asked as casually as Sina, there was no reason for Baba to say no. No reason.

Baba was sitting on the floor in the TV room, shuffling through the pages of his newspaper.

"Baba?"

"Yes?" He didn't look up. It seemed like he'd finally found the piece he wanted to read.

I tried to adopt a casual tone, but the words came out of my mouth in a high-pitched voice: "Can I have some money to go to Sari?" At the same time, I was thinking, Please just say yes and it'll be over. Please.

"Why do you want to go there?" The routine question came out almost as a mumble, automatically. His face was half covered by the paper, making it difficult for me to read.

"Erm, I want to go meet a friend."

"Oh? How do you know this friend?"

Ah, that question. There are times one needs a plan—several plans, in fact: A, B, C, and maybe even a plan D. Well, I didn't have any.

"Erm, I know him from chat—Yahoo!"

As those words came out of my mouth like links of a chain, one after the other, pulling out a bucket of foul gunk from a sewer, I already knew I had dug too deep. The stink was already filling the room. But it was too late, and my mind had frozen.

Baba had now flipped the corner of the newspaper and was looking directly at me over the top of his glasses, which sat threateningly low on his nose.

"Really? Have you met him before?"

Brain shut down, I was on autopilot, my mission being self-destruction. As if I had been given a truth syrup, I said, "No."

Baba was not smiling. His face was rigid, emotionless. I was not going to go to Sari, but that was the least of the problems

I had landed myself in. I looked at the newspaper in his hand, desperately hoping the column in the paper was really important and yearning to be read.

"I don't think it's wise to go to someone's place for the first time, in a different city, if you haven't even met them before," said my father, with concern vibrating in his voice.

What surprised me was he had given a logical answer as to why he thought it was a bad idea. He was not asking, "Who is this guy?" or "What is Yahoo! Messenger?" or "Are you freaking gay?"

My face was red with shame, beads of sweat trickling down my back. I gave an awkward smile and whispered, "OK, sure, no worries." I needed to escape again.

After years of mastering a double life, I should have known better. There was one rule: no mixing of the two lives was allowed, or possible. Everything could be ruined.

Baba continued to tell me how safety was important, what I wanted to do could be seriously dangerous, and I should never do anything so reckless. How crucial it was to meet someone first before making such decisions. Baba, unintentionally, was giving me dating advice.

I listened, head down, staring at the red floral pattern of our carpet, then I nodded and finally left the room. I knew he was still looking at me as I did. The snap as he unfolded the newspaper with an angry shake made me quicken my pace. As soon as I closed the door to my bedroom, panic crept in. What the hell was that? What was I thinking? What have I just done?

My determination to see Kian in Sari did not dampen. My dad and possibly Maman were going to suspect a slip-up. But I was in a trance. Even a shake as hard as that could not wake me from it. The prospect of meeting him made me breathless.

So, I came up with a different strategy: do it secretly. A scheme took shape in my mind, one which would involve more lies and more stealing money from Baba.

During the medical internship, we had started night shifts, staying in the hospital for twenty-four hours. I told my family I would be on a forty-eight-hour shift at the hospital, which meant I would not be coming home for two days. I bought myself a return plane ticket to Sari and took leave from work. I packed a small bag, as if going to hospital.

Next, I need to buy a gift, something unique. Kian was into history and antiques, subjects I had zero expertise in. But there was one place I could find anything: Tehran's Bazaar.

Located in south Tehran, the Bazaar was one place I had not ventured into before. The privileged bubble of the north provided everything I needed. But now I was looking for that special gift.

The early afternoon sun was unforgivingly baking the asphalt, but the Bazaar was buzzing. I joined the slow-moving stream of people as I navigated through twisted narrow alleyways lined with stalls, the goods and tat on display. Salesmen stood by them, shouting, "*Haraj, haraj!*"—"Last chance, biggest discount *ever!*"— as if the sale was only for that minute.

An older woman in a green thick scarf and with a prayer chador tied around her waist sat on a little plastic stool outside one of the smaller stalls selling tablecloths. The holes in her worn-out flat shoes revealed chipped nail polish on her big toe, and a string of prayer beads sat on her lap. She was not shouting, only picking at the dead skin of the calluses on her palm. The countless wrinkles and creases on her sun-kissed face moved synchronously as she smiled at me, revealing her one remaining tooth.

I felt out of place, instantly recalling the old lady who worked for us. There I was, in my new expensive north Tehran attire, shopping for a man I loved. As she started unfolding one of the tablecloths to show me, I immediately said, "No, no, thank you," to save her the trouble. She shook her head and the smile faded, making her disappointed face resemble a statue. She then waved her hand dismissively, shooing me away. I quickened my pace.

Stall owners got me to smell a perfume, or shoved whatever they were selling in my face, and, before I had a chance to say anything, insisted I would get a decent discount. After roaming from one corner of the maze where the heavy smell of different spices burned my nostrils to another where glass and wooden handicrafts were sold, and after asking around for a while, I finally found antiques lined up on the floor on a dusty maroon cloth. An ancient man, sporting bushy eyebrows, an unkempt beard, and a dervish hat, sat cross-legged by them. I wondered if he was for sale too. A small handmade silver box caught my eye. It was not cheap, and Gandalf did not like bargaining. I could not even tell if it was truly an antique, and when I sheepishly asked him if it was a genuine piece, his death stare shut me up. I bit the bullet and went for it, hoping Kian would like it. Thanks again, Baba.

This is a memory smelling of salt in the air as it hit my face, and tasting of mint and tobacco, when my heart shot fireworks.

The day arrived. It started with a returning guilt burden when I saw how Maman felt sorry for me, believing I was gearing up for a terrible shift at the hospital. But a much stronger feeling had taken over. As I got in a taxi towards the airport, I heard my Baba's warnings in my ear one final time. I slid my hand in the small rucksack and felt the edges of the silver box, now neatly wrapped. I smiled at the image of Kian opening it and imagined his excitement. The voice was long silenced before I took my hand out again.

And so I flew to Sari.

It was a short flight; in less than an hour, I was at Sari airport. Kian was supposed to pick me up. My heart was beating so fast, I could barely breathe. As soon as I walked into the airport lounge, I went to the toilets. I checked myself in the mirror one last time, touched my gel-hard hair, took a deep breath, and headed outside. I passed the airport security, who looked exactly like *Basij* and morality policemen, in dark green uniforms. I kept my head down, as if worried that *I am committing a haram* was burned on my forehead. Their looks lingered on me for a bit before they resumed their conversations.

It was nearly midday. As soon as the sliding doors of the air-conditioned terminal opened, the hot and humid northern air welcomed me. It was not busy, only a few cars parked—and his was one of them, the one flashing its headlights. I squinted and made out his outline in the driver's seat. I could see sunglasses and a smile. I smiled back and walked towards his car, conscious of every step I took. I was about to meet *him*.

I opened the door and got in. "Hi," I said, as I turned to face him.

He was nothing short of what I had expected. He seemed taller than me, had an athletic build, was clean-shaven, and smelt fresh. I had butterflies in my belly, hopelessly in love, and was getting more nervous. What if I'm not his type? I worried. What if I'm not good enough? How miserable will the next two days be?

He took his sunglasses off. "Hi! You're here, finally!" The warmth in his voice and the smile were reassuring, but not enough. We shook hands and touched cheeks. His skin was soft and cool, and his grasp strong.

He started the car and began talking like he did over the phone, in his typical confident and casual manner. I was thankful for it. As he drove through the beautiful lush green surroundings, I rolled the window down and breathed in the fresh, clean air, noticing the faint sea smell. I smiled to myself. As he carried on talking about his day, my mind ventured through a whirlwind of different scenarios, from us being together forever to him asking me to leave sooner. I had already made a plan for what to do if he didn't want me. It would have been costly, but doable: I'd get a flight back the same day and perhaps stay with Saam till my "hospital shift" was over, which would've been excruciatingly awkward.

I was only half listening to him when I realized we had arrived at his flat. We were welcomed by an excited Coco, the small white ball of fluff. I did not care anymore if a dog was considered *najis*. I was not going to wash my hands seven times after touching her.

Five minutes later, I was in the kitchen with Kian's back to me as he washed a plate in the sink, still talking.

I was still unsure, still on edge.

I looked at Coco's inquisitive big black eyes for answers: nothing there. Everything was simply too good to be true.

And then, in a swift move, he turned around and kissed me, wrapping me in his arms.

Within a heartbeat, all my anxiety and fear melted away. I kissed him back, eyes closed, breathing in his scent. I already knew the sweet mint-coated nicotine taste was going to hook me. He locked his hands behind me and pressed me against him. His chest against mine, I could feel his heavy breathing through his skin. He took my hand and led me to his bedroom, telling Coco to stay out as he closed the door.

Afterwards, he took me through his impressive antiques collection, a silver box its latest addition. Even if it was not a true antique, he seemed excited and found a purpose for it immediately.

His flat was my refuge from religion and his bed impervious to Allah's vengeance. I was in a dreamy place I had never imagined myself in. In awe of him, I was already scared of losing it.

I spent one of the best forty-eight hours of my life in Sari with Kian; I had to pinch myself several times.

When I got back home, already missing him, I was greeted with a comforting meal Maman had cooked for me after my "horrible forty-eight-hour shift," later making sure I got the quiet needed to catch up on sleep. It was sweet and sad at the same time. In bed, staring at the ceiling, I contemplated the past two days, repeating every memory and every minute I'd spent there, making sure they were engraved in my mind, never to be forgotten. I couldn't stop thinking about when I'd be able to see him again.

My relationship with Kian was *the* turning point in my beliefs. His influence over me was immense, life-changing.

I realized that I was not experiencing "just a phase." It was the *real* me.

The ugly hidden monster was not a monster, after all, and certainly not ugly; it was a colourful butterfly, ready to leave his cocoon and spread his wings.

At twenty-five, I was finally accepting who I was.

Part II

The Love, the Quiz and the Crush

Autumn 2005

Under Kian's influence, I had stopped praying. He never told me not to, but made me think twice about the religious routines, and, having my own doubts already, I had little to offer in defence. I was growing out of the stories I had been told when I was a child. I also found it hard to believe Allah was interested in my prayers: that time of day when I mumbled something in a different language, which I didn't understand, mean a word of, or care about. Questions danced above my head as I prayed: Why am I doing this? Does Allah really need this? Would he truly punish me if I didn't?

It was the same scene again: I was behind my desk, Baba at the door wearing his typical frown. I looked up inquisitively.

"Do you *not* pray anymore?" he snapped. The ominous tone demanded an apology.

But I was feeling defiant. In my mind, I had what I thought would be a winning argument. "No," I said.

A few creases were added to his forehead. "Why?"

Deep breath, you can do this.

"I don't see the point; I don't pay attention to it. I think—"

I was going to give him the whole argument, well thought through. But he was not there to listen. He was not there for an explanation. He interrupted my speech.

With a calm voice, he spoke slowly, allowing every word to sink in: "You may not understand why you do it, but you *have* to pray as long as you live in this house, understand?"

I nodded and looked away as he left. I pushed back my chair and walked around the room, fists clenched. I wished I could speak like Kian, demand attention.

Baba and I knew it was not going to happen; we were both defeated. He kept waking me up for morning prayers, which I deliberately did not offer. I would sit in our living room for five minutes, looking at the Ayatollah's picture on the wall. He *knew* what I was doing, and he was still angry, still disapproving. I hushed him, then went back to bed. Baba, the Godfather, may have had the final word, but it was just that—a word.

Kian came to Tehran a few times and we managed to hook up, with more lies about night shifts at the hospital. I was getting frustrated with the long-distance relationship.

I had finally come out to myself and was desperate to drown in my feelings for another man. With him, though, it was like a trapped breath in my chest, and each time I tried to release it, I feared it might be my last.

Our chats were not romantic; mostly, he would give a monologue about his day, what he had got up to, and Coco. I didn't know how he felt about me; it was as if he did not want the conversation diverted towards *us*. The uncertainty was suffocating.

I didn't dare ask. What if he lashes out? I thought. What if he thinks I am being "clingy" and dumps me? The pathetic helplessness was starting to hurt.

I needed to distract myself. I needed to stop thinking about him so much and find a safe place where I could proudly shout, "I am gay."

It drove me into the warm embrace of the one thing I knew well: the internet.

In my straight life, on the other hand, I felt more in control—a feeling which was not meant to last.

One evening in the summer of 2005, I had Ali, his sister, Saam, and my cousin Atoosa over at ours. Sina was home, but my parents were away.

When conversation ran dry, Saam came up with the brilliant idea of playing a game of truth. He always had an itch to entertain.

We spun a bottle in the middle of the carpet. The person whom the bottle pointed towards *had* to answer truthfully, no matter what they were asked. Years later, I realized how we had modified a sexual game into something so incredibly dull. How Saam would have kicked himself.

The bottle decided that Ali was to be my tormentor. I thought, There is nothing he doesn't know, so this will be quick.

"Are you interested in girls, Majid?" was the question that came out of his small lips surrounded by chubby cheeks.

Blood rushed to my head, my heart began to kick my chest wall trying to escape the scene, and a bit of my dinner started creeping up to my throat. I made eye contact with Ali, wishing he would say something funny to follow up, but his eyes were serious and there were no smiles. I looked at the others, hoping they would come to my rescue. All looked on expectantly, silent.

I swallowed and composed myself. "Y-yes. What kind of question is that?" I gave a faint chuckle.

But he was not letting go, like a lion squeezing on its prey's windpipe. "Really? You know you must tell the truth. Is that the truth?"

Not now, not like this. Not in front of all these people.

I had to stand my ground. My face was red. "I am, and it is a ridiculous question; you met my girlfriend. I'm sure you remember her well." My tone was daring, and it was effective.

He said, "OK," and narrowed his eyes. The awkward tension was contagious.

His sister came to my aid: "You got your answer, Ali. A waste of a question. Next."

It was not a waste to *him*. I could feel his eyes on me for a while afterwards. I didn't give him a chance to reopen the subject.

I thought about it later, in bed. What scared me was that I'd wanted to say, *No, I'm not interested in girls; I'm gay.* I wanted to get it over and done with and shout it out. A bit of me was excited about the confrontation, but I wasn't ready, and wasn't sure they were either. Not then.

That night, when I eventually slept, I was smiling. *He knows.*

*

In my penultimate year at university, I got closer to Pouya.

Pouya—the blurred line between my straight and gay lives, belonging to neither entirely.

My six-year-long crush on him had not faded. The random holding of my hand, the hugs and the touches became more frequent, but I never got used to them. I was beginning to think he was gay. He talked about girlfriends now and then, but I did not believe it, or I chose not to. Girls, as usual, were there to cover up a secret.

The thought made me more attracted to him. Having accepted my own sexuality, I was becoming bolder. I wanted him, and there was no voice stopping me. Religion had become powerless. I had waited long enough and now wanted to take action. The frustration with Kian only fuelled my resolve.

I invited Pouya for a sleepover at mine. As a classmate, I needed no back-up story for Maman and Baba. He delightedly accepted. I was the architect of a scheme, using every innocent loophole within our household to my benefit, and somehow even convincing myself that my intentions were pure.

After dinner, once I'd come back from the kitchen for the last time, I stood at our living-room door, looking at him. He'd forgotten to bring extra clothes and was wearing one of my oversized T-shirts.

Sitting on the chair sideways, with one elbow on the dining table and the other on the back of the chair, he was looking at his phone. I took in his black hair gelled into small spikes; his tanned skin, more prominent against the white T-shirt; his clean-shaven face with those soft-as-velvet eyes; and his lips, full and wet on the corner he usually chewed.

He saw me. "All done?"

"Yes," I cleared my throat, "all done, just need to sort out the mattresses, now."

He stretched and yawned. The T-shirt's sleeves flopped back, revealing the full length of his arms.

I swallowed. "I'll bring some water, too," I said, and went out again. What are you doing?

I brought two single mattresses and some sheets to set up on the floor. Pouya watched me neatly laying a sheet over the first mattress. He was now sitting backwards on the chair, his arms hugging the backrest and his chin resting on top of it.

"Maybe one mattress is enough," he said.

I looked up, cheeks blushed like a child seeing a candy.

He'd tilted his head to one side and was giving me a lopsided smile.

It had come much sooner and smoother than I'd anticipated. Is he joking? He must be! Although this was precisely why I'd wanted him over, doubt upon doubt lurked in my mind.

"Hah, sure, maybe one is enough." I said it as if I got his "joke" and was laughing along. What are you doing? I hated the question ringing in my head, knowing I had no answers. *Next time,* was all my brain could summon.

He laughed too and I could not tell if it was genuine or he was disappointed. I needed to rectify this. Be brave.

Once lying on our separate mattresses, I turned to face him. "So, a goodnight kiss?" I said, before letting fear take over again. The nervous giggle escaped, no matter how hard I tried.

"On the lips?" he replied, with a laugh. He was not shy about throwing opportunities my way.

I was going to take this one, heart beginning to race. "Sure."

He leaned over, kissing me on my lips—only a peck—then he smiled and lay back.

My eyes followed as he did. I was speechless. I could not even laugh.

He turned his back and said, "Goodnight," just like that.

I whispered a "Goodnight" back, but kept looking at his back for a while, not believing what had just happened, already wanting more. I didn't sleep at all that night. He *is* gay.

*

Baba had a flat outside Tehran, in the mountains surrounding the city, near the town of Fasham. It was about an hour's drive away from the capital. Situated in an incredible secluded spot, overlooking a valley, it was a quiet and romantic haven. My friends and I used to go there every once in a while, for a weekend; we played cards, smoked shisha, and watched TV—there was even a satellite feed there.

This innocent start later turned into something very different, once I started seeing the opportunity before me. The Fasham holiday home turned into a sanctuary where a lot of mischief took place.

This memory is quiet like the surroundings, hushed like a secret, and aches like a cramp in my heart.

Pouya was the first friend I took to the Fasham flat with a different agenda in mind. We had not discussed what had happened the other night when we kissed. I pretended it was "no big deal"—however, I was excited about spending another night alone with him.

As expected, Pouya fell in love with the place. The serenity and quiet it offered was truly seductive. We ate takeaway rice and chicken and watched TV. I looked at him from the corner of my eye, trying again to read him. Can he see what's going on inside my head? I wondered. Can he hear my heartbeat too? The silence felt too heavy, and any awkward word or joke was not enough to lift it.

Soon, we found ourselves on the bed, lying next to each other, looking at the ceiling. I closed my eyes and listened as he talked. He seemed comfortable, his voice soothing.

"Are you asleep already?"

I turned to face him. "No, just listening."

"Oh, I thought I was being boring."

I put my hand on his face. He did not flinch. I was surprised at my own confidence. His skin felt warm, as if blood was rushing to his cheeks. I didn't need to say anything. I slowly moved my face closer to his, looking him directly in his brown eyes.

We kissed.

It was quiet outside. The silence was more than welcome, now. Time had stopped and we were swallowed in a vacuum, where there was only us. The moment took us with it. Pouya didn't speak. I unbuttoned his shirt, kissing him over his body. He exhaled deeply. My anxiety had long diminished. His touch was gentle and his hands steady. I looked up as I unbuttoned his jeans for a final confirmation. He only smiled. He wanted it as much as I did.

About twenty minutes later, we lay next to each other, back where we'd started, both in a state of disbelief and relief, staring at the ceiling. I moved my hand closer to his, hooking my little finger into his. He squeezed my hand, turned, and kissed me on the cheek.

"Good night."

"Night."

Without saying another word, we fell asleep. Before drifting away, a thought settled in my head: Six and half years of waiting was definitely worth it.

Next morning, when I opened my eyes, I turned my head to find him still asleep. There was a flutter in my chest. As I moved to the edge of the bed, he opened an eye and mumbled a "Good morning." I smiled and kissed him on the cheek. As soon as my lips touched his face, I felt it: a spasm, a tiny wince. It was enough. I stood up quickly and left the room. Something was not right.

When he finally came out for breakfast, he was fully dressed, ready for the trip back. He did not make eye contact. There was a strange familiarity in the air: guilt.

"Erm, we need to go back soon," he said. "I have work to do at home."

I didn't reply. He had to look at me to see if I'd heard him. When our eyes met, I did not see his gentle look anymore. It was replaced with pain, with frustration.

"What happened last night…it…it was not right…I'm not gay."

I saw myself in him, a few years back, muddled and conflicted. I wanted to say something to help, something no one had told me.

"I understand how you feel. Trust me, I have been there."

Too soon. He was not ready for any of that.

"No. Listen, you are a good friend, and will always be. But I'm not gay. I shouldn't have done what I did. I feel…I feel I have abused your family's trust in me. They think I am your friend… not…not this."

It broke my heart to hear the words coming from his lips. Those same lips I was caressing with mine not too long ago. Was this how Babak had felt, back when I'd insisted *I* was straight?

I knew I could not do much to comfort him. I knew he needed to figure things out for himself. Was he at the beginning of the painful journey I had been through?

I packed up quickly and we travelled back to Tehran in silence. Six years of wait and hope ended there.

Pouya had become the only person from my straight life who knew I was gay, and he was not going to stick around. He respected me enough not to say anything to anyone, or perhaps he was worried it would have invited questions about him. My contact with him became less and less. He became visibly uncomfortable when I was around, although he masked it with silly jokes.

I avoided him, for his sake; I knew he was out of my life.

The Reveal

2006

The Kian impact on my faith had taken on a life of its own, messing up my mind and practices. Islam, on the one hand, allowed room for questions, but, on the other, drew red lines which I could not cross. We were taught that "one may not always understand why one must do something. That is our defect, not Allah's." Or, "not finding a reason for something does not mean there is none. Have faith." These were words Maman spoke again and again—no, she lived by them.

My faith was no longer strong enough to keep me going. Stories of the Prophet's miracles or the description of heaven and hell only rendered the religion more unbelievable. My life was a contradiction because I was Muslim *and* gay; the two words were not meant to exist next to each other, and I despised the hypocrisy. I felt my religion did not give me enough leeway to get away with being gay. I had to choose—and, at that point, it was an easy choice.

At home, mid conversation, Maman would occasionally drop something like "so and so has found a suitable girl…" and that "she is not very religious, you may like her…" How she tried to sugar-coat that "righteous path" and adjust it to my liking, whatever it took.

Marriage was her favourite subject, and the lectures about the importance of marriage and building a family became more frequent. My parents had been more cautious just after my disastrous relationship with Leila, but enough time had passed now for them to consider me ready to move on. My only weak pushback was, "I need to finish my studies before getting married."

With the gradual mounting marriage pressure, and since the little game of truth last summer with Ali, it was time to come clean. I wanted to introduce my best straight friends to my "Mr. Hyde."

I was almost sure Ali and Saam would not mind, but *almost* wasn't good enough. I had got close to the subject before with others, letting my guard down, and regretted it.

Sharing our passion for films, Ali and I tried watching most, if not all, of the Oscar-nominated films. Western films on VHS tapes or CDs were sold by street sellers in parts of Tehran. One could also find them walking among cars at a traffic light.

Watching a cowboy Heath Ledger luring Jake Gyllenhaal into a tent and using his spit as lube sparked an idea in my mind.

I had already seen *Brokeback Mountain*; I knew it wasn't entirely dissimilar to my life. I could relate to the secret double life depicted in it. Ali and Saam took little convincing to watch it with me. A reaction, a feel of what they thought about homosexuality, was the aim.

My nerves were firing left, right, and centre. It felt like they were watching a film about me, but I kept my composure, with an eye on both for every wince, noting every comment.

Afterwards, in my bedroom, Ali and I talked about the technical bits: acting, directing, music, and whatnot. But Saam's loud fake yawn signalled I may have been losing the opportunity to address the key question.

"So, what do you think about, you know…the gay bit?" I said.

Saam sat up immediately, as if he'd been poked with a hot rod. "I personally don't get it, but, if some people are like that, well, they are what they are. I don't care," he said.

I was about to open my mouth.

"What is there not to get?" said Ali softly. "Most men like women, but some like men. I think it's normal."

I looked up at him, absorbing the words coming from my best friend, after all these years—years I'd wanted so badly to share with him, and I now wished I had. A knot formed in my throat, a mixture of regret and pride.

I cleared my throat. "Yeah, I think it's normal, too," I said, looking at Ali.

Was that the first time *I* had said those words out loud, too?

Saam didn't disagree. The conversation carried on for an hour afterwards. Maybe it was safe to come out to them, after all. I could have said it there and then, but saying *those* words seemed impossible. That needed a plan of its own. A separate *when, where* and *how*.

Maman, also interested in critically acclaimed films, asked about *Brokeback Mountain* once, in front of my brother Saman, Mohammad.

His face twisted, as if a war had broken out in the bush which was his beard. "You don't want to watch *that* film; it's about same-sex *players*."*

That was it. The way *he* said it. The disgust filled the room like the stench of rotten fish.

I shut my half-open mouth, biting the inside of my cheek, furious and helpless. I was going to suggest she should see it. Not anymore, especially when she replied, "God forbid."

I sat quietly, my teeth clenched.

If only he knew how close he was to one of these *players*.

Once Maman had left the room for prayers, I turned to him. "I wanted Maman to see the film; can you keep your opinions to yourself?"

It was so unexpected that Saman could only stare at me as he chuckled a nervous laugh. I held his gaze, face flushed, but I could not speak or swallow my saliva.

"It is haram. It should not—"

"Oh, just SHUT UP. You and your harams," my voice broke through, trembling.

He stood up and walked towards me, narrowed his eyes, and walked past, towards his bedroom door.

I was not done yet. "Go! Go and sniff your love's T-shirt, your Payam," I spat.

---

* Since attraction to the same sex is meaningless and a grave sin in Islam, it is replaced with a derogatory way of saying the same word: "same-sex player" (or sodomite).

I wanted the words to hurt. I wanted to ease the pain in my own chest.

He turned back. The slap came harder than I expected. I welcomed the sting on my cheek as it was joined by a stream of tears. When I looked back, I saw him slamming his door shut, clenching his *Tasbih*.

I did not speak with Saman again after that.

I knew then I may never be able to broach the subject with Maman, but I decided I would stand my ground where I was able. I would not allow her or Baba to impose religion and all the extras that came with it, including marriage, on me.

On the other side of the ever-thinning veil of sharia, my love life was in a bit of a mess; I needed to move on from Kian.

We still chatted now and then, conversations which were becoming less and less frequent and more and more uninteresting. I could not recall when I'd seen him last and did not want to care. He was the only gay person I talked to, and he was not listening. I went on random dates occasionally and had hooked up a couple of times. The distraction revived a bit of normality, one which was eclipsed by a stale relationship.

The internet, my refuge from Kian's mental torment, remained my main mode of finding dates.

And with dates came the excuses, the lies. My two straight guardian angels, Ali and Saam, were who I told my parents I was with—mostly Saam.

He was less bothered with my made-up stories and did not ask too many questions. I'd send him a message, which typically read, *I'm with you—don't call and ask for me,* and his usual reply was a simple, *OK*. He thought I was seeing girls, and, when asked how I managed to find them, I laughed it away with a vague answer.

On one occasion, however, Maman called his home looking for me. He had to make up a lie on the spot, and that made him anxious, especially as he really didn't know where I was or what I was up to.

I called Saam later that night to thank him.

He huffed and puffed, "Honestly, I don't care how many girls you are sleeping with, but this was way more stressful than I expected. You didn't warn me your mum would actually call."

"Calm down—nothing happened, did it?"

That was not what he wanted to hear.

"If you don't tell me now what the hell you were up to, good luck with next time. I am not covering up for you again."

It was an empty threat, and we both knew that.

I don't know whether the sex had been good, or I was just in a good mood, but, instead of making up another story, I said, "OK, OK. I was at someone's place—"

Maybe he was looking for an argument, maybe he was surprised, maybe both, "Who? A girl from uni? Yahoo!? Tell me more."

"Not a girl."

"A *guy*?"

"Erm, yeah."

Silence ensued; he was breathing heavily.

I was not bothered, strangely; in fact, I was amused, smiling.

"You were there to do…do what?" he asked hesitantly.

"To do exactly what you think." The tease was more fun than I had imagined.

"Really?"

"Yes, Saam—a man."

"Seriously? Come on!"

"Yes, serious." I was imagining his face, cheeks flushed, eyes bulging, and jaw on the floor as the reveal sunk in.

I'd always thought Ali would be the first friend I came out to, but the moment felt right. A part of me thought Saam had an idea (he didn't), and the part which thought he didn't was pleased by his reaction.

Our conversation didn't last much longer. He said he needed to gather his thoughts and would call me back. As soon as I put the phone down, a chilling fear settled in my spine, making me shiver, extinguishing the pleasure. What if I was wrong about Saam? Had my naivety taken over again? What if he wasn't OK with it? Had I just sealed the fate of our friendship? I sat by the phone, staring at it. Scenarios started playing out in my head, each more ominous than the last. Losing my friends, Saam, Ali. I was watching them as they turned their backs on me, followed by my family. All gone, till I was left alone in a dark void, which then, too, began closing in on me. I could hear a ringing, like a bee buzzing in my ear, making me nauseous. Or was it in my head? The third ring of the phone shook me out of the daze. I realized I had been holding my breath all the while, perhaps to cling on to the only dear thing I was being left with. I let it out and picked up the phone.

"I have a question," he said, unaware of my state.

I looked up at the Ayatollah's picture, so emotionless, staring. I rolled my eyes at how ridiculously wild my imagination was. I winked at him, with a grin, challenging him.

"Go on."

I was prepared. Ready to tell Saam the story about how I came to realize I was gay, what the struggle was like, and so on. To show him the closet I was in for so long. Well, that was not exactly what he had in mind.

"Does it not hurt? You know, when you…do it?"

Whether it was a genuine question or he wanted to lighten the mood, I'm not sure, but it made me laugh, hard. A light switch had been flicked on in the dark room in my head to find everyone was still there. I knew it was going to be OK.

Saam was not the best person to be trusted with secrets. He was not capable of it. I needed to control the spillover of his excitement. He wanted me to tell Ali as soon as possible. He needed to be able to share his shock.

Two days later, he, Ali, and I were sitting in my living room. Saam had told him that I had "some important information" I wanted to share. I did want to tell Ali too, but it proved to be more difficult than I had anticipated to say the words, "I am gay." In fact, it was impossible. An hour had passed, and Ali was still waiting for the news, and I could not say it. The words just refused to leave my lips and, the more time elapsed, the more difficult it got.

"Just guess, Ali. It's something I think you have guessed before," I said eventually.

He knew exactly what I was talking about. He couldn't say it either. The taboo word had power. It had stigma. Saying it would have added fuel to the hellfire. We sat there with the big news, which everyone in the room knew by that point, hanging in the air, unspoken.

Saam suggested Ali type his guess and text it to him. A stroke of genius. And he did. Saam's mobile pinged a second later. He looked at the screen and a smirk formed on his face, ear to ear. He held his phone screen in front of me. One word: **Gay**.

I nodded, embarrassed. Finally, I was out to my best friends.

The ice was broken; for the first time in my life, I started talking about my other life with them. I told them the truth about Kian, while Saam looked at me with a half-open mouth.

Ali took the moment to pat himself on the back, saying he had been suspicious for a while and 99 per cent sure. Saam, as expected, had no clue. He did have unanswered questions, but had not been able to piece the puzzle together until now. We talked for hours that night. I had never felt lighter.

At uni, the end had come: I was becoming a doctor finally.

The feeling of graduating from medical school was a mixture of pride and the anxiety of "What now?"

Maman was teary eyed and Baba beaming with pride. Ali, his sister, and Saam accompanied us. Pouya was friendlier at the ceremony; he was relaxed and behaving naturally again. We exchanged knowing smiles. We never discussed what had happened that summer in Fasham again.

Ali and Saam were now part of my hidden life and I shared everything with them. I was not sure they really wanted that level of sharing, but they didn't get a choice. I was unburdening a lifetime of secrets.

My confidence much improved and life events seemingly beginning to fall into place, it was time to close the Kian chapter in my gay life. We had never discussed what that "thing" between us was, which made it all the more difficult to decide "it" had ended.

A few months after the ceremony I spoke with Kian for the first time in a long time. The call was meant to be a friendly catch-up. A small portion of our chat was about my graduation, and the rest quickly diverted to him talking about his life again. At that point, I was sure we were not in a relationship anymore. His monologue, which used to spark fireworks in my chest, was now only inducing a yawn.

He asked about my sex life. Him asking about anything in my life was strange, let alone sex. It made me hesitant.

"It's OK, a few encounters here and there, nothing special," I replied, honestly but with reservation.

"Oh, so you *have* been having sex with others," he spat.

"Erm, y-yes. Is there something wrong?"

"Something wrong? You have been cheating on me, and you're asking me if something is *wrong*?"

The words cut through me like a knife. My mouth suddenly felt dry, as if filled with sand. Could it be? Had I fucked things up? Did he love me back? I feared the answer.

"I…I don't understand. We haven't been in touch for months, you barely know what I have been up to. I thought, whatever this was, was over."

"You *thought*? Just because we haven't talked as often as *you* would like us to?"

"B-but you never call." My voice was betraying me.

He was not letting it go. "So? You think that makes it OK to go and cheat? Do you know how many guys I could have slept with and didn't?"

Cheat: there it was again. Each time he said it, it felt like another punch in the face. I was not going to lose it. I knew I had not done anything wrong. I had loved him. Maybe I still did? Is that why I am so shaken? Was *this* the opportunity I had been waiting for, to tell him how I'd really felt about him all along?

The words poured out of my mouth: "You knew how I felt about you all the time. My feelings were never reciprocated. How should I have known where I stood with you? You never said anything about your feelings."

"I don't need to say it; I have always shown my feelings in my actions."

That voice—just Kian's voice shook my confidence.

Actions, shown not said, but had he? Had I just been blind and not seen it? No. I didn't need to think twice to answer that question. I had loved him hopelessly and never got the reassurance that it was reciprocated.

Kian was good at many things, but he proved that his exceptional talent was making me feel petty, and I did.

"I simply didn't know. I'm s-sorry. Do you think we could try again?" I said, sheepishly.

I was beaten and bruised. Obviously, it was too late. He wished me luck and said goodbye and hung up.

I sat there for a while, paralysed, looking out of the window at the tiny snowflakes floating in the wind, dancing free. The first snow of the year, another reminder of change.

Up until then, I had given myself credit for being able to gradually distance myself from Kian and move on, but I had failed miserably. He managed to have the last word and left me feeling awful. I cried over a guy that night for the first time.

And then, an escape hatch opened. Had I still been pious, I would have looked to the sky and thanked God, and asked "Why?" at the same time.

The escape opened to one place: Café Soosan.

Camp, funny, and typically wearing a T-shirt two sizes too small, Reza was the first gay man I became friends with. He was Atoosa's university friend. I met him first when out as a group with my cousin, and later at my uncle's. He was not out officially, but his attitude and hand gestures left little room for any doubt. I suppose he could have said the same for me, as he did not waste any time coming out to me.

What I liked about Reza most was that he did not care about people's opinion of him. His friendship meant more to me than he could have imagined.

Reza introduced me to Café Soosan first. The place was an old friend of Reza's home, who did not mind being called Soosan nor his flat being called a café. "Soosan" is a name that conjures an image of a middle-aged, overweight woman, who smokes cigarettes, holds poker parties, knows the ins and outs of everyone, is neighbourhood watch and the source of the best gossip. Although this Soosan did not fit all of the above, the nickname somehow fitted perfectly, as if the stereotype should change to fit *him*.

He sucked on a cigarette or shisha pipe in the corner of his mouth while listening to the latest gossip, his eyes widening, his palm on his mouth, either out of shock or being modest by containing his laugh, belly vibrating.

Soosan had turned his flat into a hub.

Café Soosan was a gateway into Tehran's gay network. A weekly visit to the place became my routine. I smoked shisha and drank tea with other gay men, sharing stories, getting tips, finding my bearings. It was also where I met Kasra.

Kasra looked like he had stepped out of the pages of a fashion magazine. The well-groomed stubble on his angular face, perfectly shaped nose, and dark eyes made me think, He should do modelling, every time. His shirts had the top three buttons undone, at least, revealing a shaved, chiselled chest. His talent was adding colour to any story. It seemed his life was a series of dramatic events, all camp, all with exaggerated characters, and all filled with laughter—one which echoed in my ears for a few hours every time I left Café Soosan.

Our queer trio—Kasra, Reza, and I—ventured into the Tehran gay scene together. I no longer needed Kian.

And so, by the end of 2006, I was a doctor, out to my best friends, had stopped all religious practices, became a member at Café Soosan, and my relationship with my first love had officially ended.

Farid

2007

At Colombia University, President Ahmadinejad's famous remark, "There are no gays in Iran," was met with a roar of laughter from the audience.

The comment made me angry initially, but it was not unexpected. Perhaps the government's denial of our existence was beneficial, enabling us to exist peacefully under the radar.

The shame dropped, the secret revealed, and the religion having receded, I had torn through a thick black-out curtain and the light was blinding. Dates came one after the other—gossip to share at Café Soosan and stories for Saam and Ali.

Another internet date.

He'd picked me up from home just before midday, and we had been driving for a while, chatting and exchanging a few flirtatious touches and glances. My head leaned against the car window, looking at the sea of people. They took little notice of their differences from one another. From trendy, fashionable, and sometimes strange looks, to the traditional and religious—men with full beards or women in chador—they were all going about their own business. Did a gay boy fit in? Had I been walking among them with a rainbow T-shirt, would they ignore my dissimilarity too? Accept me as part of their society?

Religion had divided people enough. There was tension between the religious and the so-called liberal, and they had to tolerate each other. Perhaps homophobia united them. The open-mindedness of the non-religious had its limits too.

My date snapped me out of my daydreaming: "I want to have sex with you."

I eyed him. He had pushed his seat back as far as possible and stretched out his right arm, holding the top of steering wheel, while the other elbow rested on the windowsill. The tiny sleeve of his T-shirt stretched over his arm and revealed some of his armpit hair. There was an air of sexiness about his attitude, his straight-talking, and his deodorant, the whiff of which was tickling my nostrils. Or perhaps I was just horny.

"OK. I can't accommodate—can you?" I said, with a forced smile, contemplating whether I really did want to have sex with him.

"Nope."

"What do you suggest, then?"

He bit his lip. "I can find a secluded spot and perhaps we could do something."

Something? Fairly vague, but I was intrigued. "OK, sure."

He drove off to a motorway, towards the outer skirts of the city, in the mountains surrounding Tehran. The plan sounded risky, but I liked the idea, the adrenaline kick. It turned out I needed to ask for specifics when someone suggested doing "something."

After driving up the bendy mountain road, he stopped at one of the corners, on the hard shoulder. It was a main road, but not that busy for the time of the day. We sat in silence for a few minutes, the only noise coming from cars as they whooshed past us.

He eventually made the first move and kissed me. It was exhilarating to kiss a guy outdoors, in daylight.

"Come on," he said, after the kiss, winking at me as he got out.

Curious but nervous, I followed him to a small opening in the middle of the trees. I could still see cars passing through the trees. The *something*, which I had thought was the cheeky kiss or perhaps some fooling around, turned out to be full-on sex. There and then. Scenes of *Brokeback Mountain* flashed before my eyes.

That was the embodiment of what was written in the law—"two men caught in the act of sex"—the punishment for which was "death by hanging." Was my newly found "fuck you" attitude blunting my common sense? Perhaps.

Back in his car, he stroked the back of my neck and bit on his poking-out tongue. "Wanna do this again?"

"Yes." I smiled back. And then there was a knock on my window.

It might have been less than two seconds, but in the time it took me to turn my head towards the window, I saw my life going past me, all the colours being drained out as it gradually became grey and then black. And then I opened my eyes.

A man was standing outside my window, his hand leaning on the door. I looked at my date. He had already turned into a statue, hand frozen on the ignition key.

I rolled the window down, less than an inch.

"Y-yes?" My voice was hoarse, as if my vocal cords had been run over by a truck.

"Salaam." His eyes pointed down. For a second, I thought he wanted me to look at his crotch, but then he continued, "You have a flat tyre; better change it now, or it'll be difficult to find a spot on the bends."

I still have panic attacks thinking of the millions of "what ifs" during that outdoor adventure. I was too naïve to think it could happen to me. My limited imagination at the time was a blessing. By the end, I was sure he had done it before at the same spot. He did not look for *a* secluded place. He took me to *his* secluded spot.

A few days later, at Café Soosan, I was retelling my close brush with disaster to a bewildered Reza. Shisha smoke had created a thin fog in the room. Reza had both his hands over his mouth in shock. His perfectly plucked eyebrows, or what was left of them, were pushed up in two arcs, like the domes of two mosques. Soosan leaned back and held his big belly as it shook with his silent laughter.

Then, I heard it. Possibly everyone in the building did.

A high-pitched laugh, followed by a few squeals and screeches. Soosan shook his head and got up, while I stared at the door.

He pushed the door to the flat open, out of breath and still laughing.

A bony figure with a pointy chin and hollowed cheeks which kept his lips in a constant pout pranced in. He was carrying a man bag on his forearm, or possibly a purse, with the famous *LV* signs all over it. He had a full head of hair, meticulously blow-dried into a quiff, and a baby face. Kasra followed shortly, giggling. I was amazed how masculine Kasra looked next to him. He scanned the room; as soon as he saw a new face, me, he dried his hands on the sides of his large silky shirt and walked over, hand held out, cocked at the wrist.

"Hello. I am Farid. You must be Majid."

I wondered for a second if he wanted me to kiss the huge blue stone on his finger. I held his hand in a half handshake, mindful of the slim fingers which I thought may break with the slightest pressure. We air-kissed and then Farid hugged Reza tight.

"And I have missed you, you little whore," he said, and when he saw my widened eyes he continued, "Don't worry—it's a term of endearment among us. You'll be a whore soon, too."

"He already is," Reza whispered under his breath, nudging me with an elbow.

Farid gave me a side glance and winked.

I knew then I was going to like Farid.

Some days later, at Ali's, I retold the story to Ali and Saam, expecting them to be amused. Their reaction—particularly Ali's—was not what I had been hoping for.

"Have you lost your mind?" he said, pinching his forehead. He sighed. "Listen, Majid, I've been meaning to tell you this for a while. Do you think you're going too far?"

I was taken aback. "Too far doing what?"

"These... these random hook-ups and the risks..." He waved his hand, as if I should know the rest of it.

I did know what he meant, but I was not having any of it. "You think it is wrong?"

"No, no, that is not what I said."

"Then...?"

"You're becoming reckless, and...and maybe you're spending too much time with Kasra and Reza."

There it was. I was spending more time with the *new* friends. Gay life was taking over and Ali was losing his friend.

"You're welcome to come to Café Soosan. You'd enjoy it."

He shook his head. "Your stories are more than enough; I don't need theirs, too."

"I'll come." Saam had a grin on his face.

Ali shook his head. "OK, have fun then." I tried to ignore the frustration which engulfed his voice.

I took my phone out and left the room. I called Kasra.

"Hi, honey."

"Where are you?"

"I'm just driving to Soosan's. I was gonna tell you, actually—"

"Can you pick me up on your way?" I cut through. I couldn't let him start telling me another piece of gossip, or the call would have taken half an hour.

Ten minutes later, I sat in his car, relieved I had escaped the building tension.

As expected, Kasra had a story, laughing throughout, his usual loud shrieks. I drowned my thoughts about Ali's comments in them.

"Anyway, have you noticed Reza holding Farid's hand, by the way?" he asked, catching his breath and wiping a small tear from the corner of his eye with his pinkie.

"No, I haven't. But doesn't Farid hold everyone's hand? Hell, he's all over people, especially when he's telling another jazzed-up story."

"This was different. I think there is something more between them," he said with a mischievous grin.

"Reza has kept it quiet. I'll look out for clues tonight."

As we walked into Café Soosan, Farid's show had already begun. Soosan was in stitches. Another guy, who I had not met before, another new face, was laughing loudly, and Reza was swearing at Farid "terms of endearment."

Farid had chosen to re-enact a mullah's wife's reaction to his death, as you do. He had a blanket over his head as a chador, perfectly kept in position with his teeth, like Saman's mother-in-law, the dentist. He rocked back and forth as if in mourning, like Maman's rocking when she read the Quran. And, as if rehearsed a million times, words rolled out of his mouth, religious Arabic words which one would expect from a mullah at mourning ceremonies.

But, in Farid's version, the wife was a secret sex-worker. When her hand accidentally came out from under the chador, it revealed long fake nails and black nail polish, and packs of super-slim cigarettes and condoms fell out of her bag during prayer.

The similarities of the elaborate act to the facts of life I had grown up with should have been appalling. They should have been depressing. But it *was* funny. I remembered my childhood when the Ayatollah's pictures decorated our walls, his presence perpetual. The laughter pushed the memory away, muted it. I felt warm.

When Farid eventually emerged as himself from underneath the blanket, he had sweat beads on his forehead and a wide smile on his lips. He was pleased with his performance. He sank on the sofa next to Reza, and there it was: Reza held Farid's little finger in his hand. When he saw my look, he blushed immediately. I mouthed, *You little whore.*

He chuckled. I was happy for him. I felt I belonged among them. I did not worry about Ali. I should have.

I was safe.

President Ahmadinejad's "There are no gays in Iran" was met with a roar of laughter, one that echoed that of Columbia University, thousands of miles away, in Café Soosan.

Pink, White, and Blue

Spring 2007

A new mode of internet dating was in town: Manjam.net. It was the one dating website which all gays in Tehran, if not the whole country, used. Multiple pictures of faces and torsos were shared on it, with details about what users were looking for. I gave in to the temptation, and the competition, and created a profile eventually. Having a photo of my face on a gay dating website in Iran was as out as I could be. The freedom was a virtual one. The fear of the website being monitored by the authorities was constant, but it did not stop us. There was a desperate outrageousness which needed to be expressed.

This memory is like a spark jumping off a log fire, going rogue, and flying away. That feeling of being free, not knowing how long it will last. The spark began when I saw his profile.

His photos.

They made me dizzy—how his tight T-shirt stretched over his chiselled figure, how that side glance to the camera teased. I knew it was going to be special. His name was Soheil.

It was another Ashura day: the annual day of grief and mourning. With my usual excuses, I smoothly ditched the family and the "*majlis* crawl." Reza had invited me over to join him and Atoosa, who were supposed to be doing a uni project together. I had time, and Reza's place was closer to my Manjam date.

In the taxi, I got stuck behind a mourning procession. I lowered my window as the loud clash of cymbals filled the car. The familiar *BOOM, BOOM, BOOM* had not changed over the years. The rhythmical chest-thumping of the mourners echoed in my head. I remembered the power that day had had over me.

The harsh braking of the taxi driver brought me back. His long and hard honk was completely ignored by the woman in a black chador who had decided now was the right time to cross the road.

He swore under his breath. "They think they rule the world, arseholes."

I kept quiet, knowing he was looking for encouragement to give his monologue about the state of the world, the Islamic regime, and the religion. Judging by my spiky hair, he assumed I would be on his side. I probably was, but I was too preoccupied to want to hear his opinion. I was glad that I was almost at Reza's.

We had lunch together, gossiping about everything. Atoosa laughed at Reza's animated hand gestures, almost choking on her food.

In the bedroom, I told Reza about my date, and showed him Soheil's Manjam pictures. His envy made me more excited about the date.

"So, are you and Farid now exclusive?" I said, pushing my phone in my jeans pocket. As the phones got bigger, it was getting more difficult to squeeze them in my jeans, which were getting tighter.

"Well, kinda. Not to start with, but, for the past month, I'd say yes." He blushed a little.

"Is he the jealous kind?"

"I think so, and God, I don't want to get on his bad side. He would be a proper diva."

"I can so imagine that—he'll murder you." I laughed. "Is he out to his family?"

"Not officially. I mean, they must be stupid not to have figured it out by now, but I guess they prefer not to talk about it," said Reza, leaning back on the bed. "They are trying to send him to Italy to study fashion, of course. But secretly I think they just want him to leave Iran."

I imagined Maman and Baba trying to protect my gayness in the Islamic Republic by sending me abroad. I remembered their ultimate solution: therapy, and, when that wasn't successful, ignore it and hope for the best. Maman would carry on praying for me, waiting for a miracle. I took a deep sigh.

"Oh, well, it is probably better for him. He'd be freer, though it's hard to imagine that."

Reza laughed again, this time with a bitter undertone.

"You'd better go get ready for your hot date. Don't make a mess, please."

I jumped up, looking at my watch. The window to meet Soheil was a slim one and I needed to prepare. I ran to the bathroom, leaving a sniggering Reza behind.

Inside the toilet, I washed myself, squatting over the traditional basin on the floor. The hose had been an unintended blessing for gay men, and how to use it was one of Reza's first valuable lessons.

While pulling up my jeans, I heard a thud. Already knowing what the sound was, I watched helplessly and in slow-motion as my phone bounced on the floor, then on the sides of the ceramic basin, finally disappearing inside the latrine hole.

Fuck. Of course this would happen today, of all days, I thought to myself, stunned, staring at the hole in the floor. I was meant to text before leaving. *Damn.* Sweat began leaking from the pores on my forehead as my brain cells started working hard: I didn't know Soheil's phone by heart, or I would've used Reza's phone.

I already knew what I had to do, but was delaying the inevitable by thinking of other impossible solutions. I took a deep breath, swearing, and stuck my hand in the hole. I could feel the phone with my fingertips. Just a little bit deeper.

There, got it.

I fished out the phone, which had stains on, and dropped it in the sink. The smell made me gag for a second.

Ah, hand wash—that will definitely eliminate the odour.

I clumsily washed the phone with soap and water, and dried it with some toilet roll.

Walking out of the toilet with the shit-acquainted phone, I said, "Guys, help! I dropped my phone in the basin and it got soaked. I need to dry it out."

Atoosa sprang into action, snatched the phone from my hand, and went to the bedroom to get a hairdryer. I followed her, eyes on the phone. If only she knew where it had been. She opened the case and blew the hairdryer on the battery and SIM, and there it was again, in full force: the stench.

She turned to me. "This smells like shit. Where did you drop it again?"

"Just in the basin; you're imagining things."

She wasn't. The smell was overwhelming. I had to do something else, all the while worried that Soheil was trying to reach me and couldn't. I took the phone from her with a dismissive grunt and removed the SIM, asking Reza for his phone.

As soon as I turned it on, texts appeared, one after the other. I frantically replied.

It was too late. He could no longer accommodate.

I hopped into a taxi to go back home, shoving the smelly dead phone in my pocket. I leaned back and took a deep breath. The sound of another procession could be heard from a few streets away. Mourners would still be thumping on their chests, another nine-year-old boy mesmerized by them. Another promise of heaven drawing out tears. Had Allah sent me a warning? I was deaf to it.

Once I got home, I sent another apologetic message to Soheil on Manjam, while staring at his pictures, letting the sparks fly away from a fire that was impossible to extinguish, not even on Ashura.

A few weeks later, I was inhaling the peach-flavoured smoke as bubbles danced in the base of the shisha, singing that soothing gurgle. It was already making me feel dizzy. Soosan put the tray on the coffee table. Next to cups of tea, he had neatly arranged sticks of saffron-infused crystallized sugar: the perfect cure for the light-headedness. There weren't many of us that night at Café Soosan.

"Why don't you come? It'll be fun." Kasra had a mischievous smile on, his eyes sparkling.

I leaned back as I passed the shisha pipe to him, blowing out the white cloud. "I don't know. I mean, I'd like to. It's just…I have never even met someone like…"

"A trans?"

I nodded.

"I'll speak with Roya, I'm sure she'll be happy to have you. She won't care."

I had heard of Roya, Kasra's trans friend. To me, having only recently come to terms with homosexuality, this was the land of the unknown. The gay scene was a secret one; the trans scene in Tehran was buried in an even deeper layer—a layer I had not been exposed to at all and my comprehension of it was non-existent.

"I think you should go," Soosan shouted from the kitchen. His gentle and camp voice belied his large hairy body habitus. I thought how Soosan was a perfect nickname.

I turned to Kasra, who'd taken his phone out, texting. "What are you doing?"

"Making a decision. I just texted her. You are coming."

I nervously smiled, and picked up the shisha tube from where it was leaning against his knee. "OK," I said. "Will you ask Farid and Reza too?"

He lifted an eyebrow. "Honey, it's not an open house. Plus, those two are constantly doing one thing or the other."

Although Farid was perhaps a bit extreme in every possible aspect, looks and behaviour, I enjoyed his company at the Café. A trans party seemed like the perfect place for him to create another story.

A week later, I stood in front of the mirror, not sure yet if the shirt was good enough. I undid another button. Better. One final spray of aftershave and I was out of my bedroom.

Baba was sitting in front of the TV, leaning against the kilim cushion in his usual half-cross-legged pose, a hand dangling over the upright knee. He looked up. I immediately became conscious of how tight my clothes were, as every fibre of the fabrics started squeezing in, prickling my skin. Sweat patches were the last thing I needed before going to a party.

Maman was walking to her bedroom. Her white prayer chador was rolled up around her waist. She looked like cotton candy on a stick, with a face—a stone one. She awaited Baba's verdict on my outfit.

My hand automatically went to my shirt and pulled the edges close enough to get one button in the buttonhole. The stretch over my chest was truly testing the durability of the fabric.

Baba finally spoke: "Where to, now?"

"Out, with Ali and Saam."

Maman was praying under her breath, but kept looking, eyebrows in a frown.

"Be home by eleven," said Baba. His curfew.

Maman tutted and went back to her room.

"OK, bye."

"Don't be late!" He turned back to the TV.

Walking down the staircase out, I released the tension in my chest and let my breath out. I glanced at my watch. I've still got three hours—plenty of time.

Kasra was already outside. He stood leaning on the bonnet, fiddling with his Gucci sunglasses, as his golden bracelet twinkled.

"You look good, as always," I said. "Sorry I'm late."

Flicking his imaginary hair, he smiled. "Thanks, darling. You look gorgeous, too."

I got in quickly. As much as I loved Kasra, my best gay friend, I did not want Maman to see him. She would pass a judgement as soon as she saw his flamboyance. Kasra was not out to his family either, but they were more liberal. He was given more freedom to do what he liked. We drove off, to my first trans party.

A memory filled with contrasting feelings and colours; joy and sadness, two entities hand in hand, leaping together.

The party was at a north Tehran penthouse apartment in a posh neighbourhood. Before getting out of the car, Kasra took out a tiny travel-sized bottle from his man bag and sprayed a few more puffs on his bare shaved chest, then he checked himself out in the rear-view mirror, pouting, and got out.

The flat was large and extravagant. Huge paintings of semi-naked women in elaborate golden frames adorned the walls. They were matched with similarly heavy furniture, with golden armrests and legs, and maroon cloths. A few silk carpets covered areas of the white marble floor. I had no idea what Roya did for work, but she seemed to be doing just fine.

We walked through the hallway, which opened to the living room, another immaculately decorated area; Roman-looking statues in dancing poses stood on wooden stands and heavy velvet curtains covered the large windows. Kasra and I were the only men present among around twenty guests, all women, chatting, laughing, and dancing to Western music.

Like a confused child, I turned to Kasra. "These are all women. Where are your trans friends, then?"

"Darling, none of these were born women; everyone here is trans." He laughed.

I looked at his face for a second to see if he was joking, then turned and looked at the crowd. I blinked a few times. "All of them? Even that one…?"

He did not look to where I was pointing my head. "Everyone."

A hoarse voice from behind his shoulder called, "Kasraaaaaa! Darling!"

Wearing a tight golden leopard-print dress, which her breasts seemed to be in a tense competition to rip their way out of, Roya put her hands on Kasra's shoulders, air-kissed on each side, and swiftly turned towards me. "You must be Majid."

My mouth was half open, my breath held.

She turned to Kasra, winking. Her shiny forehead barely moved. She continued, "He is a cute one, like yourself." She gave a coarse laugh, which turned into a cough, then shook my hand with the tip of her fingers, varnished with golden false nails, and kissed the air above my shoulders.

"Welcome, darling—make yourself comfortable. Get a drink. We are just getting started." She noticed my look. "They are impressive, aren't they?" she said, cupping her breasts, then she gave another laugh and continued, "They were my thirtieth gift to myself. Fifth trip to Thailand."

I only stared. She waved her hand towards where drinks and snacks were and moved to other guests.

I turned to Kasra. "Stay by my side at all times, OK?"

"Don't be ridiculous. Let's get a drink."

A drink or two in, I started talking to a few guests. Some left me speechless merely at the sight of them—gorgeous women in elegant dresses, and wearing heels so high I had no idea how they could walk.

I was beginning to enjoy myself more than I'd thought I would: dancing, hooting, and bouncing to the loud house music with Kasra and all the girls. In the dimmed lights, I saw their faces, smiling, eyes closed, lost in the moment. Their propped-up hair was now carelessly loose, strands stuck to their sweaty faces. The sting in my calves as I hopped, the sweat on my forehead—it all felt like it belonged to someone else, someone who had never cared what people thought. I wished to stay in this fantasy land.

Could the Islamic regime, or anyone else, have foreseen or imagined the pink, blue, and white party taking place under the country's Allah-embellished flag?

Soon, the stylish guests were in a different mode.

They had formed a semi-circle on the floor, on their knees, and were vigorously swinging their heads like they were about to rip off from their bodies, hair circling in the air as if a ritual was being performed.

I stood on the outside, confused.

"First time?"

I turned around to find myself face to face with a golden-haired woman. A pale blue, short dress, matching her eyes, floated over her immaculate figure. She was showing off her slender long legs, and her high heels made her stand even taller than she was. Her skin was glowing, her voice soft and feminine.

"I said, is it your first time at a trans party?"

The question snapped me out of the trance I was stuck in. I cleared my throat. "Uh, yes. Is it *that* obvious?"

"Very." She laughed and took a sip from her drink, holding the straw with her fingertips. She looked towards the others on their knees. "I've never been into it, the head-banging."

"The what?"

She laughed even louder, tilting her head back. I was obsessively staring at her long smooth neck.

"The head-banging. That's what they do when they're high on coke and ecstasy and whatnot. They must release the energy." With a sigh, she continued, "I'm Artemis, by the way."

"Majid." I wiped my sweaty palm on my trousers and shook her stretched hand. I looked back towards the others. "It is quite amazing. I never knew transgender people existed, let alone threw such lush parties."

Artemis raised an eyebrow and huffed. There was a sadness in the smile on her lips. "It's not always like this. It has not been easy for most of us. That's why some take drugs and *need* this escape." She gestured her hand towards the head-bangers.

I nodded knowingly, not really knowing, feeling ashamed about my ignorance. I wanted to ask more, but worried I might offend her.

She must've read my face. "A lot of us don't want to transition fully—you know, have it chopped off."

I coughed a bit of my drink out.

She carried on, not taking any notice of my spluttering: "We aren't allowed to be trans and have cocks. They say, 'You are either a man or a woman,'" she said mockingly, deepening her voice.

I wondered who "they" were. "S-so, what *do* you do? Have it... chop—"

She gave a fiery look with those blue eyes.

I cleared my throat. "Cut?"

"Some risk it and don't do anything—a 'fuck you,' I suppose. Those who can afford it go to Thailand, like I did, and sort it out there. The mullahs help out the rest." She sighed and huffed again.

"Mullahs?" I was beginning to think she was high as well.

"Yes, Khomeini gave a *fatwa** or something. The government pays half of your bills if you get the op here and turn into a woman. It's their *cure* for our *condition*."

She didn't see my flinch as she said the name without the prefix *Imam*. The name for which I used to send three prayers to the Prophet whenever I heard it. But what she said did not make any sense to me. I needed to change the subject. "I'm sure you know it already, but you are very pretty," I said.

She put her slender fingers on her chest, exaggerating her humble surprise. "Aw, thanks, darling. Effort has been put into it. I'm thinking of doing some modelling," she said, as she flicked her hair back and took another sip.

"You definitely should. You have the full package."

"Thanks, you're sweet. It's not easy being a female model here, really. Don't want to have to answer to the police *again*."

The word "again" came out of her mouth with a spite, a disgust.

How many times has she had to answer to the police for who she is? I wondered.

There I was, always thinking *I* was the victim, that *I* had had it difficult. What must she have gone through? How much was out there that I did not know?

"Anyway, I'm trying to go to Turkey or Dubai. It would be much easier there," she continued.

I wanted to ask, *What would be easier? Being a model or being trans?* Or maybe both, probably both.

"Can I...can I ask something?" I said, clearing my throat.

She raised both eyebrows in anticipation.

"What does Roya do for work?" I continued hesitantly.

---

* Fatwa: an Islamic ruling. Only high-ranked clerics can give fatwas.

Artemis laughed again. "Roya? Have you met the slut?" She laughed again. "Do you think her hands have ever done any work?"

I looked back at the dance floor. Roya was in the middle, her head tilted back and eyes closed, her cleavage shiny with sweat. "But this flat is—"

"It's her husband's—well, *sigheh** husband's," she interrupted. "He is a top-ranking person in the Revolutionary Guard, or something, and Roya is *his* escape. All of this, and most of Roya, is paid for by him." She gestured towards Roya's breasts, then took another sip of her drink and winked at me. "Don't tell her that, obviously. I don't need more enemies." She smirked.

I smiled back as I was contemplating it all. My eyes wandered around the flat again: the carpets, the statues, the paintings, Roya. *His escape.*

Kasra joined us then and pulled me to the dance floor. I put my drink down and waved at Artemis while being dragged away. "Lovely to meet you! Good luck with modelling!" I shouted.

She stood there with one arm across her chest, the other holding her drink. I saw her raising her glass and nodding before my vision was obscured by another sweaty guest jumping up and down.

Moments later, maybe minutes, maybe hours, immersed in the music, the sweat and the smoke, I heard a hoarse voice whisper in my ear, "I really like you."

The hair on my neck stood on end. I looked at her droopy eyes, a bit of her mascara smudged over her cheek. Roya was clearly off her face and a wobbly smile spread ear to ear. I was speechless, again.

"Uh, right, OK."

I gave out a nervous chuckle and pretended I was dancing with her, while slowly backing off the dance floor with awkward moves.

---

* Sigheh: an Islamic temporary marriage which allows a man to marry a woman for a pre-determined period of time and have intimate relations with her.

I mimed that I needed to get a drink. She held my gaze, gave me an unnerving wink, and carried on dancing.

As soon as I spotted Kasra, I rushed to his side. He was in stitches when I told him she was coming on to me.

Around midnight, way past my father's curfew, I began to panic. I didn't want to leave. Kasra suggested staying the night there, saying he had done it many times before and "Roya would totally be fine with it."

I shivered at the thought of her creeping in my bed, mid-sleep. "No. Are you crazy? I just told you what she has in mind!"

He giggled again. "Don't be silly. She's high and, I promise you, she won't even want to sleep tonight."

I made eye contact with him, raising an eyebrow.

He rolled his eyes. "I promise, nothing will happen. We'll sleep in the same room, OK?" Kasra insisted.

I looked at the dance floor. I *did* want to stay. I bit my cheek, thinking. "OK. You promise?" I said, looking at him with pleading eyes. He gave a squeal of joy and, as he went to find Roya, I took my phone out of my pocket. I typed a quick **I'm with you** message to Saam, and another one to Maman, saying I'm staying the night at his.

Maman had always been the safer choice to approach when disobeying the Godfather. When I received her simple **OK**, I smiled and looked up to find Kasra and Roya laughing in a corner. He made eye contact and I gave him a thumbs up. He whispered something in Roya's ear and she looked at me and blew a kiss. I waved back uncomfortably and walked to a different corner, out of her eyeline. I could hear the crackly laughter behind my head. She was enjoying it.

As Kasra predicted, Roya spent all night awake, gossiping about the party with another friend of hers.

The next morning, I sat at her kitchen table with Kasra and a throbbing headache. Roya's filtered coffee and cream was more than welcome. We chatted about the night before, talking about everyone's dresses and who said what. I was conscious of how every look, every giggle, and every comment was dissected and analysed, worried I might have said something offensive I would have to answer for.

Despite the glammed and glittered surface, the small Tehran transgender community had their own gossips, conflicts, and competitions, with higher intensity. Kasra and I left there intact, with no significant mischief noted by our host.

Not long after that night, in true diva style, Roya fell out with Kasra and, since I did not back her against him, I was to follow. She insisted I owed her, as I was a guest at hers and she had made me her "special coffee."

I was excluded before being included, but the memory stayed. Roya, Artemis, and the rest.

But now I had another evening to look forward to. When I got home from Roya's party, I found I had a message in my Manjam inbox. Soheil had replied.

Text me, and let's try to meet again.

I texted instantly, Hi, **can meet tomorrow evening, I'll pick you up**, and when I pressed *send*, I looked back at the computer screen, the side-look, the stretch of cloth over his biceps.

Narnia Does Exist

Spring 2007

"So, yeah, it was a crazy night. Roya is a character," I said with a big grin on my face, still reliving the party night.

"I can tell you enjoyed it," said Soheil, spinning the teaspoon on the table. I wondered if he was intentionally flexing his biceps. Intentional or not, it worked.

I had picked him up earlier in Baba's car. An hour had passed, and he had not said much. I had done the talking, mostly about the trans party.

"We should do this again," he suggested finally, looking up, narrowing his dark brown eyes. His knee touched mine under the table. I was careful my swallow wasn't audible.

I looked around. The small coffee shop was almost empty. The red and black décor was meant to give a cosy or romantic feeling to the place, or evoke passion perhaps.

A bearded man was sitting two seats away with his companion, a young lady in a chador. They held hands on the table, their affection on display as well as their faith. He met my eyes. I automatically pulled my knee away from Soheil, hoping he had not seen that guilty touch. Soheil saw my stare and followed it to the serious face. Then he turned to face me and pushed his knee against mine.

I held his gaze and tilted my head. "Erm, sure. Let's do this again."

"Great, shall we do dinner soon, then?" He linked his legs behind my ankle under the table and pulled it towards him.

There was a small flutter in my chest, one which I had not felt for a while.

As the romantic religious couple walked past us, I looked the man in the eye again, chin up.

There are no clubs or bars in Tehran. Restaurants and cafés are the main hang-out venues, and there are lots of them. Growing up, I saw how our neighbourhoods changed face. The low-key pizza shop on the main street was the only place I knew when I was younger, and eating there would have been the event of the week.

By 2007, they had multiplied like rabbits on steroids, and style had taken over substance; modern and fancy restaurants with prices to match the look opened up everywhere.

A food court appeared on one of Tehran's busiest streets in a glitzy mall: the Jaame Jam food court. It was the first of its kind. But that didn't make it unique.

Tuesday nights were "gay evenings."

I first heard the news from Atoosa, who had heard about it from her straight friends. Stunned, I wanted to know more.

"Oh, I'm not entirely sure, but apparently, on Tuesday nights, only gays go to Jaame Jam," she said, texting on her phone. Atoosa's lack of interest in my questions had always been a blessing.

How could this be possible? How is it that straight people know about it and I don't? What is happening there, really? I needed answers, and Atoosa wasn't the right person to ask.

When my gay friends confirmed it as "common knowledge," I felt left out. It turned out it had not been a planned event to start off with, but somehow gradually gay men had claimed Tuesdays at Jaame Jam and word had spread until it became a *thing*.

There was one problem: common knowledge would have applied to everyone, including the police, and yet it was still happening. And my uncertainty was not because of the *basijis* alone. Being there on a Tuesday would have been an unofficial way of coming out, if I was seen by someone in my family.

Eventually, I mustered the courage to go a few weeks later. I took Reza with me, wearing one of my older, less tight shirts in an effort not to stand out. By then, Reza and Farid had become a couple hard to get hold of, constantly doing something together. I was glad Reza saw my ignorance about Jaame Jam as simply "unacceptable," changing his plans with Farid to "educate" me, as he put it.

My heart started beating faster as I walked into the sparkly building. Every glance, every smile, and every nod had a different meaning. Guys were on the prowl, and I was on display. Everyone could see written on my forehead: *First timer*.

We went up the escalator to the food court and there it was: a big semi-circular floor, with colourful tables set up in the middle and fast-food chains surrounding it. And among these tables were sat guys, my kind, gobbling food. The majority of the gay community were well camouflaged as part of society, and, had it not been a Tuesday night, perhaps I would not have taken notice of the shoes, the too-tight T-shirts, the jewellery, and the stares. It was gloriously absurd. We bought some chips, sat at a table in a corner, and watched everyone else. Is this what a gay club looks like? I thought. Reza waved at a few people and air-kissed a few others, before settling on looking at my face in amusement.

A "mini-pride" happened every week at Jaame Jam. I should have been scared. But I was not. Their confidence was infectious.

I once suggested going there with Saam and some of his straight friends on a different night.

"Nah, not there. It's full of fags," said one of his friends, others laughing.

Saam looked at me from the corner of his eye, coughing nervously. I gave him a reassuring look back: *It's OK.*

I didn't blame them—the blame rested upon the homophobic culture they had been brought up in: my culture. I needed the reminder.

It did have one effect: I *was* going to go to Jaame Jam every Tuesday.

April 2007

Not long after the transgender party and my date with Soheil, Reza, Kasra, and I were in Jaame Jam on another Tuesday evening, eating fried chicken and chips. I was wearing a new shirt

I had bought the week before with Kasra and was beginning to think that every bite I took from the chicken was making the shirt more likely to rip. My date with Soheil had already been dissected and the verdict was I should see him again, but not appear too keen: "Play the game" were Kasra's words of wisdom, as he checked his eyebrows in his mini mirror.

As always, Farid's voice came first: "Darling whores, there you are!"

I almost choked when he appeared in front of us. He was wearing a loose green shirt and boot-cut white jeans. His shirt had a huge golden half-Versace face printed on it and only the bottom two buttons done up. I suppose any shirt on his slim body would have been floppy.

He had golden bracelets on and there was something new, an eyebrow piercing. A diamond stud sparkled above his eye. I instantly looked around us. I had to. Meeting him at Café Soosan and laughing at his acts was one thing. But that eyebrow piercing, here, in a public place, made me uncomfortable. When I looked at the others, I was the only hesitant one. Reza got up and hugged him, and Kasra quickly found a chair for him to join us.

I shuffled on my chair. Was I being a hypocrite? I loved Farid. How was it that, after all this time, building my own confidence bit by bit, I was still ashamed to be in his company in public, even though perhaps he was not the only one looking as outrageous on a Tuesday night?

On our drive back, it was just Kasra and me. He had noticed my demeanour.

"You know, I admire Farid," he started.

"I do too, but—"

"No, you don't, honey. I saw the look on your face. You were embarrassed," he said jokingly, though he wasn't joking.

"Maybe I was. I worry about the looks, and I know he doesn't. I wish I could be more like that."

"I'm not like that either." When he noticed my raised eyebrow, Kasra continued, "Oh, shush—these are men's accessories." He sighed deeply. "Anyway, I am less stiff than you. He will get himself in trouble one day, the little whore." He laughed.

I chuckled, looking outside, lost in thought. Could I ever not give a shit about what people think? Would I ever say anything back when Saam's friends make a joke about us?

Probably not.

The impromptu Jaame Jam event came to an end when eventually the venue was ordered to close on Tuesday evenings by the morality police; I suppose too many queens in a closed space was considered a recipe for a coup against the regime.

Soheil and I met up the next day, and then the next week. "Bouncy Soheil," so nicknamed because of his love of parties and dancing, was five years younger than me and bursting with energy—he was constantly busy, not working, but partying. He lived a life which, at the time, was the opposite of mine. Already over the minimal initial struggle of being gay at the age of nineteen, he had immersed himself in the gay world. A world I had only seen a glimpse of.

A new phase of my life was about to begin. Soon, Soheil and I were going out in a new group with his friends. Having one or more of them with us became the new normal. They were different from the small group I knew from Café Soosan. A distance was beginning to form between the newly found friends and our trio—Kasra, Reza, and me.

They were all on the same deafening wavelength as Soheil's: full of energy, craving a party and a dance every day, and camp. Shortly after our second date, we decided we were in a relationship. One day, he just flicked the switch, friend to boyfriend. I did not even need to listen to Kasra's advice. There was no game. Soheil made the decision, and I was happy to follow.

Soheil took me through the backdoors of the closet I was in before, opening to another realm: Tehran's gay underground world, and what a world that was.

All the Colours of the Rainbow

May 2007

Less than a month into our relationship, Bouncy Soheil had transformed my social life, from having a secret online life for occasional dates, and weekly Café Soosan rendezvous, to going out daily with a group, all gay, younger than me, and loud. I took them to our Fasham flat often to spend a night, telling my parents I was with Ali and Saam.

Their clamour was muffling the constant nagging noise of unemployment. I kept myself busy with Soheil to forget a depressing reality was looming round the corner: military service.

Soheil was from a different world, but, unlike Kian, it was an uninspiring one. He was what one may have called *living in the moment*—well, he was, entirely. There was no wonder he looked the way he did—he was either at the gym, or out "bouncing." A beautiful shell, which was hollow within. When, on rare occasions, chats diverted to future plans, he admitted he had none with an ease which made me uncomfortable. I had only joined his loud life in a boyfriend capacity. I wondered if he had added me only to look cool, a concept: "I have a boyfriend."

Why do I stay in it? I thought to myself often. The answer was, For the thrill of being part of the gay scene.

The new world was fascinating; when with them, it felt like I was wholly myself. We gossiped about relationships, how one looked or what the other's party was like. Unlike with Saam, I didn't need to explain anything. They just got it. And, unlike with Ali, there was a palpable absence of a philosophical analysis. Nothing deep.

So Soheil and I each kept the relationship for our own benefit: a gay symbiosis.

My straight-gay life balance was tipping more and more towards the gay side.

I still went to Café Soosan occasionally, and took Saam with me. Saam, who normally couldn't stop talking, sat quietly on the edge of the sofa and only smiled, absorbing the world he had stepped into. When Farid put on his shows, shrieked, sat on Saam's large thighs and called him a "whore," I enjoyed watching his horror. It looked like a hummingbird sat on a watermelon. Saam was accepted in the clan.

He would not come out with us, though—too conscious of the turning heads and eyes. Those same looks which had once pierced through my skin like needles had now lost their power for me. I was shielded in an invisible rainbow cloak. Let them look, I thought.

Ali, on the other hand, was not interested in mixing groups. In his balanced world, one gay man was enough. I could not help but imagine Farid calling Ali a whore. How he would be sleep-deprived for a week after.

Gradually, I started cancelling more plans with my straight friends to go out with the gay ones. Ali had accepted my sexuality, but he was finding it increasingly difficult to keep up—something I failed to see. He was *losing me to the other side*, and he might have been right. I was seeing less and less of him. And then that day came.

If memories had tastes, this one would only have the bitter aftertaste, for, like all my other senses, the flavour is blunted. As if my tongue is covered in a gel coat, numbing all the buds. I bite on it and only feel it when it bleeds. The coldness is what possessed me that day.

"You will come, right?" said Ali through the driver's window as I dug into my pocket for house keys. It was the third time he'd asked.

"Yes, yes...Still not sure why you want me to be there?" I was already thinking how Soheil would be disappointed that I would not be picking him up that night.

Ali, as always, could read it on my face. "Majid, I'm counting on you. Be there, this one time."

He had invited a few girls over to his, one of whom, I later found out, he liked. To Ali, that was a huge step. He had been spontaneous, taken a risk, and plunged into the unknown, and he wanted us, Saam and me, to be there. "To balance the vibe," he'd said. But I knew it was to help him calm down.

I waved my hand dismissively as I opened the door, and he left. I texted Soheil.

An hour later, I was sitting in the car outside Soheil's gym, tapping on the steering wheel. It didn't stop the itch at the back of my head. Soheil hadn't said not to go to Ali's, but his reply read disappointment all over it.

"Sure, have fun. Bye."

I had not told Ali yet. I took my phone out and was beginning to type when Soheil opened the door and dropped himself on the passenger seat. His spicy aftershave filled the car. I closed the phone.

"Let's go—they're already at the restaurant," he said.

"Hi." I leaned over for a kiss. "Don't be grumpy."

He gave a half smile and touched his cheek on mine. His half-grown stubble tickled. "I'm not—just worried we're late. Hi."

We drove off.

Another hour passed.

I'd had two missed calls from Saam and one from Ali. Soheil and his gang were making plans for another Fasham night. I only listened. I had to tell Ali I was not going.

"Where are you?" he said, after the first ring. His voice was hushed, but coated with urgency.

"Sorry, I'm out with...with Soheil and—"

"What?" I could hear him shutting a door as his voice raised a notch.

"It's just...just...he had made plans and it was rude to cancel last minute."

I only heard deep sighs on the other end. He was definitely pinching his forehead.

I continued, "I…I can still come after."

"I need you to be here now, Majid. It is a bit awkward."

"OK, let me ask Soheil."

Another deep sigh at the other end.

"I'll call you back in a sec."

Soheil was not happy when I told him, saying I should have gone there in the first place, as he'd already said over text. I *should* have.

"Bring Soheil and his friends, but just come, please," Ali insisted when I told him I could no longer make it.

Soheil and *his friends*. I wondered if he was high. From not wanting to mix to "bring them all"? I heard the desperation in his voice, but took the chance.

"OK, I'll ask him."

What I failed to see was that he was questioning my loyalty to years of friendship. Ali wanted to believe he could still count on me. Like I had counted on him, with Leila, with Kian, with everything, before there was a gay world.

Soheil was not interested and was getting fed up with the back and forth.

"Just say yes, we are coming," he snapped.

I looked at him and everyone else. "Are we?"

"No, of course not, but he'll stop, won't he?" A few of his friends sniggered. He put his hand on mine and winked. "Just send the text. We need to plan Fasham."

I looked at the prominent veins on the back of his hand.

As if in a deep hypnosis, I did as he said, and the messages did stop.

Ali was waiting, for us.

The Fasham trip planned for the next day was a movie night, they decided. I didn't have a DVD player there, but the solution was easy: Ali.

Another hour passed.

I dropped Soheil off, then I called Ali. No answer.

Called again. No answer.

Irritated, I called Saam. "Why isn't Ali picking up his phone?"

"He's lying on his bed. Why didn't you come?"

"Soheil didn't want to. Anyway, listen, tell Ali I need his DVD player and am popping by to pick it up, OK?"

"Majid, listen—"

I did not want to hear a lecture, I did not want my fun night to finish on a low note. "We'll talk when I get there. See you soon."

Twenty minutes later, Saam let me in to an eerily quiet flat, as if someone had just died.

"Where is everyone? Where are the girls?" I said.

"They left ten minutes ago. It was…not that great."

I sensed there was more to it than just "not that great," but an arrogant voice whispered in my head, *Don't ask*. Strangely, it spoke with Soheil's voice.

Through the gap of the ajar door, I saw Ali lying on his bed, staring at the ceiling, his wrist on his forehead.

"Hi," I said, in a fake happy tone.

He looked at me and, without saying a word, turned his eyes towards the ceiling again, as if annoyed at being interrupted while watching a thriller. I shrugged and glanced at Saam. He was still waiting for me to sit down to debrief, to tell me how upset Ali was.

I was there for the DVD player.

"Going to Fasham tomorrow night with the gang; I *need* the DVD player."

Saam's mouth was half open to say something, but his eyes were resigned. I heard a mocking grunt from Ali's bedroom. I was getting annoyed. I headed to the TV room to get the player. I needed to get out of there. The air was heavy with anger, with shame.

While I was unplugging cables, Saam tried to explain what had happened, standing over me, leaning against the wall. His cheeks were rosy and he cleared his throat a few times.

Ali had asked two new girls over to what they thought was a party, and it ended up being only the four of them, sitting there, while Ali was frantically texting me.

I was half listening. "So? What's the big deal?" I stood up as soon as the player was free.

"He actually liked one of the girls."

"Well, it's done now. Invite them again with proper notice, maybe?" I said, walking out.

I shouted a goodbye to Ali, who was now sitting at the edge of his bed, leaning his elbows on his knees. He looked up and I saw only one word: disappointment. I looked away and closed the door behind me.

I had hurt Ali, my best friend. I convinced myself it was a minor thing, that he'd get over it, but he didn't, and it was not a "minor thing"—not to him.

Ali stopped talking to me after that. At first, I was angry at him for being childish, and then I started to not care. Saam did his best to get us back together, but, from Ali's point of view, our friendship was over. It saddened me, but I let it slip and carried on with my gay friends.

I was feeling like a fish which, up until then, had been in a tight bowl and now had jumped into an ocean. Ali could either join me or be left behind.

Meanwhile, I party-hopped from one gay party to another with Soheil. He was taking me through the back alleys of the underground gay life in Tehran.

In Tehran, the gay scene consisted of small groups, each with certain characteristics. North Tehran, where I lived, had a different scene from the south. The lines between these separate communities were faint, but a distinction could be made based on who one kept company with in the "gay life," as the gay scene in Tehran was called.

Like a chameleon, gay men blended in with the background, lost in the crowd, religious or not. The murals of the Ayatollahs watched over them, like they watched over everyone else. I thought of us as the Ayatollah's gays.

Farid and his type, the ones who would not contain their flamboyance, were few. The ever-judging heads turned, faces twitched, and gasps were let out, but Farid revelled in them.

Others showed their true colours where it was safe, among their own kin.

Gay men in north Tehran, known for being more upper class, mostly came from rich families; they were pretentious and precious, up to date with the latest fashion trends or design, or they pretended to be. A trip to Dubai or Turkey was enough to keep one bragging for a while, sometimes even having acquired an accent after a week's trip; however, the true "wow factor" resided in travel to Europe or America.

In the south, however, people were more grounded and more religious, and so were the gay men living there. When I used to go on dates, before my relationship with Soheil, most men were from within the north Tehran community. I too made sure I wore the latest look and didn't have a trace of my religious household on me.

When I met a guy from the south in his flat once, the sincerity of it embraced me like Maman's scent in her chador. We sat on the floor by his small *sofreh* and ate food out of metal bowls, while his prayer mat was rolled up, leaning against the wall. His religion had been on display like everything else. Could I ever be like that? He'd used slang and expressions I had rarely heard before, belonging to the "southerners". I had a mental image of Kasra tutting in the alien environment, keeping his Gucci sunglasses on.

There were undoubtedly a few "queens" among the scene with a certain mafia-vibe about them, only the assassinations were not literal, but character-based. Gossip about how one party was better than the other, or who had slept with whom, or what they wore dominated. A few were famous in the community. They had earned their reputations based mostly on the level of their outrageousness. One was known for holding regular parties, one for being a psychopath—in fact, quite a few shared that quality—and the other for their wealth. Each of these queens had a group of minions around them. "The life" had turned them into rivals.

I, new to the scene, was not yet part of any of these packs, but had heard of their leaders and met some of them here and there. Like a prize to be won, new faces always attracted attention, a potential recruit if I proved myself resourceful. Soon, I found out having a holiday home in Fasham was a "resource".

The world saw Iran as a nuclear threat, and our president denied the Holocaust and made other inflammatory comments. Sanctions after sanctions were being handed out, like gift cards from Santa, to nullify the Ayatollah's ambitions. What seemed to concern the outside world was the least of people's worries living here, especially my generation.

The youth of the country—us, gay or straight—wanted more freedom, to have an easier day-to-day life. During President Khatami's time, the religion's heavy fist pressing on people's chest had somewhat lightened. We would hear and see less of the morality police or the *basiji* enforcers.

With Ahmadinejad in power, the Islamic regime's grip retightened. More women were stopped on the street and told to fix their headscarves or lessen their make-up, and more men were stopped because of their Western spiky hairstyle and tight T-shirts. Often, cars were held at random checkpoints to see if everyone inside was behaving in line with the sharia. If boys and girls were together, what was the nature of their relationship? Heaven was being forced on us, shoved down our throats.

Laws, laws, and laws. Each meant to hold down a beast, like ropes pulling on each limb. Break them, and penalties dictated by the sharia descended like a rain of fire.

Drinking alcohol is haram. If caught drinking, one could face large fines or lashes or spending a few nights in prison.

Mixed parties for girls and boys is haram.

Dancing, haram.

Listening to women singing, haram.

More harams meant more ropes needed to hold the beast down. More laws.

Did it stop us? No.

The regime had bitten off more than it could chew.

Farid crashed on the sofa next to Reza with a high-pitched sigh, beads of sweat shining on his forehead. A few more laughs between his fast breathing and then there was silence. A few seconds of it.

It was a warm spring evening. Soheil was recovering from a hangover, providing me with an opportunity to hang out with the old gang at the Café.

Farid wore a two-sizes-too-big shiny navy shirt, its rolled-up sleeves hanging from his elbows like the drapes of a gown. A thick golden pendant in the shape of Versace's medusa head hung from a golden chain sitting heavily on his chest, bobbing up and down on his pale skin.

Soosan downed the rest of the home-brew spirit and orange juice mix and got up with a grunt.

"Is that the hooch from the new dealer?" asked Farid, slouched on the sofa.

"Yes, it's apple, this one—not bad. That previous dealer was a bastard. He charged double the price, too."

"Soooooosan, please get me some too," Farid pleaded, back in character again: that one was Faati, a fifty-year-old divorcee who'd found a twenty-year-old religious lover, a *Basij* member. As usual, he swore it all to be factual.

"I'll have to call him and introduce you; he's way too scared of being busted," said Soosan from the kitchen.

"Welllll, Faati can be very persuasive..." Farid spread his legs open on the sofa. Soosan waved and disappeared behind the counter, giggling.

I looked up at Kasra. He leaned on the wall, taking a drag from his cigarette. He seemed lost in thought and focused on the smoke he blew out.

"What's up?" I asked.

"Nothing, honey, just thinking…" His words disappeared with the smoke, as if everyone should have known exactly what his thoughts were.

Farid noticed. "Kasra *joon*, are you OK?"

"I'm fine." He sat on the arm of the sofa and dabbed his cigarette on the corner of the ashtray. "Was just thinking how things would be if there was no morality police, no *Basij*, no sharia . . ."

"Oh, that's where you were," I said mockingly.

Farid sat up, pushed his hair back from his forehead, and sucked on the shisha tube, his cheeks caving in. "*Jooni*, imagining things like a dream gets you—gets us—nowhere. It shouldn't just be that, an impossible imagination."

I had to turn to Farid to make sure this serious, rather deep voice was coming from him, as if he was suddenly possessed. Reza looked as startled as me.

Farid continued, "Last week, one of my straight friends had the arseholes barge in on his party. Most of the men have been let go, but two girls are still in custody. It's pretty shitty." Another swig from the shisha, this time his knuckles pale. "I'm not one for keeping quiet and thanking God it wasn't me, cos next time it will be."

"Honey, we all have a story. These *basijis* are rabid—what can we do?" Kasra protested, Soosan nodding in the background.

"I don't know, there's always a way, form a group, protest…" Farid trailed off. Reza put a hand on his shoulder, but he shook it away. "Don't need pity. Need that cheap hooch Soosan finished and a stronger fist."

Reza took his hand, looking at the bony fingers. "I think these only need some bright red polish, little whore."

The corner of Farid's lips formed a smile, a sad one. "One day…" he exhaled.

A life without sharia was beyond my imagination. I tried hard, but only a vacuum filled the space.

There was nothing else.

*

House parties. They had become a popular phenomenon, especially in north Tehran. The danger of the morality police was always present, like a sticky shadow. They had the power to gatecrash any party without a warrant. For them, barging in on a mixed party where alcohol was being served was like hitting the jackpot.

Stories of parties being ruined, where people were taken to the holding cells for a night or two, some being fined and some getting lashes, were not uncommon. If lucky, when they came knocking—or banging, rather—they could be paid off and would leave without causing a major interruption, and the party could carry on. But if the morality officers truly believed they were saving us from sin, that was when it could get scary. The majority did prefer the money.

The exception to those rules was us, the "non-existent" gay life of Tehran. Gay parties took place with much less hassle; they were mostly girl-free. If the police dropped by, as long as no alcohol was found, they'd have no grounds to make arrests. Regardless, being in a party and having *basijis* at the door was an unpleasant experience.

I was with Soheil and a few of his friends at one of these parties.* I did not know the host or most of the guests. I was Soheil's plus one. The "gay symbiosis."

One girl was among us. It was beginning to be considered cool among girls to have a gay friend. Her being there was the only anomaly.

At ten p.m., there was a ring. Our host answered the intercom.

As if a tap had been turned on under his chin, all the colour from his face drained away, leaving only white behind. Everyone knew who the uninvited guest was.

He pressed the buzzer and, in a panic, turned the music off and shushed everyone. "The girl!" She could ruin everything. I

---

* More a gathering, to be honest; I don't know at what point a "gathering" turns into a "party".

did not want to spend a night in a prison because of a girl. If they found her among us, the scene would have been too perfect to let it go: a gang bang.

Worse was if my parents found out; I did not even have the imagination to explain where I was and who I was with. I looked at the others; the feeling was mutual. There was no time. A few more steps and the police would be at the door. One of the guests jumped to hide the booze. The host took the girl's hand and stood her behind the thick curtain in the living room.

Knock, knock. They were here.

There were two of them at the door. One came in; the other one stood at the entrance, fiddling with his walkie-talkie, making crackling noises. The one who came in wore a green uniform from top to toe, too big for his thin frame, and he had a serious look on his face. He had a messy beard and his hair was side-parted and flat on his head, his eyes too close to one another, at a constant sad angle. I tried to guess his age. Twenty? Max twenty-one. He reminded me of someone. I rummaged through my brain for images of men I had dated. No luck. But the tickle did not ease. We avoided eye contact; the eyes were unsettling.

We were scared of that flimsy being walking among us like the grim reaper, and he knew it. He sniffed something was not right with these people, but couldn't figure us out. I sniffed something too; if not showering or using a deodorant was a badge of *basiji* honour, he got top marks. He walked towards the curtain where the real "sin" was hidden.

"Busy night?" said the host, with a cough.

The *basiji* glanced at him, his lips forming a lopsided smirk, and without answering he went towards the bedrooms. The host exchanged glances with a few of us and released a held breath.

Ten minutes later, he was at the door, giving a stern warning about the music. We promised that we wouldn't be listening to music again. I was standing at the back, arms crossed, leaning on a wall; he was a child who was indulging in his power, how he could have decided our fate. I thought to myself, If only he knew what these innocent-looking guys got up to, he'd kick himself. I smiled at that and glanced at Soheil. He was sitting and had already resumed his chat with his bestie next to him.

And then it hit me: that look, that beard, that hair. Closer than I dared to look, he was like Saman, Mohammad, my own brother.

They left and we let the young woman out. No matter how the host tried to pretend it was all OK and we should carry on, most of us didn't want to stay there any longer, least of all me. Soheil did want to stay and party, but that was too close an encounter for me. I left without Soheil and with the taste of the thin bearded man's sweat still under my tongue. I thought of Saman and his ideals on my way back and gritted my teeth.

It didn't stop me going to parties. The determination to defy a harsh and twisted system and to carry on had built a resilience and indifference towards it. I was just getting started.

The Useless Disorder

May 2007, the Café

I wiped a tear off my cheek, still laughing. My belly had begun to ache.

"How do you even come up with this stuff?" I asked Kasra, catching my breath.

"All of what I said was true, darling, and that is what he *really* does in the evenings," he said, protruding his lips out in an exaggerated pout, his hands showing where the imaginary breasts would stick out to.

Saam was shaking his head, barely containing his laugh. That evening, Kasra had taken centre stage re-enacting the relationship one of his girl friends was having with a new prince charming. Well, a prince charming who now, in Kasra's version of events, was a secret trans woman and did burlesque dancing for the mullahs. Farid had taken it upon himself to fill in the bits he felt were being left out in the impromptu act.

Getting together at Café Soosan had been a rare event since Soheil and I had become an item. Reza had insisted I join them for old times' sake, and I was glad that for once I was not listening to Soheil's friends' usual gossip, and instead was watching a quality act.

"He is so gorgeous, it is sickening," Kasra said finally, sounding more angry than jealous. "I sometimes wish I was straight," he groaned. "In fact, most of the time."

I looked at him, waiting for the punchline, my mouth frozen in a smile, the laughs tailing off.

Nothing.

Is he serious? I wondered. I waited for a debate, clearing my throat.

Silence.

I looked around the room. Saam held my gaze. Anxiety began building up inside me, the kind that an awkward smirk cannot hide. No one appeared surprised, no one protested, and what followed made me ache.

"Me, too."

"Yeah, me too. Life would have been so much easier."

"Yes, I wish it all the time."

One after the other. Despite all the laughs, all the gossip, all gay life had offered, did no one *want* to be gay? Were none of them happy with their sexuality? My friends, whom I thought were the most fabulous.

I wanted to say, *I am happy; I don't want it to be different*, and I wanted to be angry, but a knot in my throat stopped me. Was I truly happy? I imagined my life, had I been straight, blended in with the rest of society. Where would I be now? Would I be married and with children? Would I still need cheering up, or would I have found military service more appealing?

"It would be so much less hassle," said Farid finally, breaking the silence. He saw the surprise on my face. "Don't get me wrong, I like the hassle, I never wanted to be straight, darling." He smiled. The stud on his eyebrow flickered.

"You like the hassle of answering to the morality police? The *Basij*?" asked Kasra.

"The bloody wolves, attacking defenceless sheep," said Soosan from the kitchen. I was sure he meant to say it angrily, but his voice just did not allow it.

I winced at the analogy, thinking, I am not a sheep.

"Oi, Soosan…Who are you calling sheep?" Farid screeched. "I, for one, am a gazelle, and the *basiji* are hyenas. Ugly, pathetic hyenas. And when has a hyena ever caught a gazelle?"

He was standing on his toes at that point, elegantly curving his figure. He did look like Bambi.

When I glanced at Saam again, he was staring at his feet, his cheeks blushed. Was he, the straight one among us, feeling the guilt of a society which rejected the ones that were different?

My eyes stung. I got up and went to the bathroom. Standing in front of the mirror, the dismal look on my face made me laugh.

I took a deep breath. By the time I was back, conversation had moved on. I walked past them, avoiding eye contact, and headed out of the flat.

A cool draught smelling faintly of petrol welcomed me, as I stepped out into the quiet alleyway. The door to Café Soosan was just one dull black door in a row of many on the street. The gateway into a different world. I sat on the step outside and allowed the built-up emotions to stream out of my eyes. A car passed by, beats of house music blasting out of it windows, echoing against the walls.

Moments later, I heard the door behind me open and close, and felt someone sitting next to me. I turned my head away so they would not see my miserable expression.

"You know," Farid started, his shoulder touching mine, "everyone's 'me too' in there was for a different reason."

I turned to face him. He was just looking ahead. The smoke-infused breeze was flapping his silk shirt against his chest.

"Y-yeah, I guess—" I started, but he cut through.

"I sometimes wish I was straight, because of my mum." He bent his head. "Her only child, is…is this."

I was not able to say another word.

He continued, "I cannot give her a grandchild or bring a bride home. She won't be able to go wedding-dress shopping for her daughter-in-law." He half-smiled. "And she needs to spend double the amount of money on make-up."

I smiled back.

He turned and looked at me, eyes glazed over. "Does Haj Khanoom share make-up with you?" He sniffed.

It took me a moment to realize he was talking about Maman, using the religious prefix. I laughed. "Haj Khanoom does not *wear* make-up."

"Of course she doesn't. It is haram, right?" he said, biting his lower lip.

I began to protest, instinctively wanting to correct him on sharia law.

He carried on, "Anyway, that is my reason, even though I wouldn't even try to become straight. Kasra *joon* wants it because he has a straight-dick fetish, the slut. And you, darling little whore?"

"I...I don't want to be straight, not any longer. Fuck them." I was not sure who I meant by *them*.

Farid chuckled. "That is the attitude. FUCK YOU!" he shouted into the street.

I crouched in fear.

"We need to teach that to all of Tehran's gays. We...*I* should..." He said the last bit to himself, sighing. Then turned to me again, this time with a pout, back in character, the stud on his eyebrow lifted. "Let's go back in before I ruin the foundation on my face." He gave me a peck on my cheek. "They don't deserve us," he said, waving his hands towards the empty street.

Back inside, Kasra was already on another camp made-up drama. Farid did not hesitate a second before using a blanket as a chador and joining him. Everyone was giggling as if nothing had happened. That evening passed, with the dilemma floating in my mind.

I wished for the day when it would not even occur to me to be any different from what I was.

Where I grew up, tradition intertwined with religion fuels the fire of homophobia without needing the mental-illness label. Homosexuality is a perversion in the eyes of sharia, and the law punishes those who practise it. A death penalty.

A mental illness on the one hand, and a sin on the other. The lucky ones got the first label. Don't they say, "death the cure for all diseases"?

Two men *caught in the act* of sodomy is a crime which the system punishes, not the desire itself. The law says, *If two men are caught in the act, witnessed by four wise men, they shall be punished, by death.* To me, it sounds like a description of a twisted niche porn film, where Gandalf, Dumbledore, and perhaps the Ayatollahs, walk in on someone taking it up the arse. Anyway, the point is, crime or not, in Iran, same-sex desire is still considered a mental-health issue.

All men in Iran must do compulsory military service. The law which allowed it to be "bought" had been abolished by the time my turn came. So, all of us university graduates were desperate to find another way out of it, and there were a few.*

One was having a medical condition: needing very strong glasses, having one leg, being wheelchair-bound, and so on. These all exempted someone from the service. There was a list of mental-health problems too, such as schizophrenia and, you guessed it, homosexuality.

Saam had managed to prove he was the sole carer for a disabled parent, and he told me that Ali had found a medical reason; both were exempt.

I did need glasses, but my prescription didn't hit the threshold. I had one option left: use my other "condition" as an escape route from the service.

The process of doing so involved nearly ten sessions of psychiatric evaluation by a military-approved psychologist, who would then issue a letter stating one was truly gay. Detailed questions such as, *Position during anal sex: missionary or doggy style?* had to be answered to tease out whether one was lying.

Many of my friends went through this process and got the exemption from military service. It may have been demeaning, but the reward was priceless. At the time, I had no idea what it entailed.

Saam pumped me up with courage to get it done, saying, "You have to ask; you can't just let it go." He had a point.

So, there I was, in front of the military recruitment building, not knowing which department I needed to go to.

I started walking down a long corridor, offices to my left and right. Each had a plaque stuck to the wall next to their door which

---

* It is only after university that one would be recruited, unless one fails to get into uni, and then military service is done straight after school.

said what that office was meant to do. To me, they all looked the same, with different wording: **NEW RECRUIT AFFAIRS, RECRUITMENT ISSUES, DEPUTY HEAD OF RECRUITMENT.**

People in uniforms were going in and out of these doors purposefully, holding files, letters, and whatnots. I found the door I needed, took a deep breath, and popped my head in with the biggest grin I could muster.

Sitting behind a large desk was a man in a green camouflage uniform. The desk was cluttered with stacks of different-coloured files, letters, stationery, and dust. The man himself seemed lost shuffling through the papers in front of him.

"Hi, sir—can I ask a quick question about medical exemption from the service?" My voice was shaking.

"What is it?" he said, without looking up, thoughtfully reading a letter, stroking his stubble over the double chin.

"Erm, I have friend (of course) who is a homosexual and a doctor, and he wanted to know what he needs to do."

The word "homosexual" came out in a whisper, but he heard me right. He looked up, serious eyes and frowning eyebrows, obviously knowing that I had no such friend.

"He can't."

"Erm, how come? I heard—"

He stopped me abruptly. "I said he can't, he is a doctor. Does his problem stop him from being a doctor? No! I have work to do, now." And he looked towards the door.

His *problem*? My bloody *problem*? It took me a while to understand what he meant, but the conversation was already over, and I didn't dare ask any more. I mumbled a thank you and left, deflated.

Once I'd become a doctor, I'd sealed that escape hatch without knowing it.

I would be working as a medic in military barracks somewhere in the country as my service. Unless I proved I could not practise medicine because of my sexual orientation, there was no way I could get out of military service.

Fuck. Had I chosen the wrong subject to study at university?

And that was it. By the beginning of summer 2007, I was going to start military training in the Iranian army.

The first two months of military service was pure military training: drills, marches, learning to shoot a gun, all of it. But, before any of that, I had to shave off my beloved hair.

The day before the start of the service, I sat in the hairdresser's seat and told him to use the zero on the clipper. He knew exactly what it was for. Almost ceremonial, I was being prepared for sacrifice. He joked about it, trying to lighten the mood, which did not help. He did not know how precious my hair was.

Once it was all gone, I looked at myself in the mirror and had a feel of my scalp. Tomorrow I am starting military training, I told myself. It was happening.

It was time to say goodbye to my gay life, and my boyfriend. Soheil.

My relationship with him was like glitter sprinkled over my life, and it was eye-opening in many ways, but it was only a co-dependence.

He got what he wanted out of it: a driver, picking him up and dropping him off every single time we went out. We had nothing else between *us*. We almost never spoke on the phone, and, when he texted me, it was to let me know when and where the next plan was.

I knew I didn't love him, but I needed him like a strange addiction, a horrible one. The fall out with my best friend, Ali, and the depressing prospect of military service made me more dependent on the toxic relationship. I needed him as an escape and reminder of the "real world." He was an unreliable anchor to keep my sanity.

Our goodbye was also scripted: a half hug, a pretend sad face, and a "Keep in touch, darling" was all I got, as if going to an actual war. I played my part well. "I will" and "See you soon" were the answers I was expected to give, and I delivered them perfectly, and then dropped him off at his place. The coldness of that interaction ate at me like munching maggots in my gut.

I insisted on seeing Kasra. He'd always managed to make me smile. Though he did not sound that keen on the phone, he agreed to meet for a quick tea.

Kasra's hair was a mess, his eyes hollowed, and he was wearing a grey hoodie. No brands, no act. I had not seen him so flustered before.

"What happened to you?" I asked, kissing him on each cheek.

"Had an awful night," he started, sitting down. "I like your new hairstyle."

"It feels so strange on so many levels," I started, touching my head, which felt like caressing a kiwi. "Tell me, what happened last night?"

"You know, last night's gay party, which you didn't come to—"

"I so wanted to, it was just too late and past my dad's curfew, and I had been out every night with Soheil," I cut through.

He wasn't listening. "*Basijis* came to the place at two a.m."

"Fuck, what happened? Were they paid off?" I could read the answer on his face already.

"No." He pinched his eyes. "It was chaos. I bloody told them their music was too loud. I told them."

I reached out and took his hand; it was shaking. "What happened?"

"A few, including Reza and I, snuck out from the fire escape and ran," he started. "No one spoke, we just ran. It was dreadful. I left my jacket behind, with my car keys and sunglasses in the pocket."

"Is Reza OK?"

"Yes, he's home. Pretty shaken, but he's OK. I don't know who managed to get away and who stayed, or what happened to the rest. These *basijis* looked scary—they meant business."

My chest felt heavy. As if my shaved head was not testament enough to the path put in front of me against my will, this was another reality check, a wake-up call. Our colourful underground lives had always been under their shadow, always under threat.

Kasra's phone rang and, as he answered, I watched the remaining colour pigments on his face drain away. He asked a few questions, mumbled something that sounded like it was meant to be a reassurance, and hung up. I only stared at his face.

"It was Reza. He can't get hold of Farid."

The Slap of Reality

Summer 2007

Military service for a gay man may sound like a testosterone-fuelled fuck-fest, so I wished. Mine was far from it.

This memory smells of dust and melting rubber, and rings as if a bug is trapped in my ear. It is like a bucket of sand has been poured over it, all the colours buried.

On a hot summer day, Baba dropped me at the barracks, located just outside Tehran. It was where I was going to become a soldier.

My chat with Kasra the night before had shaken me. I was unable to follow up on what had happened at the party, only hoping everyone was safe. Calling Reza as soon as I got a chance was my number-one priority.

At that moment, though, I had to focus on the alien life I was about to enter and needed to adapt to. Standing in front of the pale blue gates in my oversized khaki trainee uniform with my shaved head, I looked small, I felt small. I thought of how I had got there, how my friends had got out of it and I, of all people, was the one there. The prospect of one and a half years made it gloomier; I was at day one. Before walking through the gates, I looked back at the busy road and listened to the loud honks, watching people outside who didn't look twice as these poor souls walked into the camp, like little ants crawling into a nest. How I wanted to be one of them driving by without noticing what these gates were. I shook off the idea of turning around and running away, being a "deserter" before I'd even started.

I walked in.

The camp was enormous; it contained several dormitories, sleeping ten or more squads. They were spaced out from each other by about 200 metres. A large flat courtyard was situated at the centre for marching practice and morning ceremonies. The catering area, the infirmary, a mosque, and various other offices were all yellow-brick structures with the green army emblem painted on their sides. It was a self-sufficient community. As soon as I walked in, the mood changed. Even the air smelt different, of baking asphalt.

Once I was allocated to my squad, we were given a speech by our staff sergeant. In true military style, he sucked out all hope, like a leech after a hunger strike. We sat on the hot asphalt in neat rows, taking it in. How he enjoyed watching our faces.

"This is where you will be spending the next two months, and a lot needs to be learned. Forget about home, this shall be your life."

He carried on giving a list of basic duties, from cleaning toilets to clerical jobs and getting water. Mobile phones were left at home. There was a payphone on site which could be used for emergency calls. No questioning anything he said. All facts. All to be obeyed. I scanned the faces of my squad-mates, relieved to see I was not alone. All appeared to be in a daze. The last thing I wanted anyone to know was my sexual orientation. It was time for me to put my camp Mr. Hyde back in the box and lock it; I had to become straight again.

After I found a bunk bed and a locker, in my own time, I had a wander around the barracks. I didn't go far from where my squad was, scared I may be shot or something. The place was eerily quiet, as if we were the only ones there. Tall, hay-coloured bushes surrounded the area. The outside traffic sound was completely muffled and replaced with the constant buzzing of crickets. Had it not been what it was, one could say it was almost peaceful.

Only when all the squads were gathered for classes, speeches or ceremonies did I appreciate how many of us were there. For us beginners, education degree determined what squad we were put in, and ultimately what rank we got after the two months of training. Undergrads or school dropouts ended up in the same squad, and post-uni recruits in a different one. So, I was put in a squad with men roughly around my age and post university.

A few of us were from outside Tehran—young men who had managed to pull themselves up and get a decent education. When talking to them, I felt how my life, my upbringing, and my privilege had created a gap between us. I sometimes envied their outlook on life. There was a well-camouflaged pain engraved in the creases of their faces, one which I was not familiar with. However, their attitude remained positive, happy with what life had handed them.

Unlike the rest of us, who mostly owed our success to our families and where we were brought up, they truly had earned it. I was for once standing outside my bubble and it was uncomfortable. It was hard to be friendly, to ask more about their lives and not be patronizing at the same time.

It was true that hardship brought one closer to God; religion was a big part of their lives. The same religion that, for many years, had taunted me, that I was angry with and defiant of. That gap, I couldn't and didn't want to bridge. Hence, when I made a few friends among our squad, they were all from north Tehran.

"Military service is when a boy becomes a man." Baba's words of wisdom had been repeated so many times, I had lost count. So, this was it: my rite of passage of becoming "a man." There was a hint of truth to it. To me, if anything, the service was an eye-opener: to the vast differences between people, the gaps in society caused by poverty, belief, and corruption.

Staff sergeants in charge of squads were usually military personnel who were enrolled by the army straight after high school, and again the majority came from disadvantaged backgrounds. Their demeanour said everything about how they felt about us, strolling in from our comfortable homes in north Tehran. My sergeant's eyes lingered on my neck as I passed by, burning my skin. They had power over us now. They were our bosses, and a loud "Yes, sir!" was the answer expected from us for *any* order given. The godlike power they were given over us was daunting. I needed to be in their good books.

When I'd said my goodbyes the night before, I'd thought I would not be seeing family, friends, or Soheil for two months. However, that was not entirely true. Every week, two or three people from each squad were allowed to go home for a night. The welcome speech was always meant to be disheartening and intimidating. It was the army, after all.

Our blue "leave booklets" had boxes which would be ticked off once we had used a day. There were only four or five of us who lived in Tehran and could benefit from going home for a night. After spending only two nights in the godforsaken camp, the prospect of being able to sleep in my own bed sounded like a dream.

When, that weekend, I managed to go back home for two nights, Maman and Baba were shocked. Maman prepared my favourite meal, *tahchin*, and offered an extra prayer. After dinner, with a childish excitement bubbling inside me, I called Soheil. His voice did not betray his surprise.

"Oh my God! I can't believe they've allowed you to leave."

"I know, I was not expecting that either. I already have so much to tell you."

"Of course, I bet it's not easy."

He sounded interested, or was he being polite? I was just happy to hear his voice.

"I can tell you all about it. What are you up to tonight? I could come and pick you up."

Silence followed for a few seconds, but it was enough.

"I...I'm going to a party tonight, with a couple of friends."

Of course you are.

"Oh, OK...A gay party?" I asked, already knowing the answer.

"Yeah."

"Ah, cool—maybe I could join?" I said pathetically, my balls sore from the kick they had received already.

His reply had a touch of nervousness: "I would have loved that, obviously, but I can't take a plus one."

"Really? Erm, OK...Maybe don't go? Or see me before?"

The idea of not going to a gay party, to Soheil, was like a cheerleader belly-dancing in front of the Ayatollah.

"No, sorry. I'm already late and need to go to the gym before. Maybe tomorrow? You said you have two nights anyway, right?"

His routine of "puffing up" his chest and biceps before a party was stricter than my mother's midnight prayers. Bruised, I agreed, and hung up.

I tried calling Reza next, and, when I couldn't get through, called Kasra.

Reza had become less sociable since the *basiji* raid, Kasra explained. He had not got through to Farid yet, but had heard from others that they'd seen him escape as well. I felt relieved at the news, hoping the ordeal would soon be behind us. I made Kasra promise to tell me if he heard any updates on Farid.

Soheil granted me an audience the next day—with his friends, of course. He did not appreciate it when I complained about how I had expected him to be more enthused to see me the night before rather than going to another party. The meet-up I had been looking forward to turned into a tense quarrel. A heavy silence ensued, for which I was blamed. *I* had ruined the moment.

Back at the camp the next day, and in my uniform, the face of my reality transformed again.

It is true when they say, looking back on your life, that tough events will appear insignificant and not worth the stress you put yourself through, but having that perspective when you are in it is next to impossible.

We were woken up at four in the morning, first having our bunk beds examined by our staff sergeant, making sure they were neatly made, then taking part in morning exercise: running around the main camp courtyard. The air was fresh and cool, and the sky pink with rising sun rays. Running in our white vest tops, our khaki shorts, and military boots, we repeated chants after our staff sergeant.

I was going over the argument with Soheil in my head, thinking of ways to make it up to him. Another cadence call was shouted at us, more praise for the regime and religion. I only mumbled it back, and one of the cadets jogging next to me gave me a nudge.

"What's up? Not into the Arabic chants?"

I smirked back. "Yeah, guess not, today."

Another chant by our sergeant.

I jerked my head away with a frown as the guy next to me shouted it back too loudly.

Wait, that's not what the chant should be, I thought.

I looked at him. He was smiling, waiting for the next round. Every time we had to repeat a phrase, he only changed one word or one syllable, but transformed the whole meaning into something rude. My eyebrows raised and I instinctively shushed him. He didn't seem bothered and kept it on.

The boss shouted again. I waited for my new friend's twist and shouted it with him. And the next one, and the one after. Once the giggles of the silly risk settled in, Soheil was long forgotten.

We cleaned up and changed into our uniforms for the morning ceremony, kicking off at seven a.m. It was part of the daily ritual. After the Quran recital and speech by our colonel, the head of the barracks, each squad marched in front of his stand. He was never impressed with our goose-stepping, and our group was the one which usually had to stay back to do extra runs around the courtyard, or push ups, or crawls as punishment.

Classes about the military, war, strategy, hierarchy were held in an open-air space. The crickets provided the background soundtrack. The subjects were mind-numbing and I knew, or hoped, they would never be of use to me.

I learned how to dismantle a semi-automatic rifle to clean the parts and put it back together. I cleaned a rifle, while Soheil and his friends gossiped about their latest party, while Kasra was probably planning another evening at the Café or topping up his tan in his Versace swimming briefs. The images danced in front of my eyes and were joined by the sweat dripping off my forehead.

And the blows kept coming.

My relationship with Soheil was bleak. I was still thirsty for the attention that I never got, and he was off enjoying his partying, his bouncing. *I* was turning into a nuisance for *him*.

Ali was not talking to me; I had to put up with a military routine with no escape; and Café Soosan seemed like a fantasy land which had never existed.

I was at Atoosa's place during another lucky weekend away from the barracks. I had planned to buy Soheil a gift to say sorry, again. Start over, again.

His text was to the point: **This is not working anymore. Don't contact me again.**

I stared at my phone for a while. I dialled his number.

Rejected.

Dialled again, and rejected again.

I sent texts, one after the other, as tears streamed down my face uncontrollably.

Silence.

It was over.

The end came like the beginning: quick and unexpected, like a neat slash on the wrist.

I sobbed in Atoosa's bed for a while, as she rubbed my back. If I had to point out one of the lowest moments in my life, if not *the* lowest, that would be it.

A harsh and pointless military training, coupled with a heartbreak, had taken a toll on both my lives. There was a light somewhere at the end of the tunnel. I just hadn't yet managed to see it.

With Soheil gone, I needed to gradually put myself and my social life back together, piece by piece. The gay me broke free once more. I saw more of my old gay friends again. With their help, Bouncy Soheil's short chapter was over, and the wound healed. Café Soosan became a second home.

The repetitive faces of Soheil and his gang were replaced by new faces from Tehran's gay scene who'd pop in and out. Reza and Kasra became my official crew again. Reza still mourned the abrupt end of his relationship with Farid, but was on the mend too. Kasra was the perfect therapist and the Café the perfect haven for us two broken-hearted souls.

The service, too, was about to show me a gay side.

At the camp, we trained alongside people from many walks of life. I had bonded with a group of straight cadets from Tehran. But I wondered if there was someone like me, my *true* self. I surely could not have been the only gay man there.

The infirmary was where I found the other one. It was constantly full of soldiers who wanted to get out of doing one thing or the other for medical reasons: the "sick-note hopefuls."

The clinic's doctor had been lucky—or, more likely, he knew someone who knew someone who could arrange for him to do all his eighteen months' service sitting there, having all of us at his mercy. When I first walked into his office, I did not need to think twice about his sexual orientation.

His arms swung back and forth like two pendulums on either side, his trunk was so upright it was as if he'd swallowed a walking stick, and his top buttons were undone to reveal a shiny shaved cleavage that reminded me of Roya. His puffed chest narrowed to a tiny waist, creating that V-shaped body so many craved, and his plucked eyebrows, one always raised, formed an exaggerated wonky *M* on his forehead. They sat above two white circles on a brown clean-shaved face. He must have been wearing sunglasses constantly at swimming pools, like we did.

My lips twitched as I stifled the laughter. "Hello." I waved my hand as he cat-walked by. Dolce & Gabbana *Light Blue* hung in the air behind him.

He turned his head, looking at me from head to toe. "Here for a sick note? Well, sit out till I'm ready."

I opened my mouth, but he'd walked past. I wondered what he did to get "ready."

I knew I would be visiting that place again. I could not wait for my next chance to go home to tell Kasra about him. How he would have reinvented him into one of the characters of his stories.

There was a penalty for the tiniest of mistakes or any indolence at all during the service. Anything from extra push ups and sit ups, to the worst: the leave booklet being taken away. For us Tehran residents, to be able to go home for the weekends meant a lot, and that was well known to our staff sergeant. No matter how hard I tried to befriend him, he kept that trump card over my head. *That* was his ultimate joy.

I was preoccupied with my life outside those walls, as well as what might be the best way to visit the infirmary without turning too many heads or causing people to wonder why I was there.

Sitting on the asphalt floor in our squad's yard, we had to complete another test about the lessons the week before. My daydreaming meant I was barely able to answer any of the questions. When my booklet was taken away, I didn't care initially. But then I saw them: friends leaving, one after the other, in their normal clothes, big grins on their faces and bigger plans for the weekend. I stood at the dorm's entrance, watching them. A heaviness began to press against my chest. I suddenly missed the Café, missed everything on the outside, as if I'd been imprisoned for life.

"There they go again."

I did not recognize the thick southern accent. I turned my head and looked at him. Is he in my squad? I wondered. He was wearing a white vest, Kurdish baggy trousers, and plastic slippers too small for his feet. He smiled at me, revealing deep creases in the corners of his eyes. I could not ignore the contrast to the doctor.

"How come you aren't leaving?" he asked.

I looked down and kicked a pebble, harder than intended. Dust rose. "I'm not allowed, because that arsehole has taken my booklet away."

"Oh, is that so? Well, a weekend here could be fun," he joked.
I was not amused.

He must've read my desperate face. "It's not as bad as you'd think. I haven't gone home for more than a month."

"It's different, though..." I regretted the words as they were rolling out of my mouth. How much of a spoiled brat am I? I tried correcting myself: "I mean, I bet it is hard. I just can't bear it here."

He kept looking at me, his eyebrows rising a little, but still smiling.

Stop talking, Majid.

"Here, take mine." He took his leave booklet out of his pocket.

I stared at his hand, mouth open. "N-no, I can't."

"Of course you can. They never check them at the gates."

"That's not what I mean—"

"I'm not going anywhere. Take it."

Was it shame that constricted my throat?

"Thanks."

I took the booklet from him, still brand new. I flicked through the pages, all blank. I looked at him in surprise. He nodded, offering a handshake. I squeezed his palm against mine, feeling the rough calluses against my moisturized hand.

"Bring it back in one piece. I'm off to offer my prayers."

I followed him with my eyes as he went back inside. Who is he?

That evening, I did go to the Café. As Kasra shrieked with laughter at my description of the doctor, all I could think about was the stranger I had been serving with for more than a month and the divide between us. I did not talk about him. I somehow did not want him to be the end of another joke, subject of another act. I convinced myself that would be my "thank you" to him.

Although the clinic's doctor was a walking, talking textbook gay, neither of us dared come out to the other, and it was not necessary. I did become a regular, though. He enjoyed the gossip and showing off his life outside—well, most of it: his gym routine, his trips to his family holiday home by the Caspian Sea and the ones abroad, and his drinking and partying. His stories brought a touch of Café Soosan to the clinic, and the escape was clearly a joy he indulged in too.

Having no doubts about his sexuality, I sent him a text a few weeks later.

Going to a Gol party this weekend, wanna join?[*]

I watched the screen of my phone anxiously, until it pinged: **What party?**

I stared at the phone for a second. Had I been wrong? Was it possible he didn't know the word? Then, the next thought appeared: Could he *not* be gay? I replied to that question out loud: "No, you're as much a straight as Madonna is a saint." Farid used to say that all the time. He would have said it to the doctor's face.

I saw him in the infirmary a few days later. He did not mention the text, and neither did I.

"If you need to be seen, wait outside, soldier," he said.

I had to look at his face with eyes wide. I began to utter his name—

"It's lieutenant to you, mister."

I shuffled uncomfortably on my feet and, when he did not make any further eye contact, I left the room. He had suddenly become busier, and I, another cadet, his inferior.

The friendship, if it could be called that, fizzled out thereafter. I had got too close to the subject.

The gay had no place in the army.

We were off to the shooting range the following week.

I will get back to this memory, but now a leap one year into the future.

---

[*] Among gay men in Iran, there used to be a code word for gay—*Gol*—which means "flower", of course.

Into the Lion's Den

Summer 2008

Kasra stubbed his cigarette on the railing and came in from the balcony, sliding the door closed. Soosan was in the kitchen, clearing up.

"It can be done easily. No one will know," said Kasra.

Fixing the cushion on the small sofa, I looked up. "It's too risky. Of course, I want to do it. It's just not worth the risk."

He rolled his eyes and waved his hand. "Yeah, yeah. We've heard your 'what ifs' a billion times. Just listen—"

"I *have* listened, and here we are. And *this* is as big a risk as I'm willing to take with my parents."

We were in Fasham. Last night, there had been more of us there for another sleepover. Reza had not joined, making excuses, though we all knew the main reason. At least he was answering calls and texts, which was progress.

The three of us—well, mostly Soosan and I—were finishing up the cleaning before leaving. Maman and Baba were supposed to come later; it was their weekly habit to stay in Fasham for the weekend. They thought I was with Ali and Saam.

"I agree with Kasra: we can plan everything in advance. I can even hook you up with my alcohol dealer." This time, Soosan was speaking as he tied the bin bag.

The idea of a gay party in the holiday home had been in my mind for months, if not years. It was the perfect location. The building was in a truly isolated spot. A twisting mountainous road led to the building, a route which definitely was not safety-checked and was dangerous at night or when it snowed. However, the destination made it worth the trip. It was a haven, mystical and cosy during winter, and vibrant and colourful in summer. But, even there, I didn't feel safe enough to throw a party, straight or gay.

"A plan in advance? Right, what will you do if the guy who owns the villa down the valley appears? I'm sure sound will travel that far," I said, angry.

Baba's friend, our upstairs neighbour in Tehran, the rose-water-smelling man—and, most importantly, the minister—he owned that villa. His presence in my life seemed never-ending.

"I don't know which one that is," said Soosan dismissively.

Kasra was examining his nails, as if they were painted.

"*That* one is the guy who is super religious, he's the guy who is in the government."

I was annoyed. Not at the suggestion anymore, but at the perpetual smell of rose water that followed me.

"Right, girls, let's go. I have a date later. We aren't done, though, Majid. I *will* see a party here before I die," Kasra said finally, and, laughing, went outside.

Soosan stood with the bin bag, holding his laugh, eyebrows raised. His belly vibrated. "You won't die anytime soon, given the amount of work you don't do."

I shook my head and followed, turning for one final look. A gay party? Here?

I huffed mockingly at the ridiculous thought.

"But, why wouldn't you?"

It had been a few days since the Fasham trip with the gay crew. I had been hoping Saam would agree it was an absurd idea when I rang him, making it easy for me.

"Oh, come on, Saam, don't tell me I need to explain it to you, too," I said.

"You don't. But there is always a way. Easiest solution is if you do it midweek. No one will be there then."

I chewed the inside of my lip. "I know, I know. But there are no guarantees. What if—"

"There will *never* be guarantees," he said, stopping me. "You've been talking about this for a while. Do you *want* to have a gay party there or not?"

"I think I do. I mean, it is an ideal spot."

"Then just do it. I can help."

My heartbeat began to raise. I closed my eyes tight to stop the threatening images of the *Basij*, the neighbour, Maman and Baba from appearing again.

"Fuck it, OK."

When I opened my eyes, none had appeared. I smiled.

I was about to take the leap. I had to set ground rules.

First, was the number of guests. As Kasra was enthusiastically adding names to the list, I snatched it from the table.

"I said maximum thirty, and I mean it. Who are these guys, anyway?" As I scanned down the list, my eyes widened. I turned to Kasra. "Why would you want this psycho there? You said it yourself that he's a proper diva."

"I did, but he could be fun. Also, he knows lots and lots of gays."

His naughty smile meant there was obviously more to it. "Knowing lots of gays" was not necessarily the best quality, especially in a queen known for gossip and fights. I already knew he was in deep rivalry with another diva from the scene. I for one did not want to be in his bad books. I sighed. "OK, whatever. I guess he doesn't hate me, yet."

Kasra laughed. "Don't worry, darling, no one hates you," he said gleefully.

I *was* beginning to worry, though. The numbers were still within my limits, but in Tehran's scene, word travelled fast.

"Any news from Reza?" I asked.

"I spoke with him yesterday," said Soosan. "He is going to come."

That was the best news. Reza had been up and down since Farid—mostly down. Getting hold of him was becoming impossible. The news injected me with new resolve. I was going to see this through.

It was going to happen on the safest day of the week: Wednesday. Our religious neighbour would hopefully not be there. I had decided to ignore the possibility, turning it into an acceptable hazard risk in my head.

Time for another tan top-up: the annual summer routine which I followed devotedly, like my pilgrimages to holy cities, years back. A hot summer always brought on another mission to deepen the pigments on my skin. My companions: Kasra and Reza. The venue: an open-air swimming pool. Going to a swimming pool was not part of the scene, but it was a popular daytime summer activity. By the end of summer, I looked almost black.

Baba would comment on my complexion, saying, "What are you doing? You look like a street beggar," and I would think, A sexy beggar, thank you, and head out again to top up my tan. Maman continued to mutter prayers, hoping the words would penetrate me and kill the sinful creature lurking inside. The words served as a religious kaleidoscope, distorting the image of the butterfly into an ugly creature.

Walking in the changing room, I heard Kasra's voice behind me: "Majid, wait up."

His pool bag was dangling from his forearm as he ran from his car. When he caught up with me, and after a quick kiss on each cheek, he said, "Is Reza here yet?"

"Running late, the little who—" I bit my tongue. "He should be here soon." Somehow, calling each other whores after Farid had left the group did not seem appropriate anymore.

There had been no direct news from Farid since that party nearly a year ago. Reza had tried his home a few times, calling as Farid's "concerned friend." His parents had said that he was OK and at home, but would not give any more details. After the third or the fourth call, they had become suspicious of the nature of their relationship, as Reza put it, and simply asked him not to call again. The time had come for him to move on.

We did miss the "little whore."

Giggling, Kasra and I walked in. I was used to his gasps and pinches on my arm at the sight of the tanned toned bodies of men in the changing room. Getting out of changing rooms and walking to the pool area was like a scene from a wet dream. There was barely anyone inside the pool. Guys in Speedos, the majority of whom were straight, lay next to each other, covering the surround, their bodies glimmering—a result of sweat, oil, or both.

Wearing my own tiny brief trunks with their bright orange lines, I walked behind Kasra. We spotted a gap in a corner and, as we settled, we spread olive oil and sprayed salted water over our skin to get a quicker and better tan, as if seasoning a chicken for that golden crust in the oven.

Soon after, Reza joined us. Once among the glistening men, my nerves about the party calmed down.

"Hi."

I squinted over my sunglasses at the slim figure standing above Reza's head. The blazing sun behind him silhouetted his face. His body was tilted in an *S* shape, his sunglasses swinging back and forth on his little finger. His Speedos, a florescent pink, were even smaller than mine.

For the tiniest second, I thought it was Farid, and wanted to jump when Reza answered, "Oh, hi. How're you? It's been a while."

He *was* Reza's friend, but it was not Farid, not after all that time. I lay back down as they chatted.

"Oooh, yeeees, it has been some time." All of his words seemed unfinished, as he dragged out his vowels. He continued, "I'm here with some friends, you knowww, to get the right colour." A high-pitched giggle.

I turned to my front, slightly conscious of the men around staring at him, at us.

"You look gorgeous. I like the Speedos, too," said Reza.

I raised my head slightly and looked at him, waiting for a wink which didn't come. The pink Speedos giggled again, hitting a higher note, just like Farid did. I wondered if Reza was flirting with him, his type.

"Well, thank youuu. But I need to look my best for the Fasham party, you knowww."

As if an ice bucket had been tipped over my head, I gasped and sat up instantly. He did not notice. I looked at him, head to toe. I had never met him before.

My mouth was dry. Could he be talking about a different gay party in Fasham? Before I could say anything, he was gone, his tiny bottom tilting side to side as he walked to his friends.

I took off my shades and looked at Reza. "How does he know? Have I even met him before?"

He shrugged. "I don't know. I guess everyone knows, now." And he lay back.

I looked hopelessly at him. *Everyone*. The thought gave me chills.

The invitation had indeed found a life of its own. The news of a party in Fasham had spread like gonorrhoea in a gay sauna. I had underestimated the yearning for a gay party in the community. Everybody knew about it, and everybody was trying to get an invite. If it was not for Saam's and the gay trio's insistence, I would have cancelled.

Among the flurry of self-invites, the two famous rival queens had somehow received an invitation each. One had said something about how the other looked or behaved, or both, at some point, and things had escalated from there—they were proper divas. No one knew how that clash would turn out. My friends' excitement was infectious, and I was going with the flow.

There was no concept of "bring your own booze." Soosan put me in touch with his "dealer." After a few phone calls to verify my identity, I secured the alcohol. The cheapest was the home-brew hooch. Soosan swore on his mum, like he always did, that the quality was good. At the risk going blind, I went for it.

I told my parents I would be spending the night with Ali and Saam—only it was not entirely a lie, this time. Saam *was* going to be my wingman. He even offered to make a fruit punch with the hooch in the large bowl Maman used to serve salad in.

"The size is good, we just need a ladle. Perfect."

His confidence examining the bowl was unsettling. My eyes were fixed on his face. Does he know what he's talking about? I crossed my fingers behind me, giving him an encouraging nod.

On the Sunday before the big day, three plastic gallons containing the home brew were delivered to my home, and I quickly transferred them to the boot of our car and drove off to Fasham. I whispered a verse of the Quran under my breath automatically as I started the engine. The prayer was to fend off the morality police. A random roadblock and check would mean a fine, lashes, and the party nipped in bud.

There were two days until the Fasham gay party.

"*Ya Allah.*"

I rolled my eyes. It was my brother calling Allah's name loudly as he walked in.

Saman's in-laws were having dinner at ours that night.

The shout was a warning call to women to cover up their hair—in this case, Maman. His father-in-law walked behind him, scratching his scruffy stubble over his double chin. He was followed by what resembled an upside down black cone, his wife. I worried she might stumble on something at any time, most of her face being covered by her chador. I stood at my bedroom door, out of sight. I would do the awkward greetings a bit later.

I texted Kasra to make sure he was available tomorrow morning, as he'd promised. We were supposed to go to the flat to deliver the sound and light system. I had lost count of the number of people who might show up and hoped it wouldn't exceed forty.

"Majid, come say hi." Maman disappeared as quickly as she had appeared to deliver the order.

I put my phone down and walked out.

After dinner, I retreated to my bedroom, lay on my bed, and exhaled. I was feeling in control. Preparations had gone smoothly, so far.

"We think you should do your iftar in Fasham."

The hair on my arms stood up, followed by the hair all over my body. The father-in-law was talking to Baba. I poked my head out to listen.

"Hmmm, maybe; it is an ideal place for the dinner."

Ramadan was a few months away. The famous family iftar tradition had evolved over the years. Ideal for iftar, I thought. Ideal for a lot of things.

"I think it is great. We can arrange a curtain to separate men and women."

"Yes, yes, that is a good idea. I will run it past the wife." Baba chuckled.

I did not know why I kept listening, but the conversation was twisting my gut into a knot. They were making plans to organize a religious event there, even discussing how to segregate the guests. How had I convinced myself what *I* was planning would be fine?

I was about to walk into a lion's den and pull on his testicles.

Kasra picked me up on time the following day.

"Are you OK? The bags under your eyes are reaching your knees," he said, after the kisses.

I tilted his rear-view mirror and stretched the folds down with my hands. "Gosh, they do look terrible. It's just nerves. Didn't sleep well at all."

"What are you nervous about? It will be fabulous, like Googoosh's wedding." He laughed.

"Will it?"

"Of course, darling. I haven't made this much effort to have a bad time. It'd better be amazing."

I smiled, leaning back on the seat. I imagined myself in a white dress, like the famous Iranian singer at her wedding.

"Shall we?" He gave another encouraging nudge on my leg and engaged the gear stick.

We drove to south Tehran first, to a street dedicated to sound and light systems. We picked up the large speakers, black-light lamps, sound-sensitive laser projector, and the stage flasher device.

No compromises. My party was going to have the perfect beat-matched strobe effect. From there, we drove straight to Fasham to install the hired equipment.

Driving through the gates into the grounds of the building, down the steep narrow pebble driveway, I turned to double-check everything was still in one piece. Kasra's talent for hitting all the potholes on the road was well known.

The driveway led to a wider landing, with four or five parking spaces right outside the main door to the building. There it stood, the simple faint-coloured brick structure, quiet and peaceful.

It had two bedrooms: one for parents and the other for guests. The kitchen and living area was the main feature—spacious, and surrounded with windows leading to a big balcony overlooking the valley.

I stretched as I put down the last piece of equipment and looked at Kasra. He gave out a squeal of excitement, rubbing his hands. I smiled back.

Sound system: check.

It was the day before the party.

"Pass me another roll, Majid." Kasra was standing on a chair in front of the balcony's sliding door.

I opened the box of the kitchen foil and handed it to him. "The corner, please. It's not covered."

"Yes, I know. Would you give me a minute?" And he gave me a death stare.

I enjoyed annoying him. All the windows were being covered with tinfoil from the inside. The light system was perfect, but the flat would be visible from space if we didn't light-proof it. I headed to the guest bedroom. Saam was lying on the bed.

"Are you OK?" I asked.

"I think so. Slightly anxious," he grunted.

"Oh, Saam, now it is not the time." I needed him to be on board.

"I know, but what if your parents show up? What if—"

"You really need to stop," I snapped. "Remember, you encouraged it all in the first place."

He held his hands up. "Yes, I know. Fine, I'll shut up. Just being paranoid. It will be great." He flashed a grin at me.

I tilted my head and raised an eyebrow. "If my mum and dad come, they'll join the party and dance in the middle."

"Of course. Your mother should definitely dance in her chador."

"Oh, she will! She loves how it floats behind her!" And we laughed.

BOOM, BOOM, BOOM!

The bass made the windows vibrate. We ran out. Kasra and Reza were dancing in the middle of the living room, which was completely bare now. Each *BOOM* from the speaker triggered a flash and a jump on the green laser dancing on the floor with them. They held hands as they spun in the middle.

Saam's mouth remained open at the effects. I tapped him on the shoulder and joined the other two.

We will be fine; we are ready.

Bullets and Beats

This is a memory with a full spectrum of colours, sounds, and smells, all jumbled up. It is also sliced. In the cuts, another memory has come to life, so similar in sounds and smells, yet so different. A soldier of the Ayatollah's regime versus a rebel to sharia laws.

It is a reminder, I guess. A reminder that opposites need to co-exist.

Summer 2008
It was the day of the party.

I looked at the small piece of paper in my hand for the umpteenth time: twisted lines and little arrows pointing to specific junctions, reading, *Turn here*. When I drew the map a week ago, it was supposed to be given to a couple of people who had not been to Fasham much, so they might have forgotten this or that turn. By now, I was sure it had found its way into the hands of total strangers.

"Do you think people will understand it?" I asked Reza, as he sat next to me.

He took the map and looked at it, head tilted. "Hmmm, we'll find out soon, won't we? It won't be the worst thing if some of these divas are lost and never found again." We laughed, and he continued, "Arise, Queen of Fasham. Your guests will arrive any minute now," and then he left, still laughing at his joke.

I was glad to see Reza was back to his usual self. I had missed him.

In the living room, Soosan and another friend were finalizing the playlist, meticulously arranging Iranian and English tunes, giggling at some of their choices.

"Oh my God, this is so gay!"

"Keep something classy, please. No, that's cheap."

And so on.

Saam was adding fruit juice to the punch he'd made in the bowl, and was testing it almost after every drop, like a chemist about to discover a new element. He replied to my inquisitive look with an *OK* sign next to his lips. I assumed that meant the cocktail was perfect. I smiled lopsidedly and walked outside to the balcony.

"Cute shirt, darling." Kasra puffed smoke out from the corner of his lips.

"Thanks. Thought I should wear something white—you know, black lights and all."

"I know, you'll glow like an angel." He laughed. Then, as if reading my mind, said, "I did arrange those snacks and sandwiches trays, by the way. Just came out for a smoke."

"I did not say anything, and the trays are excellent. Thanks," I said, holding my laugh back.

He raised an eyebrow and looked away with a slow-motion blink, raising his chin. "Good."

The laugh came out, this time. I turned as I saw Saam's head poking outside.

"I think your guests are arriving," he said.

Summer 2007, a year earlier

The penultimate week of military training had begun. Early that morning, we were put on minibuses to go to the campsite outside the city, in the desert. This was the field trip on which we would learn how to fire a semi-automatic rifle.

Getting off the buses, my nostrils burned as I inhaled the heat and tasted sand at the back of my throat. The beads of sweat forming on my neck tickled my back as they raced down underneath the thick uniform. Something told me I was not going to enjoy the next three days.

"Cadets! Get unpacked in the tents and be out in line in ten minutes."

I looked around inside the tent, taking it all in. Three nights. You can do this.

Ten minutes later, standing under the midday sun, the instructions continued.

"We will start in an hour, right after prayers. The practice will last two to three hours. And remember safety. We use live bullets. Twenty bullets per cadet, and all shells will be counted after the practice."

I looked at the face of my mate standing next to me. He seemed excited. I was not. *Live bullets* was echoing in my head.

2008

The excitement was hard to contain. *My gay party.*

I ran down the stairs and up the driveway to open the gate. The driver nodded as he drove through. I recognized him.

"Hi, you found the place," I said in the high-pitched voice I used to mask nerves.

"Yes, it was not that difficult. Should I just drive down?"

I was curiously looking at the other heads in the car. Three, no, four. I met the driver's eyes again, his eyebrows raised as his elbow rested against the windowsill, the back of his fist on his lips.

"Oh, sorry—yes, yes, just park behind the last car. It's the second floor," I said. I put a rock next to the metal gate to keep it open and walked back to the building, passing them again. I counted in my head: seventeen.

On my way up the stairs, I took a deep breath. The music was a bit louder than what I would've considered safe, but I had decided to leave it be. I walked back in.

Saam was sitting on a chair in the kitchen, eyes a little droopy. He'd clearly decided to let guests help themselves to his punch. The music and the effects were perfect.

Kasra walked past me and kissed me on the cheek, clicking his fingers to the tune. "Told you it would be great, hon."

I shrugged my shoulder and smiled gleefully. It was around ten p.m. This is manageable, I thought.

Reza waved at me from the corridor.

What? I mouthed.

"MORE AT THE GATE," he shouted back.

I waved back and went to the bedroom window to have a peek. Two more cars were driving through the gate. The yellow convertible was difficult to miss—it belonged to one of the famous divas. They parked on the driveway behind the earlier guests. I was glad I had left the rock at the gate. That was twenty-five, max.

I walked a few steps back towards the living room, scratching the back of my head, and then I froze.

A thought was snowballing in my brain, an image so vivid I had to squint.

I turned around and ran back to the window. They were getting out of their cars, laughing, beeping the cars locked.

The cars, the bloody cars! The line was almost at the gate.

The LINE.

I felt a lump lurch in my stomach. What if the first guests decide to leave? I counted the number of cars parked behind the first one. With each one, the lump in my stomach grew bigger. New headlights had appeared at the gate, followed by another pair. *Fuck!*

"I'm making the second bowl of punch, first one is finished." Saam was leaning against the door frame.

It took me while to answer: "Y-yes, sure, of course. Thanks."

Was he slurring? I followed him to the living room. I was greeted by new guests, just walking through the door, with kisses and hugs. I looked for Saam while touching their cheeks with mine. Leaning on the counter with one arm, he was pouring fruit juice into the bowl with the other. I guess he'd given up on the "perfect balance."

The dance floor was becoming busier. Soosan occasionally went back to his laptop to reshuffle the tracks. I was glad he'd taken the DJ job seriously. The screams and jumps to each song were testament to a job well done. The diva queen was dancing with others. I couldn't imagine why he had the reputation he did. He looked "normal."

Half an hour later, I was dancing in the middle of the crowd, which was getting denser every minute. I had stopped counting. I made no further visits to the bedroom window, blissfully ignoring the growing problem outside. From the corner of my eye, I saw Saam again, walking with the empty bowl.

I pushed my way through the sweaty crowd to get to him. "Where are you going? What's up?"

"Finished again, gonna refill, in the bathroom."

I looked at the bowl and back at him. "In the bathroom?"

"Yes, can't do it here. Too busy. It's easier there."

"Erm, OK…"

He walked towards the loo, bumping into a few guests. I was beginning to worry about his state, when he turned his head and said, "By the way, you're running out of alcohol."

2007

The crickets' unanimous buzz stabbed through my eardrum. I was no longer sure whether it was them or heat-induced delirium.

The shooting range itself was even more remote, far away from the tents. By the time we arrived, my uniform was stuck to my wet back and the rifle's sling was digging into my shoulder. We were positioned behind a temporary low hump made of stone and sand—a sangar. I could see the bullseyes about 200 metres away, a mirage glimmering in front of them. How I wished it was real, to have been able to run and jump in the lake.

"Right, cadets. In twos, you will position yourselves behind the sangar. One on the floor, shooting, and the other's job is to collect shells. Get in position, now."

I got on my knees next to my friend.

"Here we go, have you got your sock?" he said, puffing.

"My what?"

"Sock, for your face—"

"I will count down from three and you fire," the staff sergeant's shout interrupted. "I said, in position, NOW."

I lay on the floor, shards of stones poking me everywhere. I stuck my face to the heated barrel, for a split second worrying I wouldn't be able to detach it from the metal, leaving a layer of my skin behind. I squeezed one eye shut as I aimed through the sight with the other. The bullseye was winking at me. I exhaled as I secured the butt against my shoulder.

"Three, two, one…FIRE!"

I pulled the trigger. My ears began to ring as the guns sang their deafening bangs together. A pain swept down my body like lightning. The thought of my shoulder being dislocated made me nauseous.

The kick, the bloody kick!

I let go of the barrel and rubbed my shoulder.

"Push it hard against your shoulder, don't let the gun move."

I looked up at my mate spitefully as he said the words. "I know—easier said than done."

Realizing I was still in one piece, I lay back down. Nineteen to go. I dug the butt deeper into my sore shoulder and got my face close to a now even hotter barrel.

"Three, two, one…FIRE!"

OUCH!

This time, it was my face receiving the kick. Tears filled my eyes as the sting on my cheekbone numbed my face.

The sock. Of course. To cushion the kick.

"Three, two, one…FIRE!"

2008

"What are you *doing*?"

I looked at Saam, baffled. He was sitting on the bathroom floor, the bowl in front of him, and an empty tipped-over plastic barrel was in the bathtub. Small, crumpled juice cartons lay scattered around him: pomegranate. He held a kitchen knife in a reverse grip, like murderers do on TV. Rihanna was singing her lungs out in the living room.

He looked up, annoyed. "What does it look like? Making more punch. We don't have any more juice. Had to use these small ones from the storage." And he carried on, picking a new one, stabbing it at the top, and squeezing it into the bowl. The red juice splattered with every stab—on the floor, on him.

I pulled my foot back. "Need any help?"

"No, just keep them away for a minute while I'm finishing."

I turned around and found myself face to face with a guest. His shirt was completely unbuttoned, his hairy chest wet with sweat, his eyes bloodshot and half closed. This can't be good.

"Can we have m-more alcohol…please?" he said finally, after gathering the words into a sentence, and his lips formed a creepy smile.

I looked over my shoulder at Saam, deep in his stabbing action. "In a minute. You seem to have had enough already, though."

Reza appeared behind him. Reading my eyes, he put his hands on the guy's shoulders and turned him towards the dance floor. Like a zombie, and without another word, he walked.

"Thanks—the next batch of punch will be ready soon."

"He's not drunk, you know," said Reza, following the zombie with his eyes.

"What do you mean? Of course he's—"

"He's high, Majid. I've seen people taking pills and smoking in the corridors."

High and *corridors* were the only words that registered.

"N-n-no, no, no—that can't happen."

"Well, it is."

It can't, just can't. The *flat* had been secured, light-proofed and all. Nowhere else in the building. I had to get them back inside. The fear began to sink in.

Reza must've seen it in my dilated pupils. "I'll help you gather them."

I heard a grunt behind me and turned.

Saam was getting to his feet. "It tastes like shit, but it's ready. Last one. All yours." He pointed his knife to the bowl on the floor, full to the brim with a red liquid.

I took a deep breath. "OK, stand aside. I'll take it back to the counter."

I squatted next to it as Saam stumbled again, holding himself up against the wall.

"Saam, how much *testing* have you been doing?"

"Just a bit." He laughed.

Not amused, I wrapped my forearms under the bowl and stood up. The wobble in the liquid made a small splash on my chin. I closed my eyes and took another deep breath. This is going to be an interesting walk to the kitchen.

2007

BANG!

It was number twelve. I could not care less if I was hitting the bullseye any longer. My shoulder and my face were numb, and, with each count down, I swore under my breath. The thirteenth kick almost got my eye. The soreness of my cheekbone stopped me from keeping my face to the barrel.

"Three minutes' break and back on the ground."

I sat up immediately, hearing the instructions. I took a sip from the water bottle, looking at my friend. Even the hot water tasted like sand.

"You're getting a massive bruise on your face."

"I bet. It's only tingling now." I threw the bottle on the floor.

"Get a sock between the barrel and your face."

I looked at my boots. Wiggling my toes, I could feel the moisture between them. Fuck it. I quickly untied my laces and got my foot out, pulling the sock off and putting my boot back on again, my bare foot rubbing against the damp inside.

"One minute, cadets! Get back in position!" ordered the boss.

I put the sock next to my cheek and pressed it against the rifle with my face. The tart smell evaporating in the heat pulled my eyebrows into a frown. I prepared for the next blow.

"Three, two, one..."

Bloody hell.

2008
BOOM, BOOM, BOOM!

I looked at the ripple across the liquid in the bowl. My destination, the kitchen counter, was four or five steps away. Hugging the bowl, I started walking. Each step was translated into a bigger wave in the punch.

My mind was still venturing through the corridors, imagining guests in corners, taking their drugs. I gritted my teeth. I made my final step towards the counter. By now, I had a few big splashes on my white shirt and on the floor. As if famished, the guests descended on the drink, filling their cups straight from the bowl, dipping their fingers in the punch. The ladle was nowhere to be seen. I held my hands up and took a step back.

The *BOOM*s of the speakers were now digging into my brain.

Hang on, this is the third time I've heard this song.

It was an old Iranian song, which was OK when played once, for the nostalgic effect or whatever. *Once.* I looked around for Soosan. Then, I saw the culprit. He was right in the middle of the dance floor, screaming, vigorously shaking his head from side to side, eyes closed and arms above his head, showing the huge sweat patches on his tight vest top. I recognized him. It was the pink Speedos guy.

I made my way to him. "Hey, have you put this song on repeat?" I shouted, as I got closer.

Nothing. He swung his head again and a drop of sweat left his forehead, landing on my nose. I tapped him on his shoulder. He opened his eyes and stared at me.

"Did you put this song on repeat?" I said, wiping my face.

He looked confused for a second; his hands were in pause mode, wrists cocked, mimicking a T-Rex.

"Oh, yessss, this song. I looooooove it." And he gave out the familiar squeal.

I clenched my fists.

High. Corridors. The thought pressed against my temples.

Then, a tap on *my* shoulder.

"What?" I turned.

"Jeez, wanted to tell you your bowl is empty. Where can I get a refill?" he said, holding his plastic cup up.

I looked at the cup and then at him, and back at the cup. "It's finished. No more booze. Sorry."

Where is Kasra? Where is Saam?

I looked side to side and, with another apology, squeezed past his disappointed face.

More party guests appeared in my way.

"Do you have more alcohol?"

"Is it really finished?"

"No more? What do you mean?"

Their eye-wateringly sharp breath attested as to how cheap the home-brew spirit was. I repeated "Sorry" a million times as I made it past the angry voices. I was imagining the gossip taking off tomorrow: *Majid did not have enough booze*; *The non-alcoholic party*. I could not deal with that thought at that moment, though.

I spotted Kasra in a corner, giggling with someone else. I'd started towards him when the next one appeared.

"Yes, I know, and I'm sorry. No more alcohol," I said, before he could say a word.

"Erm, yeah. I don't care. I just wanted to leave and there are about ten cars behind mine."

I stopped. The inevitable had happened.

"OK, sure. Let's go down together and see who's behind you."

As we walked out, the song was playing for the fourth time.

2007

I looked back at the staff sergeant. He'd just kicked my feet as he walked by.

"Legs apart, look ahead."

I glanced at my shooting buddy and he rolled his eyes.

Last shot.

The sock was lying next to me. I had given up, taking the rifle's kick every time. My nerve endings had given up, too.

When we finally swapped places, I sat back for a second, twisting my neck and shoulders to release the tension. The ringing sound in my ears was not easing off.

About an hour later, we started packing up, bruised and battered. The useless exercise had already begun to take a toll on me. I put my sock back on and angrily shoved my foot back in the boot. I was imagining a cold shower, minutes away.

Then, his voice again: "Cadets, heads up."

I only looked up. He was walking back and forth in front of us as we sat on the floor.

"I have counted your shells. And—one—is—MISSING."

Was there a moment then, when I thought about turning the rifle to his head, or mine? Perhaps.

Everyone looked at each other with their black eyes, in a daze.

"We are not going anywhere till it is found. On all fours! The sooner it is found, the sooner we'll leave."

I could only laugh and shake my head. I put the gun down and got on my knees. Hands on the hot rocks, watching droplets of sweat fall and evaporate as they hit the ground, we started the canine search looking for that one bloody shell.

2008

I wiped my face with my arm. The once-white shirt now not only had a red stain in the middle, but also grey marks on the sleeve where I had rubbed my forehead.

Running up and down the stairs, each time grabbing a guest to take with me, I had managed to move most of the cars in the line. The next one—the last one—was the yellow convertible. The guy wanting to leave stood by his car impatiently, fiddling with his keys. I smiled at him one last time as I walked up the stairs. In the corridor, people were congregating again.

"Could you please go back inside? And don't smoke in the corridor, *please*?"

I couldn't wait for their answers and sarcastic comments, only hoping they'd listen. Back inside, the heavy air hit my face, tasting of salt. I walked on the sticky floor, looking at the stain I had left where I had spilled the punch. Where is he? The last time I'd seen the owner of the yellow car, he had been dancing in the middle of the crowd, but that was an hour ago. I asked a few people before someone finally said he was in the bathroom. A sigh of relief. He's just having a piss.

I walked to the bathroom to grab him as soon as he came out. The door was ajar and screams and squeals were coming from behind it. I tilted my head and cautiously pushed the door open.

"Hello?"

Another shriek, followed by hysterical laughing. A jet of water hit my shoes. I stood there, taking it all in; he was playing some sort of water sports with his "rival," the other queen. The toilet shower hose was on full power in his hand as he sprayed it over the other, both wet head to toe. A puddle of water on the floor splashed as they wrestled in the middle. If I'd been a gay angel, looking down from above, a sense of joy would have overwhelmed me, a tear running down my face at the sight of these divas getting back together. But *what the fuck?*

I needed to detach myself from the scene unfolding before my eyes. The first image rushing to the rescue was Maman, methodically wiping her hands and head in the same bathroom, preparing for prayer. In the image, all the edges were soft, like a halo. She was going to the living room, her favourite spot in the corner. There was a calmness to her humming, a Quran verse perhaps. A prayer rug was already spread there, a clay stone encircled by prayer beads on it. The same corner which was now covered in sweat, booze, and whatnot. She was going to be there, tomorrow night.

The next splash of water hitting my face stirred me back to the real world. I stepped in and turned off the tap. They did not even realize, still laughing mad.

"I really need you to move your car, now…please?" I said.

He looked at me, catching his breath. "Huh? Car?" he said, after a few more laughs and coughs.

"Yes, your car. The guy parked in front needs to leave."

"Ah, what a bore. *Who* wants to leave this early?" And, with a huff, he walked past me.

It was midnight. I was beginning to understand how he made enemies. Someone was in trouble. I looked at the other diva, now checking himself out in the mirror, pouting. I chewed my lip and walked back out. I ignored the mumbles about alcohol as I pushed through the crowd, this time only swearing to myself.

As I waved goodbye to that guest, who'd suddenly realized tomorrow was a work day, I stretched, and then my phone buzzed. I took it out of my pocket, immediately alarmed as I saw Saam's name on the screen.

"Come here," he said.

"Hey, what's up?"

"Come here." His voice was calm, as if he'd just woken up from a peaceful sleep.

I was about to ask again, when another guest appeared in front of me, looking flustered.

"I'll call you back in a sec, Saam." I hung up, and, pushing the phone in my pocket, I turned to the distraught guest. "Is everything OK?"

"Not really, I cannot figure out who is parked behind me. I've asked everyone. My dad has called a few times. I need to go home."

I looked at the kid's face. He was probably twenty-one or twenty-two. I was therapy-hopping, at his age.

"Where is your car? I'll find the guest."

Walking behind him, my phone vibrated again.

"What is it, Saam?"

"Come here."

"I *really* can't now." I shoved the mobile back in my pocket, annoyed at his silly games.

As the car came into view, the panic was back, heartbeat raised to max, feeling nauseous. I knew the car behind him. It was not a guest.

The car belonged to our neighbour, rose-water man, *minister*.

The memory fades. All the sounds, smells, and colours. It is dominated by the other. Taken over.

2007

I looked at my palms. The abrasions were raw and covered in blood spots. It had almost been two hours and there was still no sign of the shell. Our staff sergeant was sitting on a plastic chair, leaning back. *How did I end up here?* was a question that kept appearing in front of my eyes, no matter how hard I tried to ignore it.

He got up and had another stroll among us. I followed him with my eyes, hoping evil eye was true. Then I saw it. A twinkle in his hand as he took it out of his pocket. It dropped from his hand on to the floor. I could not mistake it for anything else: it *was* the shell. My chest began to heave. I was looking at a true sociopath in all his glory.

"Found it, sir!" a cadet shouted.

Of course you did. I got to my feet and patted my knees. Shaking my head, I went back to my rifle. As I made eye contact with the sergeant, he left his chin up and only smiled. I looked away. Day one had ended. We all headed back, with our ceremonial marks printed on our faces.

The other two days passed by quicker than the first. No more shells were "lost." I, along with a few others, also got the privilege of learning to shoot a handgun. By the afternoon of day three, we were back on our minibuses, heading towards the base camp.

A week left at the barracks and the two months of training would come to an end.

I was going home that weekend.

A Secret Service

2007
Before the party, before the chaos.

Once the two months of military training was over, cadets were sent all over the country to serve the remainder of their eighteen months in different barracks. Doctors were sent to serve as the resident clinic doctor. Some of these camps were extremely remote and in deprived parts of the country. That was when connections and acquaintances were pulled out of the bag to get a decent posting—and, if possible, one in Tehran itself.

Having just finished the worst part of the service, I for one was not ready to be sent to a lonely barracks somewhere far off for another sixteen months. Baba's connections came in handy. He knew a senior army officer, and, with his recommendations, I ended up in an army office, based in Tehran.

I started wearing a military uniform, rather than the trainee one, and no longer needed to shave my head. I made sure my shirt was tightened around the waist and body-hugging. I posed in it and took selfies, of course.

The positive shift was a motivation to begin to strike a balance between my gay and straight friends. I had found my feet in the gay life and the initial buzz had settled by then.

I had to mend my relationship with Ali as a priority. I heard about him now and then from Saam, but I wanted him back. He *was* my best friend.

Reconnecting was not easy. I realized how truly hurt he must have been when I casually strolled out of his life with a DVD player, ignoring him and immersing myself in the gay scene. I needed to dismiss my pride and accept I had hurt someone very dear to me in my self-centred quest.

I asked him out to a restaurant for a sit down and a serious chat. It took a few attempts before he agreed. There I was, with a friend I'd known for nearly ten years, and yet I was finding it difficult to get a word out. He kept his face serious, but looked tired. He wanted that phase to end too, one way or another.

"Look, I know I have hurt you, and I know I have been a bit selfish."

"A bit?"

I was about to say something which probably would have sparked another argument. I bit my tongue. "OK, I *have* been selfish, but I hope you understand, I had suppressed myself for so many years and, when Soheil introduced me to the new world, I just could not get enough."

"I will try to understand that, but I don't think *you* understand how much I counted on you and trusted you to be there when I *needed* you, and you weren't. And what is worse, you didn't care."

His soft voice—I did miss it.

"Well, perhaps. Soheil's now out of my life, and—"

"That's not my point, Majid," he cut through.

"OK, OK. You are right, and I did not realize how important the gathering on that night was to you. I was selfish and I *am* sorry. Can we move on, now?" I tilted my head.

My patience with intense chats has always been limited, and having said the *S* word, I wanted it to finish. He knew me too well. A smile formed on his face, one he desperately tried to mask with frowning eyebrows. That was all I needed. We were going to be fine; the old married couple had reunited.

Our friendship began to mend and our fall-out gradually turned into another funny story that Saam would, every once in a while, dive into, dissect, and take the piss out of.

In the gay scene, I was one of very few "men in uniform." Wearing my army uniform to go on a date was a big turn on, making them drool. Even if I went on a date in normal clothes, I would always drop the bombshell casually—"I am in the army"—and show a picture of me in uniform to woo my date. It was meant to come across as *masculine* and *rugged*, as much as I looked like one of the Village People.

By the end of 2007, I was only playing it straight with family. I even became braver expressing myself—well, almost. I confidently frequented the famous food court of Jaame Jam with my friends on the nights which everyone knew were gay nights. Prancing in with the camp crew and finding a table with a good view, I often chose a homoerotic male-model picture as my mobile home screen and made sure it was visible to passers-by. I was proud just doing that.

OK, I understand it was not exactly waving a rainbow flag in front of the Ayatollah's house, but it was still an improvement, considering.

Family, however, remained a problem. My parents knew I was not praying or fasting, but were powerless to change it. We were in a hushed agreement about our beliefs. If we didn't talk about it, it would not harm anyone. Maman tried hard to keep everything at home religiously right and sin-free, and I had decided to keep the peace. I wouldn't step on her toes and I avoided situations where she might step on mine. Nonetheless, not doing my religious routines was the extent of what I was comfortable with them knowing.

Parents provided the comfort, the money, the food, and, if we asked for it, the wives, but they never asked about our personal lives. There had always been a barrier which kept our personal lives, well, *personal*. Maman still brought up the topic: "When are you going to get married? Once you marry, I'll be at peace and happy." The line was so familiar, I sometimes finished it for her.

At the time, I enjoyed the relative privacy. Perhaps, if things had been different, if Maman and Baba had been more involved, they would have known more. Perhaps they'd learned I was gay *and* learned to come to terms with it. Maybe they did know, but an invisible wall stopped them from asking. Maybe they had accepted it in their minds but could not let me know. The infinite number of "maybes" swirled in my mind like restless parasites, creating an irritating itch. I had no answer for them. I was too scared of their reaction to the truth, for their sake: *It will destroy them* was a thought I could not argue with.

It was painful, and still is, but at least it was my pain alone. So, I carried on, as they did, in a cryptic aching silence.

Of my brothers, Saman was at his own place and had a son, which left Sina at home with me. My path and Saman's had parted long ago and our different views on Islam kept us separated. Sina, however, was not as religious. He had girlfriends and fooled around. If anyone in the household could know my sexuality and tolerate it, it would be him.

"If only you knew what he got up to in his own time," said Saam.

Ali started coughing, choking on his tea. As he wiped his face, the cough turned into a laugh. It was another evening of many, when Ali and Saam came over to play cards with Sina and me.

I shot a death stare at Saam, and immediately looked at Sina. He was fiddling with his thumbs and laughing quietly too.

To Saam, that was a green light. "If only you *really knew*."

"There are different types of people, after all," Ali said, stroking his chin knowingly.

I looked at him and mouthed, *What are you doing?* at the same time as observing my brother's reaction from the corner of my eye. He was still laughing and shaking his head.

That was not the first time Saam had teased the idea. He had planted the seeds gradually, waiting for a reaction, and when none came, he prodded more and more. He wanted to out me to my brother.

Normally, I would have hated it, as many do. But this was different. I knew I did not have the courage in me, and I did not mind Sina knowing the truth. Saam's jokes and "help" became an unexpected blessing.

The conversation did not go any further until next time, and the time after that. Sina knew that it was no longer a drawn-out joke. He knew the truth. Having lived in that home, he understood that it *should* be kept a secret, *always*. I never confirmed nor denied it, and I did not need to. We both knew we were not ever going to discuss it. The unspoken truth hung in the air, but I was content.

A few months into starting an office job in the army, I disliked everything about it. I disliked that what I did every day was a pointless chore of paperwork; I disliked that "Yes, sir!" had to become part of my vocabulary, and that every order had to be obeyed, no matter how absurd. The hierarchical system was designed to maintain discipline in the most autocratic way, which would have made sense, had we *been at war*.

What was worse was that I had started to dislike medicine. My training had been many years in the making, and this was where I had ended up. I was not practising medicine, so I was forgetting it, rendering those seven years pointless. On top of that, if I had studied anything else, I wouldn't have been there in the first place, because my "mental disorder" would've got me out of it. I would have had my passport in my hand and perhaps left the country.

Early summer, 2008

"Knock, knock."

I looked up, flustered with the amount of paperwork in front of me. My officemate, another poor soul doing his military service, walked in and sat on the only other chair, rotating on it.

I kept looking, an eyebrow raised. "Erm, do you need something? I thought you had a meeting to set up," I said, finally.

"Nah, just bored of it, needed a distraction."

I envied him. Another doctor, he was my new best friend. We'd been working in the same office for nearly a year by then. His unfazed approach to all the orders, all the stress and whatever he was assigned to do, made me anxious. It made me jealous.

I sighed. "I don't know how you do it. I have a million things to do and I'm now worried that your work will be dumped on me too. The bloody thing is happening in less than a month."

Through no choice of our own, we had become responsible for organizing a national military meeting which was to be held at our unit. Our friendship was born out of the need to distract ourselves from the dreadful task we had been assigned and the even more appalling system surrounding it.

He stopped rotating. "You are shit at your work, and Majid will take it from here," he said, mimicking our boss's voice and laughing. He often laughed, mostly at his own jokes, but his laugh was so infectious, it actually made the upsettingly lame remarks funny. He knew how unfunny he was, but that did not stop him.

I put my pen down, pinching the bridge of my nose, fighting the laugh, the sad laugh. "Seeing any new girls?" I asked.

"Don't know. Who was the last one I told you about?"

I regretted my question instantly.

He stood up and walked to the door to make sure no one was eavesdropping. His creased and untucked uniform shirt, looking too loose over his skinny body, was another middle finger to the system.

He turned around and began, "I met this new chick, she is so hot it's unbearable…"

Looking at the pile of papers in front of me, the last thing I needed was his work.

"Oh, gosh, there *is* a new one. Listen, why don't you tell me later. I can't concentrate right now," I said, grinning.

Premarital relationships and sex among a defiant youth crawled under the skin of a seemingly religious society, causing the regime an unbearable and unmanageable nuisance.

He stood at the door, clearly disappointed at my dismissal, and waved a hand. "Yeah, yeah. I'll call you later. You gotta tell me about your ones too, by the way." And he left.

I leaned back, holding a pen, tapping it between my upper and lower teeth, thinking. I shook off the image of the last one and got back to work.

Coming out had become easier. Any new person in my straight life was bound to know my sexuality. I wanted my "straight life" gone. I wanted just one life. Mine.

During the weeks leading to the event, an unexpected distraction lit a light in the dark cave I was dwelling in. It would have been a shame to go through military service with all men in uniform around me and not have an encounter, so to speak. It would have been a gay sin.

While lost in reading the minutes of yet another meeting, a deep and gritty tone vibrated my eardrum, snapping me out of the coma I was falling into. The voice was chatting with my office buddy in the adjoining room. I rolled back my seat and had a peek through the door, and there he was, sitting on the corner of a desk, one leg on a chair, making his tight uniform trousers stretch over his muscular thighs. He was tall and sickeningly handsome.

"Hel-hello," was all I could say, while staring at his full lips.

He immediately stood up and straightened his shirt. It took me a second to realize it was the stars on my shoulders that *he* had noticed first.

"Sit down, silly. This is Majid, another unfortunate doctor stuck here."

Slightly disappointed at the introduction, I got up and walked over to him, hand stretched for a shake and cheeks blushed.

"Ah, hi," he said, taking my hand, which got lost in his big palm as his embraced it, squeezing it tight.

I was beginning to wonder if what they say about big hands is true, when the picture was interrupted.

"I started here around the same time as you, I think." He smiled.

"Ah, OK, cool. It's good to have connections to get a posting in this place, right?" I said, a bit more confident, given my higher rank. But my confidence was blown away as quickly as it appeared when he spoke.

"Yeah, it is," he said, stroking his bald scalp and chuckling. "Anyway, Majid? Nice meeting you, and I'm sure we'll meet again."

"Sure, sure. Pop by anytime. We could do with the distraction, too." I looked at my mate with a grin. Both of us knew that, by *we*, I clearly meant *I*.

I couldn't stop looking at his round and muscly backside as he walked out.

As soon as the door was closed, I said, "Who was *that*?"

My office buddy burst into a laughter. "You know he is straight."

"Of course he is. Still, you never know." Pouya was straight, too.

"Don't do anything stupid. It's the army, and they can do whatever they want to you."

"Yes, yes, I know. No punishments just for looking and appreciating," I said with a wink, as I was leaving his office.

He was shaking his head in dismay, laughing to himself.

Once every month, doctors enrolled in the service had to do a night shift at the army hospital Accident & Emergency. We were given a small clinic, which opened on to another smaller room with a couch, where we could sleep the night. Other ranks, including my new crush, had to do guarding duties. Someone had to be on watch 24/7 in the army.

One of my night shifts coincided with his. I bumped into him at the beginning of my shift, and we exchanged numbers. It was an acceptable excuse: boredom during a night shift.

That same night, Kasra texted me in the evening to check if I was around to go to the Café. When I told him I was on a shift at the hospital, he said he would drop by to gossip. And so, he appeared, in his usual tight jeans and tight shirt, a few top buttons undone, showing off his smooth pecs.

We sat outside on a kerb next to the A&E entrance, enjoying the early evening breeze, and I confided in him about my crush. "He's on shift tonight, too," I said, showing Kasra a few of our texts.

"You *have* to tell him to come over."

"To do what?"

"You're an idiot. This is *the* best opportunity, and you must use it. Give me your phone, I'll take over the chat." His eyes were wild, his instincts heightened.

Reluctantly, I handed him my phone. "Don't say anything stupid, OK?"

I was hoping for a fake promise, but he didn't bother answering, and instead started frantically typing. I watched as he typed, a new sweat bead appearing on my forehead with every word. The sexually charged messages were sent in succession.

Why don't you come over and I can help you relax?

You'll enjoy it.

Have you ever been with a guy?

I was perspiring with fear, but didn't stop him, telling myself, I'm not doing this, it's Kasra.

I was envious of how easily it came to Kasra. I would think of a million possibilities before sending any of those messages, a trait that had rubbed off on me from Ali.

His replies then stopped abruptly.

No messages for five minutes.

Kasra had already changed the subject, gossiping about something else, while I had my eyes fixed on my phone in his hand as he waved it around.

Then he appeared, walking towards us, hands in pockets.

I gasped and whispered to Kasra, "He's coming."

He looked back with a mischievous smirk, meaning one thing only: *This is serious business, now.*

That familiar thumping against my chest resurfaced. As he approached, he hesitated for a second. I realized I had not told him I was with a friend, or rather Kasra had not told him he was there. I quickly jumped up and, before he could run away, introduced Kasra.

He walked over, said hi to us both, and, without mentioning the chat, cleared his throat and started talking about his shift. His hands remained in his pockets, and he avoided direct eye contact. I followed his lead and started talking about my shift and how hot the weather had been. We headed inside to my clinic to sit down.

Kasra sat next to me and said something with gritted teeth, which I could only interpret as, *What the fuck are you doing?*

I looked at him to clarify the incomprehensible growl. He gave his perfected evil look with an exaggerated smile in return. He was going to take over the conversation.

Kasra was exceptionally good at being flirtatious and provocative. Saying the most banal things, he could change his tone into a teasing one, like hypnotizing an unsuspecting prey.

Five minutes or less into Kasra's seduction, the big hands attached to toned arms pulled me aside. "Is your friend gay?" he whispered to me, his breath tingling my cheek.

"Erm, I...I don't know," I said, taken aback.

"The way he talks—it is making me horny."

Five minutes, that's all it had taken. I looked at him, at those lips, not knowing what to do or say, thinking, *What about how I talk? What's wrong with that?*

"Can we go to the back room for a little while and you keep watch?" he continued.

The chill that hit my spine made me speechless. I pressed my lips together, "Uhumm," and looked towards the room with a couch.

I saw the door into my back office closed in my face, leaving me standing outside. I was being the "guard" to their harem.

They walked out shortly. He said he was needed back at his own post and was quick to disappear, like a black-widow spider worried he might be killed after mating.

Kasra displayed a wide smile on his face and all I could do was laugh.

Afterwards, I still saw him here and there. He'd mostly have very short conversations and avoid me. My situation with him fitted well with a saying in Farsi, which translates as, "Didn't eat the soup, but mouth burned anyway." It was too familiar to me to care anymore. I had already considered him a chance missed, and had moved on.

It was a few weeks later when we went to Fasham for a weekend with my gay friends. Soosan and Maani were in stitches as Kasra retold the story in the morning. I only shook my head, containing my laughter.

Having met him almost a year ago in Café Soosan, Maani was the relatively new addition to the inner circle. "I gotta head off, need to pick up my mum," he said, still laughing. "Sorry—won't be able to help clear up."

I kissed him on the cheeks. "Don't be silly. It's easy. And I have these two, anyway."

"Bye, darling—I'm going to the balcony for a cigarette," said Kasra, waving his hands. He faced me before stepping out. "By the way, I've been thinking about it again. You really need to have a party here."

"Don't start, it's not—"

"Safe? Of course it is," he said, and walked outside.

I turned and looked at Soosan, smiling at me from the kitchen.

"Brace yourself for another speech," he said.

"Yeah, whatever," I sighed and got up.

A Queen Emerges, a Diva Falls

The world outside was going berserk about Iran's nuclear programme. President Ahmadinejad was making his usual provocative comments left, right, and centre. I had already decided I did not want to stay in Iran, and not because of my sexuality alone. I was getting tired of how the system ran. I hated the bureaucratic maze. "Stepping on someone else's head and crushing their career to progress" was an unwritten motto which belonged in a golden frame hung in every office. To get the job which one was not qualified for, lying and having connections with important people was a cruel necessity.

It was all justified by religion—or, rather, religion had facilitated it. Having a beard or a prayer-stone mark on the forehead worked wonders in getting any job, getting any application processed sooner, or jumping the queue. It happened every day in almost every encounter, and no matter how hard one tried to ignore it, it crept into daily life. The little everyday exasperations had accumulated to a suffocating level. I needed to escape—or just *an* escape, every once in a while—to breathe.

Colours, all of them pour back in, reviving this memory. I now know why it faded. It is my brain trying to delete it, but it is here to stay. Among the colours is the most dominant one: black.

Summer 2008
The party.

"Yes, yes. He lives down there, let me deal with it."

In my calmest voice, I had tried to explain who our neighbour was, trying to hide my own anxiety. Drunk, high, and now agitated, my words could not penetrate into the anxious guest's brain. Desperate to leave, he was walking down the steps with a few friends to our neighbour's gate. I was a few steps behind.

I looked back at the flat for a second, where the out-of-hand party carried on. Balcony doors were left open, the sound and the light was seeping out, like an overflowing boiling pot. I caught up with the angry guests.

"I said, wait—I'll ask him to move his car."

It was past one a.m. A few steps ahead now, as I got to the outer gate of his property, I started rehearsing in my head: *Hello, sorry to bother you—* The thought was invaded with the truth: *Could you please move your car, as these drunk gay guys from the party next door need to leave?* I could see the main door to his villa from the gate. Over my shoulder, I heard the party guests approaching. I pressed the buzzer. Once. For less than a second. Unintentionally, I hushed to myself as I heard the ring.

No response.

"Ring again."

I looked at him, impatiently shuffling. His friends behind him were giggling, eyes bloodshot.

"Could you just go upstairs and wait? I'll handle it," I pleaded.

He didn't move, only raising his eyebrow.

I buzzed again. Slightly longer. Please let this be over.

No answer.

I looked at the windows of his villa through the metal gate, waiting, hoping for a light.

A hand on my shoulder: "Can you buzz a bit longer?"

I nodded, but before I could move his hand, he went for it, putting his finger on the small white button and pushing, not letting go, as if superglued to it. The loud continuous ring straightened every hair on my body and trapped the air in my lungs.

I turned to him. "Shshshshsh! What are you doing?"

"Uh, waking your neighbour up. Isn't that the point?"

He didn't let me talk.

"Sir! Helllloooo! WAKE UP!" And he pushed the buzzer again, harder, as if it made a difference. Then, another shout: "HELLOOOO! WE NEED YOU TO MOVE YOUR CAR!"

I pulled my head away as his friends joined in with his shouts, becoming louder. I was paralysed, powerless, and hopeless. I looked at the building.

A light, finally.

I pushed his hand off the buzzer immediately. "OK, OK, he's awake. Just wait."

He stood back, huffing.

From the building, I saw him, the minister, appear—white vest top and pyjama bottoms pulled up to his chest, and that look.

I swallowed.

As he approached the gate, he made eye contact. I could not stop the sweat beads racing down my temples. If only I had melted fully before he got to the gate.

"S-salaam, sorry about this—"

"It's OK," he grunted and walked past us, saying something under his breath as he looked at them from the corner of his eyes.

I stuttered another incoherent apology, barely getting a word out. I tried to read him. Does he know about the party? Is he going to tell my parents? The music and light from our balcony were unmissable.

I opened my mouth to provide an explanation. There was none.

The thought of tomorrow whirlwinded through my brain, imagining one sequence after another, already feeling ashamed of the shame Baba would have to bear.

He moved his car and, as he headed back to his villa, looked up, eyes narrowing. I did not dare to follow his look, worried what might be on display at that point. His eyes then slowly moved and rested on me. It was the same gaze from many years ago, my childhood. The warm feeling I had felt as a child, however, when I had memorized new verses of the Quran and radiated with pride, was now replaced with dread. It was like a boa constrictor staring into the eyes of its prey as it squeezed the last gasp of air out. The prayer-stone mark above his eyebrows looked like a mini angry face, his forehead twisting and gathering wrinkles around it.

I could not miss his next whisper, the all too familiar words: "*Astaghfirullah*," I beg Allah for forgiveness.

He shook his head once more and closed the gate. I stood there, frozen, wondering whether I should call after him and ask him—no, beg him—not to say anything to Baba. But no air was left in my lungs, no willpower. All that was left was disgrace.

Seeing the back of the guest's car leaving, all I could think of was the damage that might ensue.

What I did not even think about at the time was how all those guests who were off their faces were going to drive back to Tehran, in the middle of the night, on the curvy mountain road.*

My mind was still fixed on the neighbour. What if he is on the phone to the police now?

It was done. My stupid idea of having a secret party had blown up right in my face. I needed to talk to someone who appreciated the gravity of situation. I needed to discuss it with Saam.

Damn. Where is he? I had totally forgotten about his calls.

I remembered a year back, another night out with Soheil and his friends, at the height of my gay exploration.

"And you've told your mum you're with us?" asked Saam over the phone.

It was gone midnight. I did not know who else to call. I had taken Maman's new navy-blue Toyota to pick Soheil up. Of course, I had scratched it that night. Petrified, I had dialled Saam's number as soon as I got home.

"Yes, but that is not the issue, here. I don't know what to do with this scratch."

Saam made a noise, which can only be described as clearing too much phlegm at the back of his throat. "Where is Ali?"

"Home, in bed, I'm guessing."

"Let me call him." And he hung up.

---

* Since alcohol is not allowed in Iran, there are no laws for "drunk driving," leaving it to common sense.

Twenty minutes later, the three of us were driving in the eerily empty streets of Tehran, looking for a 24/7 mechanic. Ali's hair was messy and the bags under his eyes wrinkled more as he laughed while Saam swore at me. I took it all in and laughed along. I was glad they were always there to get me out of trouble.

After coming out, their "cover up" duties had expanded to sort out my gay life mishaps on countless occasions. I had truly taken them for granted.

The thought made me smile. I felt a pang of need, hoping that Ali and Saam, when I went back up, would be sitting in the living room, shuffling cards, drinking tea, laughing.

Saam, where are you? Why don't you answer your phone? I thought, as I hung up again.

The corridors were empty, with black marks on the floor here and there, where cigarettes and joints had been stubbed out. I slowly walked up, holding the handrail. The light was flashing less excitedly to the music, thankfully turned down. There were not many guests left. Ten, perhaps twelve, mostly sitting or standing in the corners. The balcony door was half open. Tin foil on a few windows had torn. I walked in on the sticky floor, picking up a few cups, breathing in the smell of smoke and sweat. I wondered how many hours it had been since I was up here. I spotted Soosan in the kitchen, getting a glass of water.

He must have seen it in my face. "Jeez, what happened to you?"

"Don't ask. Have you seen Saam?" I asked, looking around the room once more.

"Nope, why?"

"Nothing. I'll find him."

Leaving guests passed by and kissed my cheek or tapped my shoulder as I repeated, "Thanks for coming; see you soon," with a fake smile. I opened the bathroom door. A few soaked towels with shoe marks and a few plastic cups lay on the still-wet floor. No sign of Saam.

I walked to the guest bedroom. Not there either. I looked at the bed before leaving. The creased bedcover and the pillow with a head mark in the middle were signs I did not want to interpret. I sighed as I walked to my parents' bedroom, hoping I would not find another crime scene in *their* bed.

There he was, Saam.

Lying on his back on the bed, one leg dangling from the side, he held his phone in his hand. His eyes were open and a smile was on his face. But that was not the only thing on his face. It was also covered in dried vomit, and so was his shirt, the pillows, and the sheets—my parents' sheets. I, exhausted, defeated, and deflated, had already gone past the end of my tether. I stood there observing him for a while, as if appreciating an artwork. He did not move his head, but his eyes slowly moved and found me.

"Hi. I told you to come, didn't I?" he said finally.

Drunk on his own creation, the fruit punch, he had been so dizzy and nauseous that, once he lay down, he could not get up again. That was when he had started calling me and, when the sick crept up his throat, he'd just let it loose like a volcano erupting from his mouth. To be fair, I was glad I had not been there to witness the fireworks. After the Picasso sketch, he had decided to let the "paint" dry until I found him.

Soosan appeared behind me. He was quick to get a toilet roll and help clean Saam up, while I stood there in a trance. I had forgotten why I wanted to talk to him in the first place. Eventually, I took the roll from Soosan and started wiping bits of sick from Saam's face, bearing the awful stench. He was asking how the party was and if everyone had left.

"It was great, and yes, people have mostly gone now. Thanks for your help." I did feel sorry for him. The empathy *was* there, a tiny bit.

Soosan asked if I was OK.

I looked at him. "Can you check from the windows if any police car lights are there?"

I said it in such a monotonous way, it took him a while to register it. I was ready to be arrested. Just wanted it to be over.

Soosan laughed, that camp laugh with his belly vibrating. "Why would there be any police? Get up, let me help with Saam. You sit down."

I followed his instructions, but did look out through the window first. Dark, quiet, peaceful. No red and blue flashing lights.

Soosan got Saam up and put him in the bathtub in his underwear and turned the tap on. He managed to sort the rest himself.

"Thanks," I said to him, drying my hands on my jeans. "I am assuming they're all gone."

"Yes, Kasra and Reza are on the balcony. Join us."

"Will do, in a bit. Just don't tell them about…you know…" I pointed my head towards the bathroom.

"No, not today," he said, and left.

As I followed him with my eyes, I looked at the living room, at the mess, with my hands on my waist.

I just had a gay party here.

The next day was spent cleaning and scrubbing. All the guests made it home in one piece. Saam washed all the bed sheets and pillow covers he had ruined. When I went to bed that night, all I could think of was the post-party gossip. The exhaustion put me into a long, dreamless sleep.

I peeked out from the ajar door of my bedroom. Maman was carrying a picnic basket, Baba walking in behind her. They had just returned from Fasham. I wanted the gnawing itch to be over. Have they found out?

"Salaam, h-how was it?"

Baba looked up and hesitated for a second before answering. I braced myself.

"Need to fix the tap in the bathroom, think it has a leak."

"Oh, yes, maybe." I took a breath. "Did you see any of the neighbours?" I was deliberately keeping it vague.

"No, no. I think no one was there this weekend. Why do you ask?"

"No reason. I thought I saw the minister's car when I was there, that's all." I smiled and turned to go back in my bedroom.

"Majid?" Maman called after me.

This is it; she has smelt sin.

I slowly turned. She was undoing the clip under her chin to loosen her headscarf.

"Can you go get the rest of the stuff from the car?"

The corner of my eye twitched as I walked past them without saying another word.

To this day, I don't know how many turned up, but a rough estimate would be eighty to ninety—mostly gay men, but trans women, straight guys, and a few girls were among us too. It was truly incredible, and I dare say dreamlike.

As predicted, the Fasham gay party became famous as the "alcohol-free party," and, as much as the tag was irritating, people did have a good time. The party turned into a source of gossip, and was a significant point in the gay-scene timeline. I missed most of the action and only saw the aftermath, but many cheeky kisses and hook-ups took place at the party. Relationships began and ended that night, while I was moving cars and clearing vomit off Saam's face.

I was now someone known in the scene, I had become important, and one to be friends with. The nickname "Queen of Fasham" stuck. I'd be lying if I said I did not enjoy the attention.

The chat between our religious neighbour and Baba never materialized. Astonishingly, the secret party remained secret to my parents.

Afterwards, once I had forgotten the trauma I endured that night, I set my mind to clearing my name and proving I could throw a party right. The conviction led to my second Fasham party, less than a month after the first one. The neighbour's silence made me believe he was less bothered with us than I'd thought he would be, or he respected my father enough to not say anything.

Within the "life," I thought my reputation was damaged because of the booze problem in the first party, and that people would turn a second party down. The ever-faithful gay community proved me wrong by showing up in the same numbers. Around eighty attended the second Fasham gay party. I even invited Bouncy Soheil, and he did come, of course. It was run so slickly, it was almost boring. Saam did not drink a single drop of alcohol, was on top of clearing rubbish and refilling booze. The famous punch was served from a large water dispenser with a tap. Guests all parked their cars outside, with easy escapes, and I managed to spend most of the evening on the dance floor. I was satisfied and content at the end.

I had fully established myself in Tehran's gay scene—and not as a diva. I felt I belonged. I had endorsed being gay with all its colours.

And then came *that* call.

As the palette of colours of this memory comes to the most dominant one, there is a twinkle, light bouncing off the silver bracelet in the black. And then another, this one from the tiny stone before it's covered.

I hold on to the lights, they'll keep me going.

When I saw Reza's name on my phone, two days after the second party, I ran to my bedroom and closed the door. I knew it would be about the party and that he would fill me in on all the unseen bits, the gossip, and the feedback. I had been looking forward to it.

"Hey," he said, in more of a sigh than a word.

Something about the sigh was unsettling, and my hair stood up on the back of my neck.

"Hey heyyyyy, how are you?" My voice was more gleeful than necessary. I was trying to obscure an uneasy churning in my belly.

And then, silence.

Two long seconds of nothing.

Only Reza, breathing heavily on the other end.

The goosebumps now ran all over my body, acid rising inside my chest like a volcano; I had to say something. "Reza?"

"He's dead."

Silence.

I sat down on my bed.

Maybe he's not talking about who I think he's talking about.

I was longing for some kind of reprieve, hoping for the punchline to a joke, even.

"Wh-who?" I said in a whisper, mouth dry. Please don't answer, please.

"Farid," his voice broke. "They killed him, Majid, they hanged him." He dissolved into sobs, each reeking of pain, each like a stab piercing through my chest.

Streams began to run down my face uncontrollably, a ball expanded in my throat, trying to rip free. Breathing became difficult. Walls moved in, trying to crush me.

Farid. Dead.

Farid, the life of a party, lifeless.

Loudest voice in a room, muted.

I spoke with Reza for about an hour, then Kasra, then Soosan, and then Reza again. We tried bouncing courage and assurance off each other, each more helpless than the next.

It turned out Farid *had been* caught by the *basijis* on that cursed party night nearly a year ago. His family had been made aware. They visited him in Evin, Tehran's notorious prison. He was kept there not because of the party, and not because he was gay. But because he had joined a gay activist group, doing awareness campaigns.

Farid, the flamboyant flimsy but fierce diva, was considered a threat to national security. His sexual orientation only made it easier for the judge; he was a worthless sodomite. That is, if there was any trial. His parents had intentionally shut Reza out, trying to protect him from Farid's fate, sure their phone was being monitored.

The day after my party in Fasham, in the early hours of the morning, his sentence was carried out. While we gyrated to

Western music, Farid's mum was saying her final goodbyes to her only son. The son who only wanted to make *her* happy. How it must have hurt knowing he'd failed.

The hyenas had caught a gazelle.

The images of the party evaporated before my eyes, as if it had never happened, as if it was only a dream, dreamed years ago. Another scene crept into my mind instead, one which I was never able to shake off.

Dark blue metal with patches of rust, harsh and sharp angles, zigzag lines within.

A crane.

A strip of light, tearing through the thick ever-present smog over the city.

The rising sun gives life to the ugly crane, extending its shadow and what's attached to its tip.

A rope.

He's walking in the middle, a figure in a balaclava on either side.

His hands are bound together behind his back by silver bracelets, instead of his usual gold. How he would have hated that as a fashion choice, but he could not see them.

A white cloth is tied around his head, covering those piercing eyes and the stud on his eyebrow. How it would have reflected the sunlight.

How he wishes to see the hazy dawn one last time.

Around his neck is a necklace of a different kind, now.

The sun is rising behind his figure hanging from a crane, wind blowing his tiny body around like a twig.

Farewell

Autumn 2008

The crunch of dead leaves under the feet of a busy city scurrying to work testified to the indifference of people towards the vibrant colours those leaves once displayed.

A life had been taken, but no one seemed to have noticed.

Farid's funeral was private, under strict rules. Any risk of a funeral turning into a protest nipped in the bud. His parents had to agree to the terms or they would be informed by the authorities at a later date which godforsaken cemetery he'd been buried in.

We were not allowed to go to the funeral. His gayness was his undoing and anyone representing that would have been too hard to handle for his mum, which was all of Farid's friends. Unlike me, he did not have a "straight life." His parents let Reza know where his grave was so he could visit later.

His grave.

As we drove to south Tehran, no one said a word. Behesht-e-Zahra, Zahra's Heaven, was where we were heading. Tehran's cemetery was named after the Prophet's daughter. Farid had been executed by sharia law and was now in "heaven." No choice.

Soosan was behind the wheel. Kasra sat next to him wearing sunglasses too big for his face. I held Reza's hand as I sat in the back with him. He looked tired, aged, lost. I feared he might never come out of that abyss, broken beyond repair.

As everyone walked away, one by one, from the fresh heap of soil with a single white lily on top, I stood staring. Reza was sitting on the kerb further away. The Quran was being sung in a mournful tone from a nearby speaker. A white van with a green stripe was parked further away, an officer standing next to it. He looked tired too, watching over the small groups coming and going. Farid's grave was still a threat to them.

We are taught to recite parts of the Quran when we visit a grave, while kneeling in front of and touching the soil. The sharia says it will send blessings to the dead in the afterlife. At that moment, my knees wobbled but did not give in. I could not shake the hypocrisy of it; my mouth refused to mutter the verses and my eyes stung as if shards of glass lined my eyelids.

A light breeze was shuffling the brittle leaves against one another.

I looked up and could only whisper Farid's words: "They don't deserve us."

That evening, Soosan insisted that we all reunite at his place to reminisce and remember. Reza did not join. It was a beautiful evening. Maani held my hand, clasping his fingers in mine as I wept on his shoulder. Seeing everyone around that room, I felt a warmness in my chest. I was going to hold on to that, for Farid's sake.

December 2008

Military service had ended. Once I got my Service Completion card, I immediately updated my passport and, from there onwards, I could leave the country whenever I wanted. A life-changing milestone had been achieved.

Everything I had done up until then was what I had been told to do, a rite of passage, pre-written: school, university, military service. One could sleepwalk through it. Now, all finished, I was released into society. With my upbringing, usually those rites of passage would continue to be written by the family, mainly my father: finding a wife, moving out, and getting a job.

Farid's death incited in me an anger towards the religion and the regime. I could no longer breathe the sharia air still heavy in our home. I needed to be away from home as much as possible, and the Café Soosan rendezvous were not enough. The desire to escape the suffocating mixture of religion and corruption was tiring.

My military service buddy placed an easy solution on my plate. He got a job with a private oil company who needed a doctor on their drilling sites to obtain safety-check clearance. He was flown to the drilling site in the middle of nowhere and was based there for three weeks each month, with one week back home. Ideal.

The campsite was close to the Iran–Iraq border, not far from a few small villages, where poverty had shamelessly spread her cloak over the residents. Driving through dirt roads towards the site, the ominous signs by the roadside were artfully emphasized with a picture of a skull, reading, **MINE FIELDS; DO NOT ENTER**. I wondered if the constant reminder of wartime was ever going to go away. Every once in while, the news of a child or two dying in a mine blast, or losing a limb while playing, answered that question for me.

The job itself was as uncomplicated as the backdrop: a clear skyline with nothing around, maybe a mountain in the distance, occasionally a tree. The break from the crazy life in Tehran, and the calm contrast, helped me clear my head and envisage a future.

2009

Iran was facing the most political unrest it had experienced since the founding of the revolution. The "Green Movement" was born after the disputed and controversial presidential election in June[*]—the election which kept President Ahmadinejad in power for another four years. Peaceful silent protests about the election results soon became violent, with police and the revolutionary guard cracking down on protestors. Many were jailed, beaten up, or died.

Those events, on top of how I already felt about the system running the country, and more than anything, the sharia itself, pinned the final nails in the coffin. The hope of a happy life within the system had been lost years ago, but, oddly enough, I had managed to camouflage the bitterness with the thin blanket

---

[*] The name "Green Movement" has nothing to do with global warming or the environment. The colour green was the colour chosen by the opposition for their election campaign.

of positivity which my gay life had granted. There was a sense of irony in the fact that my only glimpse of joy in the Islamic Republic had come from being gay. After Farid's death, that illusion was shredded as well. The unsettling shadow of sharia law hung over all of us.

Maani was down to earth, a couple of years older than me, and he was semi-religious—he still prayed. He had managed to find peace between his religion and his sexuality. He was not out to any of his straight friends and had drawn a clear line between gay life and straight life, living them both separately. He thought of me as *too liberal* and coming out to *everyone*. Our friendship over those few months had been taken to the next step: he became my last boyfriend in Iran.

He was not keen on staying in Iran either. Since there was a death sentence for homosexuality, one could seek asylum in a foreign country for being gay in Iran. The twisted system made the *sin*, the *condition*, the *abomination*, or whatever they labelled it as, a way to get exemption from compulsory military service, which in turn allowed us to get a passport, and it also worked as a visa to leave the country, seeking asylum.

I told my parents Maani was a friend I made during military service and introduced him into my home. It was an acceptable introduction, with no raised eyebrows. He was not camp and could easily pass as a straight man.

Apart from introducing Maani with yet another lie, all my gay life was still kept hidden from Maman and Baba. Perhaps it was true that, as we were taught in Islam, one sin fed other ones, until you were immersed in them, damned to hell for eternity.

Not long after the presidential elections and the showdown that followed, my opportunity to leave Iran finally arrived. I applied for a master's course in London and got a place. At that point, I was still working with the oil company on and off, and Maani was my boyfriend.

The time had come to close that chapter in my life too.

Summer 2010

My flight was at eight a.m. The evening had been quiet. I had been at the Café a few hours ago. With Kasra and Maani, I smoked one last shisha and drank the saffron-infused tea. We spoke of everything apart from two subjects: me leaving and Farid. I was thankful for that. I texted Reza. He did reply and wished me good luck. Maani came back home with me.

Ali and Saam popped by to say their goodbyes. While in the lift with Ali, leading him out of our building, a familiar knot formed in my throat, stopping me from saying anything. He was avoiding eye contact. We said goodbye with a small hug, a joke, and a handshake. In the lift back up, the knot was squeezing tears out. I needed to wipe them away before going back in. I looked at my miserable wet face in the mirror, sniffed and laughed. I would miss him.

Maani was adamant he would come to drop me at the airport. He stayed to leave for the airport at four, with Maman and me. They represented both the lives I was leaving behind. Maman, a symbol of religion, the one person I could not be more different from, yet who I relied on most, knowing, hoping, she would always be there for me, and my boyfriend, the face of my gay life.

In the airport foyer, after dropping my bags, we looked for a place to sit. There was time to kill, as they say. Not this time, though. These minutes, seconds, were far too precious. They needed to stretch as far as possible.

Maani pointed to a set of free seats in a coffee shop. "There. Should we sit there for a bit?"

I got a glimpse of his pointing finger before he quickly retracted it. Is he shaking? Both hands were now in his pockets, shoulders tense. How I wanted to hold him. I looked at Maman, walking on my other side, looking at me, smiling. I smiled back. I wondered if she saw Maani's nervousness too.

Once sitting down, he kept talking about the most random things, with a few laughs here and there. Lost in thought, his hand grabbed mine under the table and squeezed. The warmth of his skin spread, encasing me.

I looked at him. He held my gaze for a second. The smile on his lips could not hide the pain in his eyes. It was more than enough. Neither of us could look any longer. I pulled my hand back and faced Maman. She was tapping her fingers on the table, impatiently. She was not ready for this either. I carried on the conversation, whatever it was about. Maani cleared his throat and followed.

Moments later, I was standing at the gate. Maman gave me a hug and a kiss on a cheek, a prayer in my ears and a pat on my shoulder. I made a silly face and turned to him.

I was only a step away and yet there was a valley between us. We *needed* that touch. I needed to smell his skin, to feel his lips against mine, one last time.

It was beginning to hurt.

I hugged him. He hung on to the hug, just a second longer, just with that extra squeeze. That was how he said all he wanted to; that was all we could afford.

I looked directly into his glossy eyes one last time and turned away, breathing out. Once on the plane, it all suddenly became too real. I didn't know where the tears had come from, but I was unable to stop them once they started streaming down my face.

And so, in June of 2010, at twenty-nine, I left Iran, for good.

A New Beginning

London; city of wonders, musicals, fashion, the Underground and gays, lots of gays. The moment I stepped off the plane, I knew my life had changed, not only because of all the opportunities on offer, but because of the independence. I had managed to leave my family home without a wife. I was the anomaly, set free on the world, single. I was glad, in Baba's eyes, career was the most important thing in life, even more important than marriage.

My life in London kicked off with a room in a student hall, centrally located, and near the school. It took a while to adjust to my new life, but I didn't mind it, taking it all in. To explore London's gay scene, I went back to Soho.

I found myself standing outside the same bar I had stood in front of years back, when I had been scared to go in, scared to be seen. The rainbow flag danced above it.

I looked around. No one was staring. No one tutting.

A man walked past me and pushed the door open. He held it open, looking at me expectantly.

"I…I…I'm good, thanks," I said, putting my hands in my pockets and tensing my shoulders. He shrugged and let the door close.

I wanted to move, but my feet remained glued to the floor. *What are you waiting for?*

I reached for the door handle slowly. It opened again, from the inside this time. I looked at the smiling face.

"Oops, sorry, you first," he said, making way for me.

I walked in, whispering a "Thanks."

I was getting my bearings with the new life, one where I was not living a double life anymore, just the one was good enough: a gay man.

August 2010

Less than a month in the UK and I was checking the Brighton Pride's website. Excited and scared. I feared the unknown—that it was too *gay* or too *obvious*, and I had never been either of the two.

The train to Brighton was full. A mix of enthusiasm and shame bubbled inside me: enthused to feel what it was like to join a parade of gay people on the street, and ashamed of being associated with them. It was the remnants of my double religious life in Iran; I knew this may be a feeling I needed to learn to live with, no matter how much I glitter-coated it.

I tried to imagine my family coming to a festival such as that with us all as children, and it made me giggle and made me sad. The contrast to the Quds rally I used to go to with my parents, chanting, "Death to America, death to Israel," was more than apparent.

Though I was there on my own, not for one second did I feel awkward. I felt I belonged.

My life in the UK has been a fulfilling one. I re-established myself in my profession, and specialized within the National Health Service. I have found a partner, and I am living the life I always wanted.

Maman and Baba—I do want my parents to be part of my life. Despite the deep differences in what we believe, we still have common grounds and love each other. In my heart, I know the day will come when I will muster the courage needed to jump this final hoop, coming out to them both.

I look back to my life in Iran often; I am content with the experiences which got me here, and because of them I became who I am today. From the teenage boy who worried about being punished for a stain on his pants, to a confused and conflicted adult who tried every avenue to "rescue" himself from his desires, to where I stand today is a triumph.

With no further sense of remorse, I can now say I am an Iranian *and* I am gay.

June 2018, London

"Are you drunk?" Ben is looking at me with raised eyebrows.

"A little tipsy, maybe. Carry on."

And he does: a story at work, plans for the weekend, his next project, and so on. I am only half-listening. I look up. Pink and purple clouds are floating like random brush strokes against a blue canvas. The early evening breeze is rustling tree branches, as if dancing to the pub music, which is faint in the beer garden. It has been a good second date so far.

Earlier today, as I dropped my bag on the floor and rushed into the shower, I was cursing under my breath. Though Ben's **No worries, see you there** was supposed to be reassuring, I was still annoyed that explaining syphilis was never as quick as I expected it to be.

To my surprise, I arrived early. I got a gin and tonic and sat on the orange seats outside, hoping my red T-shirt was not too intense. When he arrived, his first comment was about the yellow lemon piece in my gin and tonic.

"Yeah, no lime, apparently," I'd said lamely. It was the first drink of a few.

I am now looking at his green T-shirt, matching his eyes.

I joke, "We are wearing Iran's flag colours, almost."

"Ha, yes. Or Italy's?"

"Yeah, yeah, or probably many other countries," I say, rolling my eyes.

The waiter appears and asks if we are eating, leaving the blue booklet of the menu on our table.

I'm starting to look at it when Ben asks, "So, Iran, what is it like there? I mean, being gay?"

I look up and meet his inquisitive eyes. His knee is touching mine. Neither of us moves our legs. Prince's "Purple Rain" is playing in the background. I look back at my drink and the floating piece of lemon. Faces appear in front my eyes: Babak, Leila, Ali, Artemis, Farid…Maman. I close my eyes for a second and a thought gives me goosebumps: all the prayers, the fasts, and the beliefs suddenly seem so distant, belonging to a different person.

I sigh and smile. "Where do you want me to start?"

And so, the memories flood back in.

Memories. The big hands that shaped me with care, colours, and calluses.

Epilogue

"So, how's things? I've missed you," I say, stretching on the sofa. It has been a while since I last spoke with Kasra.

"Same old. I still go to Café Soosan now and then, much less than before. Work is a bit much; my delicate hands aren't used to it yet. New faces appear every once in a while." He sighs.

"What news of Reza? It's been even longer since I spoke with him than it has since I last spoke with you."

"Well, honey. That is your problem. He's OK—happier."

Reza moved to Amsterdam, claiming asylum through Turkey. The Islamic Republic had taken a part of him, which would never be replaced.

Kasra tells me he has changed his name to Marc. "He didn't want the name to attract attention, for people to ask where he is from."

"And you? When are you going to leave?" I ask.

"Me? I'm not going anywhere. I won't survive anywhere else." He takes a deep breath. "It can be shit here, but I love it anyway. I have a job, my family, and my friends. I don't think I'll ever leave."

Later in the evening, once I've finished ironing my shirt for work tomorrow, I lie in bed, staring at the ceiling, thinking of Kasra and Reza, or Marc, my best gay friends—so similar, but so different. A thought makes me smile: Gay life in Iran will survive. It will thrive.

*

Iran: what does that word bring to your mind?

Gay men in Iran live in a vacuum, a black hole, where their existence is denied and their stories go untold. Although the fear of death is a real one, they still live, party, and exist. I was part of that scene. *The Ayatollah's Gaze* is a shout out to all of them. A voice that has been kept silent for too long.

This is my journey through the ups and downs of religion, tradition, and my sexuality, and the interplay between them. The decisions I made during life, some of them tough ones, got me to where I am; however, this is not to say it would work out for everyone in a similar situation. Throughout my life in Tehran, I came across people who dealt with their sexuality and religion differently. I understand how striking a balance between the two works for some and keeps them at peace with themselves, and I respect that. The views I have on God, Islam, and sexual orientation are mine and mine only. This is simply my story, and how I got through all those years, and I am sure there are many other variations of how one grows up as a gay man in Iran.

I hope my story will spark a flicker of hope in those in a similar situation, as I know there are many. I wish my story to be a constant reminder that, however much life may feel and appear gloomy at a particular time in a gay man's life, his true self will always find a way to set him free. Looking back at my life, I want my message to be: "Give it a chance, and you *will* be fine."

As for my country, where I grew up, Iran holds a deep place somewhere in my heart and I am still connected to it. I am hopeful change in Iran will come one day, and hence, in true prayer style, after a *majlis*, where a mullah recites prayers: let's hope the death penalty for homosexuality is removed from Iran's law, hope that one day Gay Pride parades march the streets of Tehran and other cities, and let's hope that "coming out" will no longer be a "thing", *anywhere*. Amen!

Majid Parsa is not the author's name; it is borrowed.

This is Majid's real story:

There was once a boy. He lived in south Tehran. He came from a religious and seemingly simple family. Simple: that is the word which could describe everything in his life. Everything, apart from one thing. He was gay. Nothing simple about that. He struggled, like his peers. More than his peers. His unpretentious life did not offer him solutions. His traditional surroundings did not offer him any support. His religion only promised him shame and punishment. Depression loomed. He began to fall. He tried to reach for help, but no hand came to hold his. The darkness swallowed him. He lost the battle. Suicide was his only way out. Maybe everything would be simple again after that, like he always wanted it to be. He took it. He was free. He died in 2001, when he was twenty-two. His name was Majid.

Acknowledgements

The idea of this book came to me in 2018. From tapping the very first (bad) draft on my keyboard to publishing it seven years later, *The Ayatollah's Gaze* would have not seen the light of day if it wasn't for encouragement and support of many. My first thank you should go to the Ayatollah himself and his henchmen. There would be no book if it was not for them, but I doubt they would read it, so I'll move to the more important people.

Thank you, Archna Sharma and her amazing team at Neem Tree Press for taking a risk with a debut author and supporting me throughout this journey. Publishers who involve their authors in the process as much as you do are a rare breed. To Anna Simpson and the Unbound team, my heart skipped a beat when I first saw the book on your website. Thank you for including me in your family. Special thank you to my lovely editor, Marissa Constantinou. Your creative thinking, attention to detail and the care you gave this book was heartening.

To Penelope Price for your meticulous work on *The Ayatollah's Gaze*. English is not my first language; I hope you enjoyed the challenge! Sorry and thank you. Thank you, Luke Bird, for creating the most vibrant *chador* I have seen for this book.

To Michela Wrong, Jana Sommerlad and Mez Aref-Adib, I am truly grateful for your incredible and kind feedback. Writing about gay life in Iran was a daunting experience, especially trying not to lose hope when reading each redraft. Your enthusiasm and fascination helped reignite the spark every time I doubted myself.

My friends and family around the world: Kyle, Tamara, Pirouz, Reza and Mitra. Thank you for your eagerness when I first told you about the book, it made me strive to make *The Ayatollah's Gaze* the best it could be. Your continued excitement was a delight and meant more than you can imagine.

Thank you, Benjamin. From the title itself to reading multiple versions of the same sentence, making me laugh at my mistakes and tolerating my tantrums, you have been there, every. step. of. the. way and you *know* I could not have done it without you. I am glad, mostly, you don't fail to remind me of this either.

And finally, to gays of Iran, this book exists because of you. Because *you* exist. So, thank you for having me as part of your colourful family.